DATE DUE

Best American Short Plays Series

THE
BEST
AMERICAN
SHORT
PLAYS
1994-1995

edited by

HOWARD STEIN
and
GLENN YOUNG

APPLAUSE
NEW YORK • LONDON

An Applause Original

THE BEST AMERICAN SHORT PLAYS 1994-1995

Applause Theatre Book Publishers

211 West 71st Street
New York, NY 10023
Phone: (212) 595-4735
Fax: (212) 721-2856

406 Vale Road
Tonbridge KENT TN9 1XR
Phone: 0732-357755
Fax: 0732-770219

First Applause Printing, 1995

Printed in Canada

CONTENTS

To Marianne and Priscilla

INTRODUCTION

When Thornton Wilder made his auspicious entrance into the American theatre with *Our Town* in 1938, the theatre was not especially hospitable to Wilder's poetic consciousness. *Our Town* is devoted to the mystery of the human predicament, spanning tens of thousands of years. In production, however, its savage irony was tamed and reduced to the scale of a moving, yet unthreatening, domestic drama. The audience was satisfied with the popular and indisputable recognition that human beings don't realize what they have; people don't talk to each other enough. Thousands of Americans left the theatre determined to spend more quality time with their parents, children, and spouses. As laudable as such a resolution may be, the sentimentalization of the play would forever relegate it to the junkheap of prosaic drama. In thousands of subsequent productions, in every backwater in America, the play's Stage Manager, whom Wilder wrought as a cryptic mythic potentate, comes across with all the cold, omniscient grandeur of the Pepperidge Farm man.

Wilder, whose play *The Wreck of the Five-Twenty-Five* appears in book form here for the first time since its discovery in Yale's Beinecke library in 1994, was not alone in this genre warp. O'Neill was commercially most palatable when his plays could be reduced to domestic drama—*Desire Under The Elms*, *Strange Interlude*, even *Mourning Becomes Electra*. Although Maxwell Anderson's poetic impulses had been triggered for more than a decade, and Clifford Odets was looked upon by Harold Clurman and others as America's Chekhov, the American theatre was essentially hostile to dramatic realms beyond their own backyards.

Our American theatre aesthetic had been firmly articulated by the establishment, in 1918, of the Pulitzer Prize in Drama:

> A prize to be given annually for the best original play to be performed in New York, which shall best represent the educational value and the power of the stage in raising the standards of good morals, good taste, and good manners. $1000.

The most exalted levels of the prevailing prosaic consciousness were represented by Philip Barry, S.N. Behrman, Lillian Hellman,

Kaufman and Hart, Lindsay and Crouse, Elmer Rice, and Robert Sherwood. These were also the playwrights from whom O'Neill separated himself when he stated that his plays were not about man's relationship to man as much as they were concerned with Man's relationship to God. His famous declaration came with the following excerpt from a letter to George Jean Nathan:

> The playwright today [1930] must dig at the roots of the sickness of today as he feels it—the death of the old God and the failure of science and materialism to give any satisfying new one for the surviving primitive religious instinct to find a meaning for life in, and to comfort one's fears of death with. It seems to me that anyone trying to do big work nowadays must have this big subject of his plays or novels, or he is simply scribbling around the surface of things and has no more real status than a parlor entertainer.

The poetic spirit was uncomfortable with the parlor entertainer, just as the parlor entertainer was uncomfortable with the poetic spirit.

But in the sixties, the theatre of this nation opened its heart, and mind, and soul to playwrights with a poetic flair and sensibility. The new wave of Edward Albee, Jack Gelber, Arthur Kopit, and Jack Richardson possessed that poetic quality of imaginative leaps, flights of fancy, and language of rich imagery, in conjunction with content that was filled with resonance, mystery, irony, paradox, and ambiguity. Everything was inspired by a sense of audacity. Pedestrian prose gave way to outrageous riffs of expression.

The poet's anarchic spirit was received off Broadway, off off Broadway, and even on Broadway despite the unconventionality, even the inaccessibility, of the poet's drama. *Who's Afraid of Virginia Wolfe* was rejected by the Pulitzer Committee in 1962, but the play was hailed on Broadway; Albee's *Delicate Balance* was not only hailed on Broadway in 1966 but did indeed win the Pulitzer Prize.

We welcomed a host of talents who used the poet's tools and who dramatized the poet's vision. Their major subject, as it has always been with poets, is living and dying, loss and love. For a brief moment at this time even Thornton Wilder returned to the theater, off Broadway, with a group of one-acts. No longer was the poetic consciousness totally alienated from its native soil.

Glenn Young and I continue to recognize and nurture that poetic environment with this year's volume. Earlier poetic spirits such as Wilder and Ribman and Schisgal are joined here with a new generation of courageous talents. Schisgal will be at home with Steve Martin, Rich Orloff, and Elaine May; Ribman will be at home with David Mamet, J.e. Franklin, and Jules Tasca; Wilder will be at home with Jaqueline Reingold, Craig Fols, and Max Mitchell.

Many of these writers exercise their wildest thoughts and ideas in the laboratory of the short play. They incant unconventional desires in ways they would never dream of venturing in a commercial, full-length venue. Witness the surreal "fugue for five actors" (*Lot 13: The Bone Violin* by Doug Wright); or the strange menu of a Bavarian cafe in 1923 (*The Cannibal Masque* by Ronald Ribman); or the farm where Kenneth harvests a love he never planted (*Dear Kenneth Blake*, Jaqueline Reingold). Christopher Durang wields his Aristophanic wit and genius to burlesque the playwriting of his peers—Sam Shepard, David Rabe, and David Mamet—in the writing of his own play (*A Stye of the Eye*). Similarly, the short play offers David Mamet the opportunity to exercise his sardonic wit, outrage, and poetic sensibility in burlesquing his own society (*An Interview*). All of these fourteen plays have for their appeal the virtues of a poetic consciousness: originality, imaginative leaps, audacity, imagery, irony, and inventiveness. The editors are proud to have that spirit as companion for Thornton Wilder in the posthumous publishing of his play. I hope we have caught up with him.

—HOWARD STEIN
Columbia University
November, 1995

Christopher Durang

A STYE OF THE EYE

Christopher Durang

Christopher Durang has had plays on and off-Broadway including *The Nature and Purpose of the Universe, Titanic, A History of the American Film, Baby with the Bathwater, Beyond Therapy*, and *Laughing Wild*.

His play *Sister Mary Ignatius Explains it All for You* won Obie Awards for him and actress Elizabeth Franz when it originated at Ensemble Studio Theatre. A subsequent production by Playwrights Horizons on a double bill with his *The Actor's Nightmare* transferred to Off-Broadway, where it ran for two years. *Sister Mary* has had productions around the country and the world.

His play *The Marriage of Bette and Boo* also won him an Obie Award, as well as the Dramatists Guild's prestigeous Hull Warriner Award, when it premiered at the New York Shakespeare Festival. Mr. Durang also played the part of Matt in that production, sharing with the other nine actors an Ensemble Acting Obie Award. The play's director, Jerry Zaks, and designer, Loren Sherman, also won Obie Awards for their work on that play.

His most recent work was *Durang Durang*, an evening of six one-acts directed by Walter Bobbie at Manhattan Theatre Club. Included in this evening were *For Whom the Southern Belle Tolls* and *A Stye of the Eye*.

Mr. Durang has also acted in movies, such as *Housitter, The Butcher's Wife*, and *Mr. North*. He sang in the Sondheim revue *Putting it Together*, which starred Julie Andrews at the Manhattan Theatre Club. He also performed with Sigourney Weaver in their co-authored cabaret, *Das Lusitania Songspiel*; and with John Augustine and Sherry Anderson in the *Chris Durang and Dawne* cabaret.

He has written a new play for Lincoln Center called *Sex and Longing*. Several of his plays are published by Grove Press. Smith and Kraus Publishers is soon to put out collections of all his plays.

Mr. Durang is a graduate of Yale School of Drama; a member of the Dramatists Guild Council; and with Marsha Norman is the co-chair of the playwriting program at the Juilliard School Drama Division.

CHARACTERS:
Jake
Ma, *Jake's mother*
Dr. Martina Dysart, *a psychiatrist*
Beth, *Jake's wife*
Meg, *Beth's mother*
Wesley, *Beth's brother*
May, *Jake's sister*

SCENE:
A desolate prairie. Wind-swept. Maybe a couple of discarded truck tires piled on one another. Or maybe it's a highway in the midst of a prairie. Anyway, not much scenery. Desolate, isolated, out west somewhere.

On one part of the stage we see JAKE, *who is on a pay phone. He is tall, in his thirties, and dressed in dungarees, boots, and a t-shirt or work shirt. He is masculine, and has a raging temper.*

JAKE: Answer the phone, damn it. Answer the phone. [*Bangs the phone receiver on the side of the phone, or any other surface.*] Come on, come on! [*Into receiver.*] Hello! Hello!

[*Lights up on a different part of the stage. MA is discovered next to a phone, or enters calmly over to the ringing phone. MA is between forty and fifty, and dressed in a sloppy, comfortable print dress. Her hair is not fussed with, just pulled back out of her face. She is a no-nonsense woman, tough, matter-of-fact, sounds like a Cracker.*]

MA: Hello?

JAKE: Hey, Ma?

MA: Who is this?

JAKE: Ma, it's your son.

MA: Who?

JAKE: Your son, ma.

MA: I got two sons. Which one are you?

JAKE: I'm Jake.

MA: Jake?

JAKE: Jake!

MA: You're not the other one? What's his name?

JAKE: Frankie. No, it's not Frankie, Ma. It's Jake.

MA: Jake?

JAKE: Stop saying Jake, or I'm going to come over to your house and punch you in the mouth.

MA: [*Her voice warming, friendly.*] Oh, now it sounds like Jake. How are you, baby?

JAKE: She's real bad, Ma.

MA: Who, Jake?

JAKE: She's all red and blue and purple.

MA: Who you talkin' about, Jake?

JAKE: I had to hit her. She was dressin' real sexy like, and goin' off to rehearsal.

MA: Who is this you're talkin' about, Jake?

JAKE: It's Beth, Ma. My wife.

MA: Are you married, Jake?

JAKE: Ma, you know I am. You wuz at the wedding.

MA: Why didn't you marry your sister, Jake, she always liked you.

JAKE: That would be incest, Ma.

MA: No, it wouldn't. Incest would be if you married me. If you married your sister, it would be ... sorority.

JAKE: Shut the fuck up, Ma. I'm tryin' to tell you I killed Beth.

MA: Who's Beth?

[*Note: MA's lapses in memory are complete. When she says something like "Who's Beth," she has no recollection whatsoever that she heard the name Beth a few seconds before. So all her questions are asked innocently, trying her best to get information. There is no "what was that thing you said a moment ago" tone to any of her repeating questions. And thus when JAKE seems irritated with her forgetting, she has no idea what is the cause of his frustration.*]

JAKE: She's my wife.

MA: I didn't know you were married.

JAKE: You have the attention span of a gnat. Ma, we've been through this. Beth is my wife, you wuz at the wedding, and I just killed her.

MA: [*Suspicious.*] Who is this calling me?

JAKE: It's your son, Ma! I just killed my wife.

MA: Well, I never pay attention to the tramps you start up with. She probably asked for it.

JAKE: She was goin' to rehearsal, Ma. She's into actin', Ma, and she's goes off to fuckin' rehearsal, and every day she dresses more slutty like, and I just know that she's doin' it with some fuckin' actor on her lunch break. And I seen her in a play once. She stank.

MA: [*Upset.*] Whatcha goin' to plays for, baby? I didn't bring you up to spend your time goin' to plays. You're gonna end up like that Sam Shepard boy down the road. Why don't you settle down and marry your sister?

JAKE: Stop talkin' about incest, Ma. I just killed my wife.

MA: Well, did anyone see you?

JAKE: No.

MA: Well, there, you see. Go get a good night's sleep, and in the morning we'll get you another one. Why don't you marry your sis ... Oh, that's right, you don't like that idea. You're stubborn like your father. I hate his guts. I wish he were dead.

JAKE: He is dead, Ma.

MA: Well, good.

JAKE: I didn't want to kill her, Ma, but she asked for it.

MA: Who you talkin' about, baby?

JAKE: Beth, Beth! How many times do I have to say it!

MA: Thirty-three. I'm getting bored with this conversation, Jake. Is your good brother Frankie there?

JAKE: What?

MA: Put Frankie on.

JAKE: He's not here.

MA: Put him on.

JAKE: He's not here.

MA: Frankie, is that you?

JAKE: Wait a minute, Ma.

MA: Did you hear what Jake told me?

JAKE: Hold your horses a minute, Ma. Hey, Frankie! Ma wants to speak to you! Frankie! [*Changes personalities, and switches phone hands; sounds more polite and reasoned though still has a temper.*] Hey, Mom, how are you?

MA: Oh, Frankie, I love it the way you call me "Mom" and Jake calls me "Ma." It's so differentiating. Frankie, did you hear that Jake killed his wife?

JAKE: He told me, Mom. He's a crazy, spoiled, mixed up kid. If only Pa weren't a drunk and a skunk and dead.

MA: Is he dead?

JAKE: You know he's dead. We were all at the funeral, and you spit on his grave.

MA: Was that your pa? Well, he never was no good. But he sure could ride a horse, and shoot a rifle, and wear boots and dungarees.

JAKE: Mom, what are we gonna do about Jake?

MA: Why did I spit on his grave?

JAKE: I don't know. You wuz angry. Everyone in this family has a fierce temper.

MA: [*Proudly.*] We do. We're fierce, us Faberizzi's.

JAKE: Mom, we're not Italian.

MA: Well, what's our last name then?

JAKE: We don't have a last name. Mom, what are we going to do about Jake?

MA: Who?

JAKE: Jake.

MA: Jake's dead. His wife just killed him.

JAKE: You got it backwards, Ma. I mean "Mom."

MA: You know you and Jake sound so much alike that sometimes I think you're both two different aspects of the same personality. That means I gave birth to a symbol, and me with no college edjacation.

JAKE: I'm not a symbol, Ma. I'm a westerner looking for the big open expanses, but they're gettin' smaller and smaller. There's no place to hope, Ma.

MA: You sound like a symbol. But not some prissy Ivy League-type symbol. My children are virile, masculine symbols who carry guns and beat up women. You all got so much testosterone in you, that you got a native kinda poetry in you, even when you spit. Why don't you go kill a woman like your brother?

JAKE: But what woman is like my brother?

MA: That's not what I meant, stupid. The verb was implied in that sentence, as in "Why don't you go kill a woman like your brother *did,*" "did" in imaginary bracket signs. And me with no college edjacation. Put Jake back on the line, honey, I'm bored with this conversation. No, never mind, I got an idea. Why don't you go try to find Beth.

Maybe she's not dead. Maybe she's only brain damaged, and *you* can marry her. That might have symbolic value of some sort.

JAKE: But what symbolic value would that have, Ma?

MA: I don't know, I'm not a writer. But if we put some jazz music under it, or some good country sounds, it's bound to mean somethin' to somebody. I gotta go now, Frankie, the cactus is whistlin' on the stove. But you keep an eye on your brother, and if you wanna marry your sister, just let me know. [*Hangs up, exits; lights fade on her part of the stage.*]

JAKE: Goodbye, Mom. [*Switches to* JAKE *personality; grabs for phone from himself.*] Hey, I ain't done talkin' to her yet! [*Switches back to* FRANKIE, *hangs up the phone.*] Well, she's done talkin' to you. Why'd you go and kill her, Jake? [*Switches to* JAKE.] Ma? [*Switches to* FRANKIE, *annoyed.*] No, not Mom. Beth. [*Switches to* JAKE.] I don't know. She just kept goin' to all them rehearsals and ... well, it irritated me. [*Switches to* FRANKIE.] I can understand that. [*Switches to* JAKE; *vehement.*] Especially this one play called "Agnes is Odd" or some such thing, all about this flakey nun who killed her baby.

[*Lights change. We see the play* JAKE *is remembering.* JAKE *either exits or stays on the side and watches with the audience.*

The sound of Stravinsky-like music, or Carmina Burana. *Startling, mysterious, otherworldly.*

Enter DR. MARTINA DYSART, *in a crisp business suit, smoking three cigarettes, one in her mouth, two in her hands. She takes the one in her mouth out, and addresses the audience. She is intense and concerned, solving a deep mystery.*]

DR. MARTINA: The baby was discovered in a waste basket with the umbilical cord knotted around its neck. The mother was unconscious, next to the body. The mother was a young nun called Sister Agnes, Sister Agnes Dei. During the night she had given birth and then seemingly killed her baby. Then she went out to the convent stables and blinded eight horses with a metal crucifix. That much is fact. But she is also a musical genuius along the lines of Wolfgang Amadeus Mozart. Furthermore, my life as a psychiatrist is drab and depressing, and even though I think it unappealing that she killed her baby and blinded the horses, still I envy her passion. You wouldn't see *me* getting up in the middle of the night to go down to the stables. And furthermore, I'm a lapsed Catholic who wishes I had her faith, and I wish I had a horse, and I ... wish I was a composer. In short, there are many ideas and subtleties to think about here, so stop rattling your programs and let's move on with it.

My first meeting with Agnes, I thought she was brain damaged.

[*Enter* SISTER AGNES, *the sensitive nun. Dressed perhaps in the strange white nun's outfit Amanda Plummer wore in the Broadway version of "Agnes of God," which is the same design Sally Field wore in "The Flying Nun" tv series. Or a more conventional nun outfit is okay too.*

JAKE's *wife* BETH *is playing* SISTER AGNES. BETH *is written to be played by a small, sensitive young man.*]

AGNES: Look, stigmata. [AGNES *holds out her palms, which at first glance have gaping red holes in them. A second later one notices that she seems to be holding red rubber things in her palms, with reddish centers to them.*]

DR. MARTINA: Nonsense, those are plastic Dr. Spock ears. Look, I'll show you. [DR. MARTINA *removes the "plastic stigmata" and puts the Dr. Spock ears on her ears. She leaves them there for the rest of the scene.*] People sell these at Halloween. Do you like Halloween, Agnes?

AGNES: Pooh. Pooh.

DR. MARTINA: Pooh. Winnie the Pooh? Do you like Winnie the Pooh?

AGNES: Pooh. Pooh. Puer. [*Last word is pronounced "Pooh-air."*]

DR. MARTINA: Puer. That's Latin for boy. Do you like boys, Agnes?

AGNES: Pooh-ella.

DR. MARTINA: Yes, puella. Latin for girl. Maybe it's Latin you like. Do you like Latin, Agnes? Hic, haec, hoc, and all that.

AGNES: Puer. Puella. Eck, eck, equus! [*Momentarily mimes blinding horses, then pulls herself together again.*]

DR. MARTINA: Boy, girl, horse. This isn't a very intelligent conversation, Agnes. Don't they make you speak sentences in the convent, Agnes?

AGNES: Agnes Dei.

DR. MARTINA: Yes, that's Latin for Lamb of God. [*With a shock of recognition.*] Oh my God, your name is Agnes Dei, isn't it? Good grief, I wonder if that means you're some sort of sacrificial lamb to God, and that maybe your giving birth was an immaculate conception, and that the father is God Himself!!! Good Lord, what a shocking idea, oh my mind is running, let me try to breath deeply for a moment. [*Puffs on several of her cigarettes.*] Goodness, what dreadful rubbish I was just speaking. Rather like speaking in tongues. Do you like tongues, Agnes?

AGNES: We had tongue sandwiches at that convent, and it made all the Sisters menstruate.

DR. MARTINA: [*Pause.*] I think that's rather an obscene remark you've just made, Agnes. Did you mean to be obscene?

AGNES: Children should be obscene. And not furred.

DR. MARTINA: Furred?

AGNES: Furred like a bird.

DR. MARTINA: What is the matter with you exactly? Are you a saint or are you brain damaged?

AGNES: [*Sings, lasciviously.*]
　　Erotic, erotic,
　　Put your hands all over my body!

DR. MARTINA: I see. Well, if you're going to sing, I think I'll go now. By the way, which member of the convent is it who won't let you watch MTV? [*Shudders to herself.*] What a sharp remark of mine. I'm definitely in the right profession.

AGNES: No do with MTV.

DR. MARTINA: Of course, it do. Does. That's the kind of song that's sung on MTV.

AGNES: Noooooooo. Who *sing*, Doctor?

DR. MARTINA: I forget. That slutty woman who changes her look all the time, whats-her-name ... oh my God, her name is *Madonna*, which means "Mother of God!"

[*AGNES has a screaming fit at this scary coincidence, and falls to the ground rolling around in circles, going "Whoop! Whoop! Whooop!"*]

AGNES: Whoop! Whoop! Whoop! Whoop! Whoop!

[*Lights fade on AGNES and DR. MARTINA, and they exit.*
Lights back up on JAKE.]

JAKE: [*As JAKE; explaining to FRANKIE.*] It was after that terrible play that I took Beth out in the parking lot and I beat her to a pulp. "Your play was pretentious!" I said, and then I punched her. "You were unconvincing as a nun, and I didn't know whether you were supposed to be crazy or sane," and then I kicked her in the side. "And I don't like the previous play you wuz in, "The Reluctant Debutante," either, and then I took her head and I put it under the tire of the Chevrolet, and I dropped it on her. And that's how I killed her. [*Switches to* FRANKIE.] Oh, Jake. The play couldn't have been that bad. [*Switches to* JAKE.] It was. It was. I fuckin' hated it, man. It made me wanna puke. [*Switches to* FRANKIE.] Yeah, but to kill someone. [*Switches to* JAKE; *big baby, teary.*] Oh, Frankie, I miss her already. I wish she was alive so we could go on a second honeymoon together. [*Switches to*

FRANKIE.] I got some land in Florida I could sell ya. [*Switches to* JAKE.] Oh yeah? [*Switches to* FRANKIE.] It's called Glen Gary Glen Ross. [*Switches to* JAKE.] Oh I don't want to go there. [*Switches to* FRANKIE, *who now speaks in a fast, staccato rhythm, with a lot of aggressive salesman energy.*] Why the fuck not? The place is good. Not great maybe, but what I'm sayin' is, it's good. Not great maybe, but good. That's what I'm sayin'. It may be swamp, it may have bugs, but fuck, Jake, what's perfect? You tell me. No, don't tell me, I'll tell you. It's not great, good. Am I right? Do you understand what I'm sayin'? Should I say it again? What I'm sayin' is, fuck shit piss damn, it ain't half bad. Half good, half bad. You gotta settle. It ain't perfect. Settle. Gotta. You gotta settle. A negotiation. Give and take. You know what I'm sayin'? What I'm sayin' is ... [*Switches to* JAKE, *frustrated and angered by* FRANKIE's *irritating sales pitch.*] Shut up! I know what you're saying, you sound life-like, granted, but you repeat yourself and you're monotonous, and you're ... insensitive to my upset about my wife. She is dead, you know. I deserve sympathy. [*Switches to* FRANKIE.] Yeah, but you killed her. [*Switches to* JAKE.] Hmmmmm. I wonder if she's not totally dead. [*Switches to* FRANKIE.] Okay, listen here, Jake, I'm gonna go out across the prairie or the highway or wherever we are, and I'm gonna see if I can find her, and if she's alive or not. [*Switches to* JAKE.] Hey, Frankie, one more thing. If it turns out she's alive, I don't wanna hear you been doin' it with her. [*Switches to* FRANKIE.] Now, Jake, don't start gettin' crazy on me. [*Switches to* JAKE; *violent.*] I don't wanna hear it. [*Switches to* FRANKIE.] Okay, you don't gotta hear it. [*To himself.*] I'll say it real soft. [*Switches to* JAKE.] Whaddit you say? [*Switches to* FRANKIE.] Nothin', Jake, relax. Nothin'. See ya around. [*Switches to* JAKE; *suspicious, hostile.*] See ya.

[*They exit.*

Lights change to another part of the stage.

It is the home of MEG, *who is* BETH's *mother. At Manhattan Theatre Club, we set this scene outdoors, in front of* MEG's *house. There was a screen door that led into the house; and there were tires on the outside yard, which people could sit on, or fall on.*

It would be easy, with tiny line adjustments, to set this scene inside MEG's *house if you preferred that.*

But my references here are to the "outside" setting.

MEG *enters the yard through her screen door, which closes behind her.*

MEG *is 35 to 45, blowsily attractive. She is based on the character Ann Wedgeworth played in "Lie of the Mind."*

Along these lines, she has red hair, kind of trashy jewelry, tight jeans and boots, and a feminine, off-the-shoulder bright blouse. She is sensual, and has a charming drawl to her speech.

She might look like a going-to-seed country western singer.]

MEG: My, it's hot in that house today. I need some air. Ooo. [*Sound of a sheep from off-stage.*] Baylor? Is that you?

[WESLEY, *a young man in jeans and a t-shirt, comes outside through the screen door. He is the son of* MEG, *and the brother of* BETH. *He carries two large paper grocery bags.*

He is spacey, and mysterious. His speech is often lacking in emotion, and he seems to have his own thoughts going on a lot.]

MEG: Oh, Mike, I thought you wuz your father.

WESLEY: The baby sheep has maggots in it. I brung it in the kitchen.

MEG: That's nice. Where is your father? Is he still out hunting deer?

WESLEY: I guess so.

[WESLEY *puts his two grocery bags on the ground.*]

MEG: He's been hunting deer a long time. Fifteen years, is it?

WESLEY: I dunno. I went shoppin'.

MEG: Oh, that's so thoughtful. Your sister Beth should be comin' home from the hospital any minute—Jake didn't kill her after "Agnes Is Odd," he just damaged her brain a bit, I meant to tell ya. And I want to make her a nice home-cooked meal. [MEG *starts to empty the two bags. The entire contents are artichokes.*] Oh, an artichoke, how nice. Oh, another one. Oh, another one. Mike, honey, we gotta teach you how to shop better.

[MEG *continues to empty artichokes onto the yard, or inside the tires.* WESLEY *just stares.*]

WESLEY: I think I saw Pop in the hunter's cabin. He didn't got no clothes on.

MEG: Lord, how many artichokes are there here? [*Suddenly hearing it.*] What did you say about maggots and the kitchen?

WESLEY: The lamb has maggots. I brung it in the kitchen.

MEG: Mike, honey, you don't bring a critter with maggots into the kitchen. Didn't they teach you home economics in school?

WESLEY: Why is Pop naked in the hunter's cabin?

MEG: I wonder if your sister Beth even likes artichokes. Oh, I think I hear her now. Beth, honey, is that you?

[*Enter* BETH, *same actor who played Agnes.* BETH'*s head is wrapped in an enormous bandage, and she's in a hospital gown. She also limps, and carries a small suitcase.*

Due to her brain damage, her speech is peculiar now. She often speaks nonsense syllables, but as if they make sense to her. From time to time, she stares off oddly.]

BETH: Monga raga. Luga mee.

MEG: Oh, Lord, you look awful. Doesn't she look awful, Mike?

WESLEY: My name is Wesley. [*Exits.*]

MEG: Oh Beth honey, the doctors said you had brain damage. Is that right?

BETH: [*Greeting her mother, telling of her recent experiences.*] Mummy. Mommy. Custom. Costume. Capsule. Cupcake. Candle. Campbell. Chunky Beef Soup. Ugga wugga meatball.

MEG: Oh! Well, that made sense. Mike, she's makin' sense to me.
[*Enter* JAKE.]

JAKE: Is Beth still alive?

MEG: Oh my God, he's come to finish her off! Mike, do somethin'.

BETH: [*Excited to see him.*] Jake? Joke? Kill me, joke? Jake?

JAKE: I'm not Jake, Beth. I'm his good brother Frankie.

BETH: [*Disappointed.*] Jake? I want Jake.

MEG: Goodness, he nearly killed her, and she wants him. Isn't the human heart peculiar?

JAKE: [*To* MEG.] I'm sorry about what my brother did to your daughter, ma'am, and I hope you don't mind my comin' here.

MEG: Oh, an apology. I've never been spoken to kindly before. Oh my. [*Cries.*]
[*Enter* WESLEY. *He's only wearing underpants now, and untied work boots. He has two more bags of groceries, also with artichokes. He puts them down on the ground, and exits.*]

MEG: [*Cont'd.*] Oh good, more artichokes.

BETH: Jake?

JAKE: No, Beth, I'm Frankie.

BETH: I want Jake.

MEG: No, honey, that's not healthy. Jake plays too rough.

BETH: Need. Bleed. I am a Jake Junkie.

MEG: [*Sound of lamb bleating.*] Mike, I hope you're getting that lamb outta the kitchen, honey.

BETH: [*Sudden fear; feeling of significance.*] Lamb? Lamb of God? Agnus Dei?

MEG: What? I guess so, honey.
[*Enter* WESLEY.]

WESLEY: Do we have any mint jelly?

MEG: I don't know, honey. Have you said hello to your sister Beth?

WESLEY: No. [*Exits back into house.*]

BETH: [*To* JAKE.] Jelly. Junket. Jacket. Jake.

JAKE: I'm not Jake, Beth. I'm Frankie.

BETH: Frankie? Funky. Fatty. Patty. Head woooound.

MEG: Oh, it's going to be hard to cast her in plays now. No Restoration comedy for you, young lady!

JAKE: I just wanted to see that you were alright, Beth.

BETH: Wait. Love. Life. The Call of the Wild. Coyote. Aa-wooooooooooooo! I want to marry you.

JAKE: But you already have a husband. You're married to my brother.

BETH: You be my husband. I be your wife. You be, I be, we be.

MEG: She's so much more interesting to listen to since her accident, isn't she? And a wedding, what a good idea. Excuse me, I want to see if there are maggots in the kitchen. Mike! [*Exits.*]

BETH: We become one together, Frankie, and we make a baby out of paper mache maybe. Baby maybe.

JAKE: I'm in love with you, Beth, but I feel such guilt at betraying my brother.
[*Enter* MAE, JAKE's *sister. She wears a tight, sexy red dress, and stands provacatively.*]

MAE: And what about betraying your sister?

BETH: Oooh, pretty dress.

MAE: Here, you can try it on.
[MAE *takes off her dress and gives it to* BETH, *who runs happily into the house with it, very excited.*
MAE *is now dressed in an attractive slip, and high heels.*
JAKE *and* MAE *kiss passionately, then rush to opposite sides of the room, banging into the walls, or sides of the stage.*]

JAKE: Why'd you come here, Mae?

MAE: I can't get you outta my head, Jake. You run around my brain like a haunting refrain. I love ya.

JAKE: I'm not Jake. I'm Frankie.

MAE: Oh, ain't you realized yet, you're two aspects of the same personality. And you and I are two aspects of the same personality, only we're male and female, and you're male and male, so I wish you'd get yourself into one person so you and I could combine into one person also. But if you remain two people, then when you and I combine, we'll be three people, and that's not what I want.

JAKE: What?

MAE: I can't say that all again. What part didn't you hear?

JAKE: Mae.

[*They rush from opposite sides of the yard and embrace. She beats his chest. They roll about on the floor. They are very passionate.*]

JAKE: [*Cont'd.*] How'd you know where to find me?

MAE: Ma tol' me.

JAKE: Ma. She's a sick lady.

MAE: Do you know how to spell Mae? You spell it just like Ma, but add an "e" to it.

JAKE: What the hell's that supposed to mean?

MAE: I don't know.

[*They run from opposite sides again, and embrace passionately. MEG enters.*]

MEG: Sorry to interrupt, but I have something to tell you. [*Points to her eye.*] I have a stye in my eye. And it hurts when I close my eye and see nothing, and it hurts when I open my eye and look around. No matter what I do it hurts. This stye in my eye is a symbol. I have a symbol in my eye. [*Smiles.*] I just wanted you to know. [*Exits back into house.*]

MAE: I was in the school orchestra in Texas when I first started to lust after you, Jake, and you know what instrument I played? The cymbals.

JAKE: We come together like two cymbals crashing, don't we, Mae?

MAE: Yes. Let's you run to that side of the yard, and I'll run to the other side, and then we'll run together again.

JAKE: [*Excited.*] Okay.

[*They run to opposite sides. Just as they are about to run together, enter BETH, now dressed in MAE's red dress, but with lots of jangly jewelry and a purse, purple stocking, high heels, and a strange, teased wig. It is a demented person's attempt to look attractive.*

She kind of looks like "Carnaby Street" London fashions of the sixties, which is most incongruous for this prairie setting.]

BETH: I feel like the jewelry counter at Woolworth's.

JAKE: You look like the jewelry counter at Woolworth's.

[*Enter MEG, carrying an American flag. She now wears an eye patch over her eye with the stye in it.*]

MEG: I found this nice flag in the kitchen. I think it's American. [*Sees* BETH.] Oh, don't you look nice? When's the wedding?

MAE: What wedding?

JAKE: I told Beth I'd marry her. [*Switches to* JAKE.] Frankie! What did you say? I thought so! The minute I turn out not to have killed her, the two of you try to betray me! [*Switches to* FRANKIE.] Now, Jake, stay calm. [*Switches to* JAKE.] I can't stay calm. You been doin' it with my wife. [*Switches to* FRANKIE.] We ain't done it yet, Jake. [*Switches to* JAKE.] Yeah, but you were gonna! Yippie-i-o-ki-ay, that makes me mad! I'm gonna have to take out my gun, Frankie! [*Switches to* FRANKIE; *in fear for his life.*] Don't take out that gun. Jake! Jake! Don't shoot me! I'm your brother! Jake! [*Sound of a GUN SHOT.* JAKE *falls to the ground, dead.*]

MAE: He's dead. Jake shot him.

MEG: *Who* shot him? I didn't follow that visually at all. Maybe it's because of the stye in my eye. Oh dear, I think I'm developing a stye in my other eye. [*The eye patch MEG is wearing on her eye is a double one, and she moves the top one over to cover her remaining eye. She now has eye patches on both of her eyes.*] Oh, Lord, I can't see anything now.

MAE: Jake, Frankie. Jake, Frankie. We can't be one together. Now I'm just half. Or three-fifths. I need two-fifths.

BETH: [*Chipper.*] Well, I don't care. These clothes make me want to go back on the stage. Goodbye, mother. Goodbye, Jake. I'm going to star with RuPaul and Charles Busch in Edward Albee's "Three Tall Women." In Act II, I get to be in a coma. Goodbye! [BETH *exits.*]

MEG: She really is brain damaged.

[*Enter MA.*]

MA: Hi, everybody. I was just on my way to work at the Roy Rogers chain of restaurants, I'm the French Fries girl, when I set my house on fire and decided to come on over here for a nice little set-down and heigh-ho, how are ya?

MEG: Oh, you're just in time to help me fold the American flag.

MA: What American flag?

[MEG *and* MA *start to try to fold the American flag.*]

MEG: I found it in the kitchen. I hope it doesn't have maggots in it.

MA: Maggots in the flag? Oh. That sounds serious.

MAE: Do you have any cymbals in the house? Oh, there they are.
[MAE *gets a pair of cymbals easily from somewhere hidden on the stage; at Manhattan Theatre Club they were inside the two tires. To the dead body of* JAKE.] Jake, Frankie. Do you remember that song we used to play in highschool? [*Sings.*]
> Blue moon,
> It hangs up high in the sky,
[*Bangs the cymbals.*]
[*Sings.*]
> Without a dream in my heart,
> Without a stye in my eye ...
[*Bangs the cymbals.*]
I love you, Jake, Frankie. I'm desperate without you.
[*Enter* WESLEY. *His underpants are now splattered with some blood. Not too gross, but noticeable.*]

WESLEY: The baby lamb is dead.

MEG: Well, please get it out of the kitchen. [*To* MA.] I'm sorry. Do you know my son Mike?

WESLEY: My name's Wesley.

MA: How ya doin'? I like your bloody underpants. Oooh. Something's wrong with my eyes.

MEG: Are you developing styes?

MA: Don't think so. I think I'm going blind. [*Puts on dark glasses.*]

MEG: Well, we'll just have to fold the flag as best we can.

MA: Alrighty-dighty.
[MEG, *with her two eye patches, and* MA, *with her dark glasses, try to fold the flag some more. It's not easy for them.*]

MAE: You're blind, and you're folding the American flag.

WESLEY: There are maggots in the American flag. Pop is naked in the hunter's cabin. The baby lamb is dead.

MAE: Why does all this information make me want to crash the cymbals again? [*Crashes her cymbals.*]
[JAKE *stands.*]

JAKE: Would you stop that god awful racket? [*Stands, brushes himself off.*] I'm sorry I killed Frankie, but maybe I can be free now that he's dead. Did I kill Beth too?

MAE: Beth has gone back to theatre.

JAKE: That's a kind of death. [JAKE *looks out. A lone jazz instrument plays in the background. Moody, yearning. The characters notice the sound of the jazz.*] I'm gonna go out west and look for open spaces. I've been lookin' for love in all the wrong places. I'm sick of women.

MEG: Well, I certainly think Beth was a transvestite anyway. [*Jazz music fades out.*] I always presumed that's why you beat her up. Or maybe I'm the transvestite. Oh, we forget the things we don't want to remember. That's a theme of the play. Oh the meaning, the meaning. Who am I talkin' to?

JAKE: Me, but I want to talk again. [*Jazz music starts up again.*] I'm sick of women. I'm gonna find me some Mexican whores and some tequila, and I'm gonna drive me down some highway with open spaces on either side of me and I'm gonna sit in the car with my legs spread open real wide so my peter can breath, and I'm gonna live like a real man, away from civilization and from styes in the eye. [*Exits to his new life; jazz music fades out.*]

MAE: He's gone. Love and hate is mixed up in my heart. What'll we do?

MA: We got to stick together. We got to go back to our roots. We got to get our heads examined.

WESLEY: I want to have a speech.

MEG: Honey, we gotta wrap this thing up. Make it short.

WESLEY: Could I have jazz music please? [*Jazz starts again.*] Artichokes. There are three different words in "artichoke." There's "art." And there's "choke." And there's "ih."

MAE: What does that mean?

MA: You're the one holding the cymbals, not him.

MAE: I don't think they are cymbals.

MEG: No?

MAE: I think … they represent somethin' else.

MEG: I wonder … if they're connected to … [*Importantly, mysteriously.*] … the styes in my eye.

[*Everyone looks out in the distance, and stares importantly. Lights dim. The sound of wind whistling through the prairie. A coyote's howl is heard. End of play.*]

Craig Fols

BUCK SIMPLE

Craig Fols

Craig Fols is an actor, playwright, director and producer. Born in Jamestown, New York in 1960, he wrote—and starred in—his first play at the age of eight. As an actor, he has worked in stock, dinner theatre, regional theatre, off- and off-off-Broadway, film, commercials and television. Favorite acting assignments have included playing Charles Ludlam's roles in *The Mystery of Irma Vep* and creating the role of Kenneth Halliwell in Lanie Robertson's drama *Nasty Little Secrets* at the Walnut Street Theatre, Philadelphia and later at Primary Stages, New York, under the direction of Stuart Ross.

Resident in New York City since 1980, he participated in the development of many new plays as an actor, director or producer at theatres including The Actors Collective (an off-off-Broadway group he helped run in the early eighties), The Actor's Studio, WPA, and the Circle Repertory Company. While at Robert Redford's Sundance Institute in 1990, he returned to writing plays as an adult. *Buck Simple* is his first script.

With the author playing Buck, *Buck Simple* has been presented in New York at Theatre Club Funambules, Club Trocadero, the West Bank Theatre Bar and as an Equity Fights AIDS benefit at Steve McGraw's. In September 1994 *Buck Simple*, together with a companion piece, *Comeback* (the further adventures of Lois and Buck) opened the season at La MaMa E.T.C. "The Club."

Three other short plays, *Only Repeat, Identical Houses Overlooking the Water,* and *Rosie in the Shadow of the Melrose* were presented at the Currican Theatre in New York in July 1994 and at the Williamstown Theatre Festival in August 1995. Craig Fols is a 1995 recipient of the Berrilla Kerr Award for playwriting.

CHARACTERS:

Buck Harwood, *a very handsome movie star in his early thirties*
Leo, *his agent*
Announcer's Voice
Lois, *a wholesomely beautiful movie star, around thirty*

SCENE:

Backstage at the Hollywood Bowl. A storage room has been turned into a dressing room. A televised benefit performance, summer, 1955.

A swinging door on the stage left wall leads to the stage. Down left is a dressing table and chair with indications of a large vanity-style mirror on what would be the fourth wall. A piano under a cloth is upstage center. Throughout the room are brooms, cleaning equipment, music stands and other miscellaneous items that might be found backstage at a concert hall.

Downstage of the door on the stage left wall is a sound monitor through which we sometimes hear what is going on onstage.

AT RISE:

BUCK HARWOOD *is discovered alone. He is a very handsome movie star in his early thirties, dressed formally in a white dinner jacket and black tie. He is waiting for someone and passing the time playing a game. Using a broom handle as a golf club, he's putting a roll of masking tape into a waste basket. He's crooning to himself as he does this.*

After a few moments, LEO *enters in a panic.* LEO *is thirty-five, fat, obsessive, and very sweet above everything. He's dressed in blue blazer, grey slacks, white shirt with French cuffs, natty cuff links, and a prissy Ascot tie. He carries his briefcase and also a large brown paper bag.*

LEO: Is she here yet?
BUCK: Not yet, Leo.
LEO: Oh boy oh boy oh boy. She was due an hour ago.
BUCK: Take it easy, chum.
LEO: You go on national television in twenty-nine minutes.
BUCK: I know, Leo. What do you think I'm all dressed up for?

[LEO *has put his briefcase and the brown paper bag on the dressing table. He now runs to the monitor and switches it on. We hear loud applause and a band playing intro music.*]

ANNOUNCER'S VOICE: Good evening Mr. and Mrs. America. This is Bob
Delano, coming to you live from the Hollywood Bowl ...
[LEO *switches off the monitor, runs to the dressing table and begins hunt-
ing through his briefcase.*]

LEO: Forty million people, Buck. Forty million live television viewers are
tuning in to see you and Lois live at the Hollywood Bowl. Think what
that means. Forty million Americans sitting in their living rooms
waiting for you and Lois to appear. Sitting in their parlors after
Sunday supper. Forty million honest, hardworking folks, Buck.
Recreating in their cozy domestic surroundings. [LEO *has located
what he was looking for: an index card with notes. He reads from it the order
of the show.*] Xavier Cugat is on now with his band. Then it's two numbers of Judy Garland, Marilyn Monroe singing "The Star Spangled
Banner" and Charles Laughton reading the "Gettysburg Address."
Then it's supposed to be you and Lois.

BUCK: Relax. It will be.

LEO: I called her house in Bel Air. There's no answer.

BUCK: See? She's on her way.

LEO: I called my house in Beverly and left a message with my mother that
if Lois called she should tell her to get herself down here as soon as
possible. My mother sounded worried. She said she and all her friends
have been looking forward to this for over a week.

BUCK: Don't worry, we will not let your mother down.

LEO: What are we gonna do, Buck? What are we gonna do if she does-
n't show?

BUCK: Come on. Do you think Lois would miss out on a thing like this?

LEO: She was pretty mad this afternoon.

BUCK: She wasn't mad. She was just upset.

LEO: She was so upset she was foaming at the mouth is how upset she was.

BUCK: You don't have to tell me, Leo. I was there.

LEO: I'm talking about after she left your dressing room. I'm talking she
slapped a makeup girl and knocked her to the ground.

BUCK: I heard all about that.

LEO: I'm talking she ripped open her dress and ran into the studio com-
missary screaming "I've been betrayed."

BUCK: Everyone in Hollywood knows that by now.

LEO: I'm talking she climbed the entrance gate and swung from it, shouting "I'll get Buck Harwood back if it's the last thing I do."

BUCK: I wish you wouldn't let it upset you this way.

LEO: I ran into Walt Disney in the lobby. And Greta Garbo's in the front row.

BUCK: That Greta's a swell gal.

LEO: Hepburn and Tracy are here. And Roy Rogers and Trigger.

BUCK: It's always nice to have your friends in the audience.

LEO: And Solomon Huron, Buck. Sol Huron is here tonight!

BUCK: Sol Huron is here? What are you trying to do, Leo, make me a nervous wreck? [BUCK *abandons his golf game and goes to the dressing table mirror. He scrutinizes himself, takes a comb from his jacket pocket and goes to work on his already perfect hair.*] When did you see Huron?

LEO: I just saw him coming out of the stage door.

BUCK: What was Sol Huron doing backstage?

LEO: Brace yourself, Buck. I think he came back to speak to Judy Garland about singing the theme song for his new picture.

BUCK: You mean he came back to speak to Judy without saying a word to me? What about my part?

LEO: Maybe it slipped his mind. Maybe he meant to stop by and tell you you've got the part, but it just slipped his mind.

BUCK: Nobody's got a mind that slippery. You don't think the part's been cast, do you?

LEO: Oh, no. I'm sure you're still being considered.

BUCK: I'm tired of being considered. I've been being considered for over a year now. All this consideration's beginning to get to me.

LEO: Don't worry, Bucko. My mother read that novel from cover to cover and she said she'd rather see you play that part than any other leading man in films today.

BUCK: Your mother's a nice woman.

LEO: Gee, I'm happy you feel that way.

BUCK: But Sol Huron isn't. What's wrong, Leo? Why do you think he hasn't cast me yet?

LEO: You know these producers. Never content with a sure thing. Always chasing after the latest pretty face.

BUCK: But I thought I was the latest pretty face.

LEO: You, Buck? Oh, no. You're much more than that. You're an all-around talent! You're a great big triple threat! Why, you're a multiple personality!

BUCK: Do you really think so?

LEO: Sure. You're my favorite movie actor.

BUCK: You're not just saying that because you're my agent.

LEO: Not at all.

BUCK: Because I doubt myself sometimes, Leo.

LEO: You, Buck?

BUCK: Not often and I get over it immediately but occasionally I do.

LEO: Why, you have no reason to doubt yourself. You and Lois are America's Sweethearts. You're the third biggest box office team in America. Two years running.

BUCK: But I want to be number one.

LEO: The Girl Scouts of America voted you and Lois the most neckable couple of 1955.

BUCK: Sure I'm glad to have the Girl Scouts behind me but I want more out of life than that.

LEO: You want the Boy Scouts, Buck?

BUCK: I want everybody. I want the world to be my fan club and I don't want them to love me for being Lois's boyfriend, either. I want people to love me for my own sake.

LEO: I love you for your own sake.

BUCK: Sure you do, but you don't count.

LEO: I don't?

BUCK: No you don't.

LEO: If I don't count then who counts, Buck?

BUCK: Huron. Huron counts. If he would cast me in his picture I'd be the leading leading man in Hollywood.

LEO: You'll always come first in my book, Buck.

BUCK: Thanks. What time is it?

LEO: You have twenty-four minutes left. Buck, where's the watch I gave you?

BUCK: What watch?

LEO: The gold watch. The gold watch I gave you for our anniversary.

BUCK: Anniversary? What anniversary?

LEO: The fifth anniversary of our signing together.

BUCK: Oh, that anniversary. Gee, did you give me a watch for that?

LEO: You remember, the gold Rolex with "Forever Your Agent" inscribed behind the dial.

BUCK: Oh yeah. The Rolex. What about it, pal?

LEO: Where is it?

BUCK: On my wrist I guess. Isn't that where a watch belongs?

LEO: That's where it belongs but if it's on there why did you have to ask me what time it was?

[BUCK *pulls up his sleeve to find there's no watch on his wrist.*]

BUCK: Wadda ya know. I coulda sworn it was on there. I guess I must have left it at the apartment in Brentwood.

LEO: I haven't seen you wearing that watch for about a month now.

BUCK: I guess I must have left it at the house in Malibu. Yes, I remember, Leo. That's where I left it. Malibu.

LEO: I haven't seen you wearing that watch ever since you hired that Norwegian guy to be your personal trainer.

BUCK: Malibu! That's where I left it. You know how forgetful I can be. Golly, I'd forget my head if it wasn't attached to my body by a lot of big bulging muscles. You know what a silly lunkhead I can be.

LEO: Yes, I do. You know, I've seen that Norwegian wearing a watch that looks a lot like yours. A big gold watch encrusted with diamonds.

BUCK: It is a beautiful watch, Leo.

LEO: Well, I've seen that Norwegian wearing a watch just like it.

BUCK: Sven is a Swede, actually.

LEO: He's a very attractive man. He has a very attractive body.

BUCK: He's a fine athlete, yes, but I know him only barely.

LEO: I hear you've been seeing a lot of him lately.

BUCK: Only because he's been living in my apartment.

LEO: He's been bragging all over the backlot that he's your best buddy now. He's been showing people that watch and saying you gave it to him.

BUCK: No. Has he really?

LEO: Buck, did you give our Rolex to that ice skater?

BUCK: Of course not. I categorically deny doing anything like that. I can't imagine what would make Sven say such a thing.

LEO: You really can't?

BUCK: Of course not. When I get home I'm going to give him a spanking he'll never forget.

LEO: Whew! That's a relief.

BUCK: Yes, it will be. Feeling better?

LEO: Much. I was really worried there for a minute.

BUCK: You oughta have more faith in your buddy Buck than that.

LEO: I know I should. I'm sorry. You know how I get sometimes.

BUCK: Let's just forget it.

LEO: Sure thing, Bucko. I'm sorry it even came up. [LEO *crosses to the dressing table and opens the large brown paper bag. He reaches into it and removes several smaller brown paper bags. He begins removing food from the paper bags and assembling a meal on the table top.*] Would you care to join me in a snack, Buck? A little snack my mother packed for me? I think you'll enjoy it. My mother always packs a nice snack.

BUCK: Okay, if it'll make you happy. Although to tell you the truth I'm not that hungry.

LEO: Oh, I am! Thinking about that Norwegian always makes me want to bite something.

BUCK: I thought we weren't going to talk about Sven anymore. Let's just eat the snack and talk about something else. What time is it?

LEO: You have twenty minutes. Look!

BUCK: What?

LEO: Mother always wraps my sandwiches in *Daily Variety*. That way when I have my snack I can read all about what's going on in the business. Isn't that thoughtful of her?

BUCK: Your mother's a very thoughtful woman.

LEO: Gee, I'm glad you think so. [LEO *begins chuckling to himself as he sets up the snack.*]

BUCK: What's so funny? What is it?

LEO: Just this crazy idea I have in my head.

BUCK: What idea?

[LEO *cannot stop laughing.*]

LEO: You wouldn't want to know.

BUCK: Sure I would. Tell me.

LEO: No, it would make you angry.

BUCK: Oh, come on, Leo, let me have it.

LEO: [*Stops laughing abruptly.*] Okay. I had it in my head that maybe that's what happened with Lois.

BUCK: What do you mean, what happened with Lois?

LEO: That maybe she saw you with that Norwegian.

BUCK: I don't see what's so funny about that.

LEO: Wasn't he in your dressing room with you when Lois went berserk?

BUCK: Yes he was, but I don't see the connection.

LEO: Did Lois see the connection?

BUCK: I don't know what you mean. Sven just popped by to give me a quick massage. You know how these Swedes can be.

LEO: No, I don't. How can they be?

BUCK: I'm not to blame if Lois imagines she saw something she didn't.

LEO: You're not?

BUCK: No I'm not. Is it my fault she didn't knock before coming into a room?

LEO: Then she did walk in on the two of you together?

BUCK: Hey pal, I don't know what you're suggesting.

LEO: I'm suggesting that if your fiancée caught you in the act with that Norwegian …

BUCK: Stop right there. Sven is a Swede. And you know as well as I do that Lois is not my fiancée.

LEO: But you've been engaged to Lois for a year and a half.

BUCK: Don't be ridiculous. Everyone knows that Lois is my fiancée only in the gossip columns and in her own imagination.

LEO: Well, you did give her that ring.

BUCK: Merely a platinum token of friendship. If she misunderstood it, there's nothing I can do.

LEO: And there was that time you told her you loved her.

BUCK: When did I say that?

LEO: At that party in Pickfair. In the moonlight. In the heart shaped pool.

BUCK: Can I be held responsible for what I say in a heart shaped pool?

LEO: And you did get down on your knees and propose.

BUCK: When did I do that?

LEO: At the Academy Awards Ball.

BUCK: Don't be silly. I would never get down on my knees at a ball. I don't know what you can be thinking of.

LEO: I thought that if you and that Norwegian, I mean that Swede, were … you know, in your dressing room, that maybe that's why Lois was so upset.

BUCK: I've no idea why Lois was so upset. And as to what you think is going on in my dressing room, I confess I draw a total blank.

LEO: Oh, Buck. You know. Like that time you called me from Carmel to wire that hotel bellboy a ten thousand dollar tip.

BUCK: That was for professional services rendered.

LEO: And that time you called from Palm Springs to pay off that parking lot attendant.

BUCK: A dry climate always makes me do a lot of parking.

LEO: And that script we bought from that biker in Pomona.

BUCK: He was a very promising screenwriter. I was only interested in developing his property.

LEO: And like ... you know ... that time with me.

BUCK: What?

LEO: That time six years ago. When you first came to see me in my office.

BUCK: What time?

LEO: Before I decided to become your agent. You remember.

BUCK: No, I don't.

LEO: Don't worry. I won't tell anyone. That memory is sacred to me. Those were ten of the happiest minutes of my life.

BUCK: Oh, Leo ...

LEO: I don't judge you for them. I didn't judge you for them at the time. I thought: that's wonderful! Here's a young actor who wants to get ahead!

BUCK: Leo, I ...

LEO: I signed you the next day and the rest is movie history.

BUCK: Leo, if you go blabbing this story to anyone else, that's all I'll be in movies, history!

LEO: That will never happen.

BUCK: It had better not happen. Listen, you've got to forget all about that. They're after me, pal. Louella Parsons, Edward R. Murrow, the whole dirty lot. If they get something on me, I'll never be in Huron's picture or any other picture. You've got to keep your mouth shut! You've got to give me your promise.

LEO: I'll give you my promise. I'll give you whatever you want, you know that.

BUCK: All I want is your promise.

LEO: Are you sure you don't want anything else?

BUCK: Leo, you're my best friend and you're my agent. Isn't that all the intimacy two people can handle?

LEO: I suppose so. If that's the way you want it.

BUCK: It is. Now can we please not talk about this anymore?

LEO: Sure. Let's have a sandwich and forget about it.

[LEO *hands* BUCK *a sandwich wrapped in newspaper and they begin eating.*]

BUCK: Oh no!

LEO: What is it?

BUCK: It's here! In *Daily Variety*!

LEO: Our ten minute affair six years ago is in today's *Daily Variety*?

BUCK: No, not that. It's about my part! My part in Huron's picture.

LEO: What does it say, Buck?

[BUCK *reads from his sandwich wrapping.*]

BUCK: "Sol Huron, international playboy and legendary film producer, announced today that casting has been completed on his upcoming pic, *The Ideal American Male*, based on the bestselling novel by Edna Mae Fitzjohnny. Huron will reveal the winner of a year-long talent search for the most masculine actor in America tonight at the Hollywood Bowl. Speculation about who will play Fitzjohnny's dashing paragon has all of Tinseltown in a twitter. Although the identity of the leading man to be is still a well-guarded secret, Huron's lawyers were quoted as saying they were asked to draw up papers on a three-picture, seven-figure contract with ... with ..."

LEO: With who, Buck?

BUCK: I can't make it out. There's a giant mayonnaise stain right where the name should be.

LEO: Oh, that's too bad.

BUCK: What do you mean it's too bad? Don't you think I'll get the part?

LEO: Sure you'll get it. I mean it's too bad about the mayonnaise.

BUCK: Huron's been stringing me along for a year now. If I don't get that part I don't know what I'll do.

LEO: You'll get it, Buck.

BUCK: But they should have cast me a year ago. Why haven't they cast me already? What could they still be looking for?

LEO: They're looking for the most masculine guy in America, Buck. I'm sure you'll wind up getting it in the end.

[LOIS O'DARE *enters. She is around thirty, very attractive in an All-American way. She wears a raincoat over a strapless semi-formal evening gown. Her head is wrapped in a sequined scarf and she wears sunglasses. She carries a tiny evening bag. She crosses into the room without greeting the two men. She seems very upset under a fragile veneer of dignity.*]

LEO: Well hello there, Lois.

LOIS: Hello, Leo.

LEO: Gee, I'm happy you made it, kid. We were starting to worry.

LOIS: Shut up and give me a cigarette.

LEO: Why Lois, I didn't know you smoked. Wouldn't you like a snack instead?

LOIS: Give me a cigarette, I said.

LEO: Sure thing, angel.

[LEO *gives her a cigarette from a silver case. She holds it, trembling, while he lights it.*]

BUCK: Good evening, Lois.

LOIS: Did somebody say something, Leo? Is there somebody else in the room here with us?

LEO: I think it's Buck, Lois.

LOIS: Buck? Buck? Do I know someone named Buck?

LEO: Well of course …

LOIS: There must be some mistake. I'm sure if I'd ever met someone named Buck I'd remember it. It couldn't have slipped my mind. I think you and I are alone in this room together. I don't think there's anyone named Buck here at all.

LEO: You're such a kidder tonight, kiddo.

BUCK: Lois …

LOIS: Did you hear something, Leo? I thought I heard a noise.

BUCK: Lois, darling I …

LOIS: What could it be, I wonder? What could be making that terrible racket if it's only you and I here alone? Did someone else come in, Leo?

LEO: We're not alone. Buck's here.

LOIS: Oh. We're not alone.

LEO: No, we're not. We're with our friend Buck. Your co-star, my client. Buck Harwood. America's Sweetheart. Are you okay?

LOIS: Actually I've been feeling kind of down today.

LEO: I'm sorry to hear that, angel. May I take your coat?

LOIS: I don't think so. I think I'll leave it on. I'm not staying.

LEO: You're not staying?

LOIS: No, I'm not. I'm on my way to the Brown Derby. I'm being interviewed there by Edward R. Murrow in seventeen minutes. I just dropped in to say goodbye.

LEO: Goodbye?

LOIS: Goodbye. It was nice knowing you.

[LOIS *turns on her heels and heads for the door.* LEO *runs to the door and blocks her way.*]

LEO: Wait a minute. What's going on here?

LOIS: I'm on my way to the Brown Derby. Let me pass.

LEO: Why are you going to the Brown Derby?

LOIS: Because Chasen's was booked. Let me out of here.

LEO: Don't you think you're being a little hasty?

BUCK: Leo ...

LOIS: I'm going to tell Edward R. Murrow how I've been treated. I'm gong to tell America what kind of a sweetheart it has.

LEO: Do you think that's really wise?

LOIS: Out of my way.

LEO: I can't let you do that, Lois.

LOIS: You can't stop me.

BUCK: Leo ...

LEO: I can try.

LOIS: On my way in here I ran into Judy Garland in the green room. I told her if I wasn't out in five minutes to call the police.

[LOIS *and* LEO *start to tussle.*]

LEO: Please, I just want you to think about what you're doing.

LOIS: Let me out of here, you lousy ...

BUCK: Let her go, Leo. [*Loudly, strongly.*] Let her go!

LEO: But Buck, she'll ...

BUCK: I said let her go. She's a free woman. And I'm a very lonely, unhappy man.

[LEO *frees* LOIS. BUCK *crosses to the piano.*]

BUCK: [*Cont'd.*] Go ahead, Lois. Go tell America all about me. Goodbye. It was nice while it lasted. Think of me sometime with kindness.

[BUCK *begins to play a very romantic melody just as* LOIS *heads for the open door. Hearing the music she turns back.* LEO *and* LOIS *listen to the music for a moment transported.*]

BUCK: [*Cont'd.*] Do you remember this, Leo? This was the theme from our first picture together. Yours and mine and Lois's. Those were happy days. I'm going to miss those days. I'm going to miss that girl.

[LEO *looks from* BUCK *to* LOIS, *who is removing her sunglasses and scarf.*]

LOIS: Leo, would you please leave us alone for a moment?

[LEO *smiles and turns to go. As he does, he checks his watch.*]

LEO: Ten minutes, kids. [LEO *exits.*]

LOIS: Oh, Buck. Buck. Buck. Buck. Buck.

BUCK: What is it, baby?

LOIS: How could you how could you how could you how could you?

BUCK: What are you talking about, honey?

LOIS: I'm talking about us. Don't call me honey.

BUCK: About us?

LOIS: About you and me. Our hopes. Our dreams. Our Academy Award nominations.

BUCK: Well, what about us?

LOIS: That's what I'd like to know.

BUCK: What is it you're having a problem with?

LOIS: Oh, Buck. Buck.

BUCK: What's on your mind, cupcake?

LOIS: How can I say it?

BUCK: Just spit it out.

LOIS: Buck, you've changed towards me.

BUCK: Have I?

LOIS: You know you have.

BUCK: That's interesting. In what way do you feel I've changed?

LOIS: Buck. I'm talking about this *afternoon*.

BUCK: This afternoon.

LOIS: Oh, this is so hard to say.

BUCK: Just give it a good honest try, kid.

LOIS: I'm talking about what I saw in the dreh dreh dreh dreh dressing room.

BUCK: What are you getting at, sweetheart?

LOIS: Don't call me sweetheart. I'm getting at us, Buck. You and me. I said you've changed.

BUCK: Well, gosh. I'm just the same old Buck. You're the same old Lois. It's hard to see how we've changed.

LOIS: I'm saying that YOU'VE changed, Buck. I'm saying that after what I saw this afternoon in your dressing room you'll never be the same old Buck to me again.

BUCK: Now how could that be?

LOIS: Oh, for Christ's sake! I'm saying that I caught you this afternoon on your knees in your dressing room performing a degenerate act with a Norwegian! That's what the hell I'm talking about!

[BUCK *stops playing the piano.*]

BUCK: Oh. That.

LOIS: Yes. That.

BUCK: Well now that we've got that out of the way, what do you want me to say?

LOIS: I think your actions speak for themselves.

BUCK: Do they?

LOIS: Don't they?

BUCK: Aren't you even going to give me a chance to explain?

LOIS: Explain what? I thought it was pretty clear.

BUCK: You shouldn't always judge by appearances.

LOIS: What should I judge by?

BUCK: You shouldn't judge at all, if you can help it.

LOIS: Oh, you're infuriating. I want to know where I am, Buck. I want to know where I am with you.

BUCK: You're right where you always have been.

LOIS: And where is that?

BUCK: You're here with me at the Hollywood Bowl.

LOIS: Oh, this is humiliating! I'm a movie star, I deserve more out of life than this!

BUCK: Lois, can't we just go on as we have been? Why do there have to be so many accusations, so much probing? Why don't we just say that I love you and you love me and leave it at that?

LOIS: You love me?

BUCK: That's what I said.

LOIS: Then marry me.

BUCK: Let's not get carried away.

LOIS: So you don't love me.

BUCK: I didn't say that.

LOIS: You said you didn't want to marry me.

BUCK: That's not what I said, either.

LOIS: Then you DO want to marry me?

BUCK: I know I didn't say that.

LOIS: Then what did you say?

BUCK: It's hard to remember now.

LOIS: I can't go on like this. I need to know what I really mean to you.

BUCK: That's very complicated.

LOIS: Is it bigger than a breadbox?

BUCK: You mean ... very much to me.

LOIS: How much?

BUCK: Very much.

LOIS: Very very much?

BUCK: Awfully much.

LOIS: My God, why don't you just say it?

BUCK: Say what?

LOIS: That you don't love me. That you've never really loved me. That you've only been using me to further your career.

BUCK: That's an awfully strong word, Lois.

LOIS: Which, career?

BUCK: How can you say I've been using you?

LOIS: What do you call it?

BUCK: We're a team. We always have been.

LOIS: But you've been lying to me. You've been pretending to be my boyfriend when all along you've really been interested in that Norwegian.

BUCK: Swen is a Svede. I mean, Sven is a Swede.

LOIS: I don't care what he is.

BUCK: If you only knew how little he really means to me.

LOIS: It's how little I really mean to you I'm thinking of now.

BUCK: Honey, I know this is a pretty tough break. It is for me too. But you've got to see my side of the whole thing. It wasn't my idea to lead you on. Golly, the whole darn country wants us to be boyfriend and girlfriend. Can you blame me if I got a little carried away too?

LOIS: But you lied to me.

BUCK: I'm sorry.

LOIS: Is that all you have to say?

BUCK: I'm very, very sorry. I'm sorry I led you on. I should have told you I was a fairy.

[LOIS *bursts into tears.*]

LOIS: But you're not a fairy, you're not!

BUCK: Oh, but I'm afraid I really am.

LOIS: I won't let you say that about yourself. You're as masculine as the day is long!

BUCK: I'm afraid it isn't that long, Lois.

LOIS: No! I won't listen! You're confused! You don't know what you're saying!

BUCK: I thought you wanted me to be honest.

LOIS: I don't want you to be honest. I want you to be mine.

BUCK: That can never be. I can never belong to anyone but myself and the American moviegoing public. Face that and we'll just be friends.

[LEO *pops in.*]

LEO: Five minutes, kids.

BUCK: Thank you, Leo.

[LEO *is gone.*]

BUCK: You're a very important person to me, Lois. I care for you more than I've ever cared for any other woman. With the possible exception of my mother. Although if my grandmother could hear me say that she wouldn't be very happy about it. God rest her sweet soul. And I did have a favorite aunt I was always crazy about. She was a large woman ...

LOIS: Buck.

BUCK: But you're the woman I became famous with. All over America they can see how much you mean to me just by popping into the local drive-in. There we are. Buck and Lois. Together forever for everyone to see. Isn't that all the intimacy two people can handle?

LOIS: That depends on which two people you're talking about.

BUCK: Sure I wish I could be to you everything you want me to be. Sure I wish I could really be that man in the movies that everyone is so crazy about. Why, half the people I come across in my daily life don't know the real me. Gas station attendants and truck drivers and life guards and delivery boys and washing machine repair men and ...

LOIS: That's enough, Buck.

BUCK: They all think the real Buck Harwood is the same guy up there on the screen. But maybe that's not me, after all. Maybe the real Buck Harwood is someone very different. Maybe, Lois, just maybe, the real me is someone I haven't even met yet.

LOIS: Well, if you ever do meet him you can tell him from me that he's a jerk. You can ask him to let me know sometime why he got engaged to me in the first place and why he let it go on a year and a half. You can tell him from me that ... that ... that I still love him. [LOIS *breaks down.*] Oh my God Buck why have you forsaken me?

[LEO *pops his head in.*]

LEO: Four minutes, kids.

LOIS: Thank you, Leo.

[LEO *is gone.*]

LOIS: What did I do, Buck? Why wasn't I good enough for you?

BUCK: I wish you wouldn't put it that way.

LOIS: What is it about me that made you debase me this way?

BUCK: You don't know what you're saying.

LOIS: What have I done that's made you hate me, what?

BUCK: I don't hate you. I love you. Like a sister. I do.

LOIS: Like a sister? What the hell is that?

BUCK: Like a very attractive sister.

LOIS: But why can't it be more than that? Why?

BUCK: It is more than that. And ... it isn't.

LOIS: Oh God, I wish I was dead. I wish I was still living in Cincinnati! I wish I'd never set foot in this modern day Babylon!

BUCK: I'm sure you'll see this differently in the morning.

LOIS: I don't care if I live till morning! I don't care if I ever see the light of day!

BUCK: Sshh, Lois, please, they'll hear you onstage.

LOIS: How is it possible I could endure such pain and live? How is it possible the man I loved turned out to be you?

BUCK: There's no sense getting all worked up right before we go on.

LOIS: You go on, you asshole. I'm staying right here. I'm going to Edward R. Murrow and tell America what a creep you are. I'm going to walk down Santa Monica Boulevard barefoot with a sign on my back that says what you are. I won't rest until the whole world knows I'VE BEEN WRONGED!

[LEO *pops his head in.*]

LEO: Three minutes, kids.

LOIS and BUCK: Thank you.

[LEO *is gone.* LOIS *and* BUCK *go to the makeup mirror and start adjusting themselves.* LOIS *removes her raincoat, gets her handbag and fixes her makeup.* BUCK *straightens his tie, combs his hair, and worries about his complexion.*]

LOIS: [*To herself in the mirror.*] People warned me. I just wouldn't listen.

BUCK: [*To himself in the mirror.*] I'm there for you. I just want you to know that.

LOIS: He can't be a pansy, I'd say, he loves me.

BUCK: I want you to know there will always be someone who cares.

LOIS: There are rumors, of course, but there are about everybody.

BUCK: If you ever need a shoulder to cry on.

LOIS: Sure I had my suspicions occasionally, but who wouldn't?

BUCK: Or wait a minute. Maybe I could fix you up with somebody.

LOIS: Yes there were moments when the red lights should have gone off, but hey, I was in love.

BUCK: There are one or two eligible men I happen to know.

LOIS: I guess now that I think about it the toy poodles were a dead give-away.

BUCK: There's Charlie ... no, on second thought, he's out.

LOIS: And nobody keeps that much Butchwax in his medicine cabinet. Why didn't I let myself see the truth?

BUCK: Does he have to be an actor?

LOIS: Why didn't I deal with what was really happening?

BUCK: Does it have to be someone in the movie business?

LOIS: Why oh why did I let myself be duped?

BUCK: Would it bother you being with someone who has a slight speech impediment?

LOIS: What a fool I was. What a silly fool girl.

BUCK: You mustn't blame yourself.

LOIS: I don't blame myself. I blame you.

[LEO *pops in.*]

LEO: Two minutes.

LOIS: I'm not going on.

LEO: Huh?

LOIS: I'm not going on.

LEO: What? What are you saying?

LOIS: I'm going to Edward R. Murrow at the Brown Derby. When I've told America what I saw this afternoon, you'll have to change your name and move to Alaska. If that's the way you want it.

BUCK: You're quite a woman, Lois. My fate is in your hands.

LOIS: That's one thing we can both agree on.

LEO: What's going on here? You only have a minute and a half.

BUCK: Shall I get down on my knees and beg?

LOIS: That won't be necessary. You've spend enough time on your knees for one day. [LOIS *picks up her handbag, opens it and removes an expensive pen. She places it ceremoniously on the dressing table.*] You are the luckiest man alive. [LOIS *takes out a huge CONTRACT from her tiny handbag.*]

LEO: Uh oh. I think I just got it.

LOIS: [*To* BUCK.] This is for you. [LOIS *hands* BUCK *the huge contract. She then takes out another contract, very skimpy this time. She hands this to* LEO.] And this one's for you.

LEO: Lois, these are contracts. You shouldn't be handling contracts without my knowing about it. That's what I'm for, honey, I'm your agent.

LOIS: Not any more, sugar. Sign that and we'll just be friends. [LOIS *hands* LEO *the pen.*]

LEO: Lois, what is this?

LOIS: These are the non-negotiable terms under which I am willing to remain in the partnership of Buck Harwood and Lois O'Dare. Hereafter to be referred to exclusively as Lois O'Dare and Buck Harwood. This is just one of the many changes you can read about at your leisure after you agree to them. I think you have a few surprises in store for you: salary, casting, the use of Swedish masseurs, etc. Everything subject to my approval! It's just too much to go into right now. I'll have Sol fill you in on all the details tomorrow.

BUCK: Sol?

LEO: Who's Sol?

LOIS: Solomon Huron, Leo. He's my new agent.

LEO: I didn't know Sol Huron was an agent. I thought he was just a producer and an international playboy.

LOIS: He's everything, Leo. At least he's everything to me.

BUCK: Since when?

LOIS: Since this afternoon. I went to see him after my little scene with you, and while I was sitting in his office he just whipped out this big seven figure deal. Imagine my surprise and delight Buck, when he put that on the table. Especially after waiting so long for a firm offer from you. I might as well tell you that he's my new fiancé! And not only that, but he's just persuaded me to play the lead in his new movie!

BUCK: You're going to be "The Ideal American Male?"

LOIS: No, but "The Ideal American Male" has got to have a girl-friend. And that's who I'm going to be. I'm going to be her!

BUCK: But ... but ... what about that platinum ring I gave you?

LEO: What about that heart shaped pool?

BUCK: You said you loved me!

LOIS: Oh, Buck. I hate to have to break this to you, but I've been ... negotiating with Sol Huron for a full year now. You know how that is. One party makes an offer, another party makes a counter offer, and what's a girl to do? Mother always said I should have someone to fall back on. I hope you didn't think your option was exclusive.

BUCK and LEO: It wasn't?

LOIS: Oh, no. I've had two or three other things going the whole time I've known you. I had a real hard time making up my mind. But finally I decided to go with Sol. Hurry up and sign boys, we have a show to do!

BUCK: I'm beginning to see this all very clearly.

LOIS: Don't be too disappointed. We're holding auditions for *The Ideal American Male* tonight after the show in my trailer. If you're very very nice to me, there might just be something in it for you.

BUCK: Darling, I ...

LOIS: Sign the paper. There's time for that later.

[BUCK *and* LEO *sign their contracts and return them to* LOIS, *who somehow manages to return them to her tiny bag. She snaps it shut, turns to go, stops.*]

LOIS: [*Cont'd.*] Leo, do me a favor and call Murrow at the Derby. Tell him not tonight. See you out there.

[LOIS *is gone. Pause.* LEO *looks at watch.*]

LEO: Ten seconds, Buck.

BUCK: Do I look okay?

LEO: It's as though I'm seeing you for the first time.

BUCK: Maybe they won't notice under light. Well, here goes nothin'.

[*Slowly, as if facing the firing squad,* BUCK *exits to the stage.*

LEO *crosses to the monitor and switches it on. We hear intro music and applause, then an announcer's voice.*]

ANNOUNCER'S VOICE: And now ladies and gentlemen, America's Sweethearts, Buck Harwood and Lois O'Dare!

[*Band plays a fanfare. Pause.*]

ANNOUNCER'S VOICE: [*Cont'd.*] Excuse me ladies and gentlemen, I had that wrong. That's Lois O'Dare and Buck Harwood!

[*More intro music and loud applause.*]

LOIS' VOICE: Thank you all you kind people everywhere! You don't know how happy I am to be here!

[LEO *crosses to the dressing table, resumes eating his snack as we hear* LOIS *and* BUCK *performing a ghastly routine to an adoring public as ... Lights out.*]

J.e. FRANKLIN

TWO MENS'ES DAUGHTER
A Ten-Minute Play

J. e. Franklin

J. e. Franklin is a native of Houston, Texas, and a graduate of the University of Texas. She is the author of the non-fiction book, *Black Girl: From Genesis To Revelations*, an autobiographical account of the development of her first major work from video to stage and screen. Her plays have been performed at major theaters across the country, including The New Federal Theatre, The Theatre of The Open Eye, The Second Stage Theatre, all in New York City, and The George Street Playhouse in New Jersey. In 1984, The Second Stage produced *Black Girl* as part of its American Classics Revival Series.

Ms. Franklin's other plays include *The Grey Panther Decatets*, a body of "Ten Minute" plays which focus on Elders in American Life, and an octet of plays which deal with the adolescent pilgrimage.

Ms. Franklin has been a full-time member of the faculty at the University of Iowa and the City University of New York. In addition, she has been Resident Director at Skidmore College and Resident Playwright at Brown University. She is a member of the Dramatists Guild, the Organization of Women Writers of Africa, The American Center of PEN, The League of Professional Theater Women, N.Y., and The International Platform Association.

Her awards include a Rockefeller Fellowship, two fellowships from the New York State Council of the Arts and The New York Foundation for the Arts, two fellowships from The National Endowment for the Arts and a New York Drama Desk Award.

Ms. Franklin is the 1992–93 winner of The John F. Kennedy Center New American Play Award, a joint project of the American Express Company and The President's Committee on the Arts and the Humanities.

As a Resident Scholar at The Arthur A. Schomburg Center for Research in Black Culture, Ms. Franklin researched and wrote a decatet of elder-centered ten-minute plays on African-American life under a Fellowship from the National Endowment for the Arts.

Ms. Franklin is a 1994 Fellow of the US/Mexico Artists' Exchange Program.

CHARACTERS, IN ORDER OF APPEARANCE:
  Goldie
  Addie

SCENE:

AUNT GOLDIE's *place has the look of a monastic cell, but it is not drab or claustrophobic. In fact, there is a good deal of light in the room. We are simply given to know that all of* GOLDIE's *activities take place in this room: toileting, cat-bathing, religious activity, etc. This is because* GOLDIE *can't get around like she used to.*

She is a woman of around sixty; it is important that she be light-skinned enough to pass for white.

She is sitting on the bed at the start of the action. She takes her snuff can, stretches her bottom lip to form a cup, and taps some snuff into the space.

GOLDIE *is spitting into her spittoon—a rusty lard-bucket near her bed—when she hears someone come in, and instinctively reaches for some object (ashtray, hairbrush, book, etc.). She goes through a few choices before* ADDIE *shows herself, a young woman of around twenty.*

ADDIE: Don't shoot, Aunt Goldie, it's me—Addie!

GOLDIE: Don't tell me they done sent you over here 'bout that mess, too!

ADDIE: No-mam, Aunt Goldie, not me! I'm on your side.

GOLDIE: Next one come over here devlin' me 'bout goin' to some funeral, I'm gonna throw something at 'em and try my best to kill 'em!

ADDIE: Then there'll be two funerals, huh, Aunt Goldie?

GOLDIE: H'it shore will.

ADDIE: I just got through telling 'em they better leave you alone.

GOLDIE: Don't tell 'em nothing ... let 'em keep it up. They the ones always saying "one monkey don't stop no show," so let 'em c'ary on without me.

ADDIE: They over there saying they can't, Aunt Goldie. They saying according to the will, you knocking them out-a their parts, too, by not going to the funeral.

GOLDIE: Yeah, h'it's a part, all right! I bet h'it ain't nothing but chicken-feed!

ADDIE: That ol' Avrill-Morrow come calling 'em while 'ago, said the lawyer told him Aunt Tootie and Uncle-Cecil-David was left $10,000 a'piece ... say you was left the most but he wouldn't say how much.

GOLDIE: Bet'cha he didn't tell how much him and them others was left. Why'n he tell that? Naw, let him bury all of it with his so-called daddy to keep him in cigars down in hell.

ADDIE: They saying even if their part ain't but ten dollars, if their daddy left it to 'em, they want it. They real mad at you, Aunt Goldie.

GOLDIE: You ever knowed your auntie to care 'bout somebody being mad at her?

ADDIE: N'ome.

GOLDIE: Well, then! Let 'em be mad and sad, and scratch up their ass til they get glad. They daddy! Which one of 'em over there calling him "daddy?" I 'members the time he was Old-Low-Down-Peckerwood-Cecil-Morrow and any other name they could think of, but they was too chicken-shit to say it to his face, too busy putting me up to doing it.

[ADDIE *busies herself with tasks, performed routinely for her aunt: emptying wastebaskets, dusting.*]

ADDIE: When I was little, I remember I used to hear y'awl! That's why they could-a knocked me over with a feather while 'ago when Aunt Tootie and Uncle-Cecil-David told me that, all this time, Old-Mister-Cecil-Morrow was y'awl's daddy!

GOLDIE: What y'awl? He might'a been your Aunt Tootie and your Uncle-Cecil-David's daddy, but he wasn't no daddy 'a-mines. The onliest daddy I ever recognized was *Mister* Emmanuel Henry Randall!

ADDIE: I hear you, Aunt Goldie!

GOLDIE: And Daddy Randall is the onliest daddy they ever knowed, too. Would you call some "white grasshopper" daddy just cause he gave you a few nickels ever' now and then ... just cause you *heard* he was your daddy?

ADDIE: N'ome. I wouldn't.

GOLDIE: See, you got sense. Them fools over there ain't got none.

ADDIE: You better tell 'em not to be putting your name on that obituary, Aunt Goldie.

GOLDIE: Say they puttin' my name on the 'bituary?!

ADDIE: As one of Old-Man-Morrow's children.

GOLDIE: My name done already 'peared on the 'bituary as one-a Daddy Randall's chill'un ... how I'm gonna be two mens'es daughter?

ADDIE: I don't reckon you can be, 'less'n you got a holy-ghost daddy.

GOLDIE: Where 'bouts they at puttin' my name on a 'bituary? I'll roll out this bed and roll over 'em like the rock'a-ages!

ADDIE: I ain't calling no name, Aunt Goldie. I just heard a certain person on the phone telling Sister Hayes their daddy ... I mean, Old-Man-Morrow is survived by five children and ...

GOLDIE: H'it was old Tootie, wasn't it? You ain't gotta tell me ... I know that heifer the ring-tail leader ... old ass-licker! I done told her to keep my name out-a her dev'lish mouth.

ADDIE: I ain't saying she called your name, Aunt Goldie, but there's ol' Avrill-Morrow and Miss Pam by the white mother ... where do five come from if they ain't counting Aunt Tootie and Uncle-Cecil-David ... and you?

GOLDIE: I swear on my dead mama's grave, I'll show up at that church-house, all right, but not for the reason they want! I'll stand up and give a testimony'll make they so-called daddy rise up out that casket and curse the day he ever laid eyes on my dark mother!

ADDIE: I know you shore will do it, too, Aunt Goldie!

GOLDIE: You think your auntie is playing?

ADDIE: N'ome. I remember that time Rev. Hill come preaching at every-body about fornicating, and you got up and told the whole church you saw him sneaking out the back door of Sister Leach's house.

GOLDIE: Well, then! I'm too old a cat to be called a kitten!

ADDIE: I was just a little bitty thing, but I remember it.

GOLDIE: That's why auntie don't hardly go to none'a these churches like she used to ... they filled with hypocrites and 'publicans!

ADDIE: You something else, Aunt Goldie!

GOLDIE: I ain't never set-foot inside no white church-house before, but this'll be one time I'll set-foot in one ... they put my name on that 'bituary, you gonna hear auntie preach a sermon they won't never for-get.

ADDIE: I shore would stand by your side while you preached it, too, Aunt Goldie. But I can't pass for white like you and Aunt Tootie and Uncle-Cecil-David, and they might not let me in.

GOLDIE: I ain't never tried to pass for white, me. Old Tootie n'em they walk in a white place just as big-and-bold and act like they white ... I don't wanna go nowhere all my peoples can't go ... I tell's 'em in a minute, I'm Colored and proud of it.

ADDIE: I'm surprised Old-Man-Morrow wanted y'awl at his funeral ... be more likely he'd-a tried to hide the fact he had outside children at all, and especially by a Colored woman.

GOLDIE: Hide it from who? His wife? Ha'ha!

ADDIE: She knew?!

GOLDIE: I wish I had a nickel for every white woman what knows her husband is fooling 'round with Colored womens! He want us at his funeral to get back at her for something ... trying to get back at me, too ... mad cause I wouldn't bow down to him in his life and figure that mess he got in his will gonna make me do it, but he got another thought coming!

ADDIE: This put me in the mind of that big case years ago of that white man in Louisiana, died and left a whole pile of money. His will said his white children couldn't get any of it, either, unless his Colored children came to his funeral.

GOLDIE: So he done tried to copy off-a that! That was him, all right! Old copy-cat!

ADDIE: Seem like he should-a known better then to try to tempt you with money, Aunt Goldie! But I guess he didn't know you ain't never cared nothing for money. Ever' since I was little, I've seen how you just give it away. Anytime one of us needed it, if you had it, we had it.

GOLDIE: I 'member one time I gave this woman the last pair good drawers I had 'cause the rubber in hers had popped. 'Cause I shore don't care. We all come in the world n'eked and although we sees people with clothes on when they gets funeralized, I done heard tell they digs them graves up after everybody leave and takes even them few rags off they ass.

ADDIE: I guess Mr. Cecil-Morrow didn't think you'd stay away and keep the others from getting their money, huh, Aunt Goldie?

GOLDIE: What I wanna put myself out for them for? They ain't never did nothing for me. What little money they do get it all go downtown to that bail-bondsman to get Sonny Jr. out-a jail for something he done got into.

ADDIE: Uncle-Cecil-David gonna gamble his all away ... his'll be gone in a week.

GOLDIE: Sooner than that, honey ... then all of 'em be over here begging me for whatever I had.

ADDIE: And you'd give it all to 'em little by little until it was all gone ... cause you just good'hearted like that, Aunt Goldie ... you good as gold. That's why I'll do anything in the world for you.

GOLDIE: Aunt Goldie shore do love you, honey. You the onliest one understand.

ADDIE: At first I wished you would go to Mr. Cecil-Morrow's funeral so you could get that money. But I'm glad you ain't gonna show up 'cause that'll keep ol' Avrill-Morrow from getting his share. That'll pay him back for what he did to me last week.

GOLDIE: What he done to you?

ADDIE: He goes out to the University now, and last week he saw me scrubbing the floors in one-a the buildings and got a cupful-a dirt and threw it on the floor, then said, "Clean it up, nigger," in front of a whole bunch of people ... they laughed at me.

GOLDIE: Why, that little pissy-ass bastard! Why'n you come tell auntie?!

ADDIE: You always say every dog'll have his day and a good dog'll have two days ... I just asked my supervisor, let me clean inside the rooms.

GOLDIE: Next time he call you a name, ask him ain't he the one shit on his'self when his pappy brought him out here one time, wouldn't c'ary him home to his own mammy to clean, naw, wanted my mama to do it!

ADDIE: Did Grandma Randall clean him, Aunt Goldie?

GOLDIE: Mama was just good-hearted like that ... Daddy Randall always said I took after her, but I know I wasn't fit to eat her doo-doo! When people did mama wrong, she'd forgive 'em ... me, I'd lay in wait for 'em for years, killing 'em in my heart long after they be done forgot about it. Then I'd make 'em sorry they ever crossed me!

ADDIE: One day I'll be walking across that campus with books in my arms, just like ol' Avrill Morrow, cause the papers say Colored can go to school out there, come next semester. I hope he still be going there by the time I save enough money to go. If I had the money, I'd enroll out there now.

GOLDIE: I believes I did see something in The Informer 'bout they gonna let Colored go out to the University!

ADDIE: Come next semester, Aunt Goldie. Miss Kemp's daughter gonna enroll in the nursing school, and Sister Williams' nephew, Isaac, say he gonna study engineering out there.

[*After a beat.*]

GOLDIE: Well, bless they hearts!

ADDIE: I would study the law ... but they say that cost more than any of the other courses, 'cause it's so many books to buy.

GOLDIE: [*A beat.*] Bless your heart! Wanna study the law!

ADDIE: Has anybody in our family ever gone to college, Aunt Goldie?

GOLDIE: None that I knows of. Mama wanted me to go to missionary school, but, honey, I ain't wanna be no nun. And they said I'd have to give up my snuff, too! Bad enough I'd have to give up my chuchie!

ADDIE: I'd give up almost anything to get to go to college. But I wouldn't want you giving up your pride and going to no ol' funeral just so I could go, Aunt Goldie. I'll find a way.

[*A beat.*]

GOLDIE: How much do it cost?

ADDIE: A whole lot, Aunt Goldie ... two thousand a semester for state residents. And I would study hard, day and night ... and make you proud of me ... make the whole family proud.

GOLDIE: That'll show the little puny-ass Avrill something, all right, and make you-know-who turn over in his grave. He didn't mind sleeping with Colored women and having us crying over his casket, but just say white and Colored settin' in a school-room together and he'd have a fit!

ADDIE: From what I heard about him, though, Aunt Goldie—and I know I didn't hear much—seem like he respected the ones who stood up for their rights. Seem like he shore respected you.

[*A beat, as* GOLDIE *communes with some moment.*]

GOLDIE: How they say they planning on gettin' to that thing?

ADDIE: Avrill-Morrow told 'em over the phone a car is being sent to pick everybody up and bring 'em back here.

GOLDIE: No doubt it's gonna be some ol' piecy trap they got off the junk-yard.

ADDIE: N'ome. Aunt Tootie say they told her it's gonna be a Cadillac ... brand new!

GOLDIE: No doubt they gonna put us at the back-a the whole funeral-train.

ADDIE: N'ome. They say Mr. Cecil-Morrow's will want the car with you and Aunt Tootie and Uncle-Cecil-David right behind the hearse.

[GOLDIE'*s muscles twitch reflexively. She averts her look, communes with a private moment.*]

GOLDIE: Think I'm gonna feel something for him in his death that I didn't feel in his life ... humph! I say!

ADDIE: I always wanted to ask you why you hatred him so, but I was scared to. I just figured he must-a done something to you he had no business doing.

GOLDIE: All of 'em should-a hated him, the way he treated Daddy Randall, never puttin' no handle on his name, coming out here like he owned mama ... !

[*This beat is longer than the others, as* GOLDIE *struggles with her feelings.*

ADDIE *is at a loss initially, unsure of exactly how she should respond to a* GOLDIE *she is seeing for the first time.*

She sits next to her on the bed and gently takes her hand.]

GOLDIE: Mama wasn't nothing but a kid when she went to work for him. Everywhere she turned, there he was, even after Daddy Randall married her. Ain't many Colored men wants a Colored woman got white men's chill'un, but Daddy Randall loved us just like we was his'n. Old Cecil-Morrow wanted to get even, cheated him out-a some money, mad cause he married mama. What could a Colored man do back then? He didn't have no rights a white man was bound to respect. I hadn't even quit peeing-the-bed yet the first time I cussed him. I didn't know what I was saying ... just repeating words I'd heard the grown-folks use. He told mama to beat me but she wouldn't. That let me know I could keep it up, even after he told me he was my daddy. I told him, "You might-a been the one sired me, but you ain't my daddy. If I pass on the road and see you laying in a gully dying, I'll pass on by like I don't even know you and let you die!" Me being the baby, I could get away with anything, but even after I got grown. Tootie and Cecil-David thought he'd sic the Ku-Kluk-Klan on me, but he didn't. I didn't care. Something had a-holt'a me. Mama'd say, real quite, "Don't do evil for evil, baby. When somebody do you evil, do 'em good." But I knowed her heart ... or thought I did ... 'til one day she told me I had ways just like him. I'm shamed to even repeat what I said to my mama. I know I hurt her to her heart cause she just left me to God then. The Bible tell you not to cuss your mama ... and your daddy ... or your lamp be put out in everlasting darkness. That's why I stays in this room, guess I'm just waiting for the lamp to go out ... cause God don't like ugly. He just don't!

ADDIE: [*Quietly, respecting* GOLDIE's *mood.*] Back in high school, Aunt
Goldie ... we had to learn this Langston Hughes poem that put me
in the mind-a you, and went:

> *My old man was a white old man*
> *And my old mama was black.*
> *If ever I cursed my white old man*
> *I take my curses back.*
>
> *If ever I cursed my black old mother*
> *And wished her soul in hell*
> *I'm sorry for that evil wish*
> *And now I wish them well.*

[GOLDIE *weeps quietly.* ADDIE *kisses the top of her aunt's head and*
then enfolds her lovingly in her arms.]

ADDIE: Aw, Aunt Goldie, they forgive you ... both of 'em forgive you ...
I know they do!

[*CURTAIN.*]

David Mamet

AN INTERVIEW

David Mamet

David Mamet's play, *Oleanna*, enjoyed a sucessful Off-Broadway run at the Orpheum Theatre where it was directed by the playwright. It also had a sucessful run in the West End. Mr. Mamet's play *Glengarry Glen Ross* won the Pulitzer prize for drama in 1984 and a film version of the play was recently released for which Mr. Mamet wrote the screenplay. Other plays by Mr. Mamet include *American Buffalo*, *A Life in the Theatre*, *Edmond*, *Lakeboat*, *Reunion*, *Sexual Perversity in Chicago*, *The Water Engine*, and *The Woods*. His plays *The Shawl* and *Prairie Du Chien* inaugurated the new Lincoln Center Theatre Company in New York City. His play *Speed-the-Plow* enjoyed a successful run on Broadway at the Royale Theatre in 1988 and his play *Bobby Gould in Hell* was produced (together with Shel Silverstein's play, *The Devil and Billy Markham*, in an evening titled *Oh! Hell*) at Lincoln Center in the fall of 1989. Mr. Mamet's adaptation of Chekhov's *Three Sisters* was produced at the Philadelphia Festival Theatre for New Plays in association with The Atlantic Theatre Company, and again in New York City by the Atlantic Theatre Company in 1991. Also, his adaptation of Chekov's *Uncle Vanya* has recently been made into a film entitled *Vanya on 42nd Street*. He has taught acting and directing at New York University, The University of Chicago, and The Yale Drama School, as well as being a founding member of The Atlantic Theatre Company and Chicago's St. Nicholas Theatre, of which he was also the first Artistic Director. Mr. Mamet is the author of four books of essays, *Writing in Restaurants*, *On Directing Film*, *Some Freaks*, and *The Cabin*. He wrote the screenplays for *The Postman Always Rings Twice*, *The Verdict*, and Paramount's *The Untouchables*, as well as Orion's *House of Games*, which marked his directorial debut. Mr. Mamet directed his second film, *Things Change* (co-written with Shel Silverstein), in the fall of 1989 and *Homocide* in 1991. His feature screenplay, *We're No Angels*, was released by Paramount in December of 1989. Mr. Mamet has completed the screenplays *Ace in the Hole* and *Deerslayer* for Paramount, and *High and Low* for Universal. He wrote the screenplay *Hoffa* for Twentieth Century, Fox, which stars Jack Nicholson; and his latest work, *The Cryptogram*, which was first produced in London, had its US premiere at the American Repertory Theatre. It was also performed Off-Broadway at the Westside Theatre and received the Obie Award for Best New American Play. Currently, David Mamet's one act play *An Interview* is running off Broadway at the Variety Arts Theatre as part of *Death Defying Acts*.

CHARACTERS:
  A Lawyer
  An Attendant

SCENE:
  At rise: a LAWYER *and an* ATTENDANT, *sitting in hell.*

ATTORNEY: Well. Alright. Shall we begin? [*Pause.*] Mmm? No? [*Pause.*] What is the issue? [*Pause.*] Alright. Is, um, well, fine. I'll begin. Fine. Did, I, I *put* it to you: did I not serve others well.

ATTENDANT: … did …

ATTORNEY: Yes. Did I not act *honorably*, and …

ATTENDANT: … did

ATTORNEY: … I'm not finished.

ATTENDANT: Forgive me.

ATTORNEY: … honorably, in the discharge of *all* duties *remotely* contained under the Laws Governing Agency.
  [*Pause.*]

ATTENDANT: I'm afraid you'll have to expl …

ATTORNEY: … did I not?

ATTENDANT: … Did …

ATTORNEY: … in all matters affecting the Welfare of Another.

ATTENDANT: … waal …

ATTORNEY: … excuse me, *which he had put in my charge.*

ATTENDANT: … which he had put in your charge.

ATTORNEY: Yes. Professional, or personal, or … [*Pause.*]

ATTENDANT: For example?

ATTORNEY: Well, well, they're not lacking.

ATTENDANT: Alright. [*Pause.*]

ATTORNEY: An example?

ATTENDANT: Yes.

ATTORNEY: Alright. An Example—of acting in others' best interest. For example: Fine: A Loan.

ATTENDANT: A Loan. Of … ?

ATTORNEY: … of … of … of. A loan, of: a *lawnmower.*

ATTENDANT: Alright.

ATTORNEY: ... When ...

ATTENDANT: ... did someone actually loan you a lawnmower?

ATTORNEY: ... did they ...

ATTENDANT: ... yes.

ATTORNEY: I'm sure they did. I ...

ATTENDANT: ... can you ... I don't mean to *antagonize* you ...

ATTORNEY: Go on ...

ATTENDANT: ... but ...

ATTORNEY: Did they Loan Me a Lawnmower.

ATTENDANT: Yes.

ATTORNEY: ... in contradistinction to, to ...

ATTENDANT: ... to your...

ATTORNEY: ... my, yes, my merely *hypothesizing* such a loan, as ...

ATTENDANT: ... that's right.

ATTORNEY: ... an example of ...

ATTENDANT: ... that's right.

ATTORNEY: ... a picturesque example of ...

ATTENDANT: ... the "sort" of transaction ...

ATTORNEY: ... yes. yes. yes. Did Someone Loan Me a Lawnmower. [*Pause.*] I am prepared to ... I don't know. I don't ... wait. I don't know. I am prepared to *stipulate*, mmm? Whichever you ...

ATTENDANT: ... I don't ...

ATTORNEY: ... that I *did*, or *didn't* ...

ATTENDANT: ... didn't... ?

ATTORNEY: Borrow ...

ATTENDANT: ... mmm?

ATTORNEY: You see?

ATTENDANT: No.

ATTORNEY: I am prepared to ... whichever you, ... *choose*. Do you see? Choose. Choose. Mm? I don't remember. [*Pause.*] I don't remember, *if, in fact,*

ATTENDANT: ... but ...

ATTORNEY: Yes. Alrig ... yes. Fine. Alright. I *was* lent a lawnmower.

ATTENDANT: You were.

ATTORNEY: Yes.

ATTENDANT: You were?

ATTORNEY: Yes. How about that. In my youth. It seems. I mowed "lawns" with it. Yes. I did. I borrowed a neighbor's "lawnmower" on one occasion.

ATTENDANT: Why?

ATTORNEY: Well, it would have been mine was broken ...

ATTENDANT: ... mmm ...

ATTORNEY: ... and I'm sure that I returned it, in Better Shape—no, I won't be grandiose—in a state *as good as* that in which I'd found it. And I'll Tell you Why! That man, my Father's Friend, the man next door, from whom I'd borrowed it—isn't it strange what we recur to? As I *took* it, I told him. "I'll treat it like it was my own." And he said, "No. Treat it as if it's mine." Now: can I think that that comment didn't *influence* me? Over the Years ... ? And I cite the Very Fact that it was buried, to support my thesis.

[*Pause.*]

ATTENDANT: What was buried?

[*Pause.*]

ATTORNEY: I'm sorry?

ATTENDANT: What was buried? [*Pause.*] The Lawnmower?

[*Pause.*]

ATTORNEY: You're joking.

ATTENDANT: What?

ATTORNEY: You're joking.

ATTENDANT: No.

[*Pause.*]

ATTORNEY: ... was the lawnmower buried?

[*Pause.*]

ATTENDANT: Yes.

[*Pause.*]

ATTORNEY: ... you're joking. [*Pause.*] Who would bury a lawnmower? [*Pause.*] Do you see my point?

ATTENDANT: Who'd Bury a Lawnmower?

ATTORNEY: Yes.

ATTENDANT: I don't know. [*Pause.*] Who *would* bury a lawnmower?

ATTORNEY: [*Pause.*] No one I know.

ATTENDANT: But you said that it was buried.

ATTORNEY: ... mm ...

ATTENDANT: ... you said ...

ATTORNEY: I said the *comment* was buried.

ATTENDANT: ... the comment.

ATTORNEY: Yes.

ATTENDANT: What comment?

ATTORNEY: The "thing" the man said.

ATTENDANT: It was buried.

ATTORNEY: Yes.

ATTENDANT: What do you mean?

ATTORNEY: ... it ... I *forgot* about it.

ATTENDANT: Yes. I'm sorry. I've forgotten it, too. Could you ...

ATTORNEY: He Said "treat it As If It Were Mine."

ATTENDANT: Yes. Yes. Yes. I'm ... he lent you the lawnmower, and *you* said ...

ATTORNEY: I said I'd treat it as if it were my own.

ATTENDANT: Yes.

ATTORNEY: And *he* said: "No. No. Treat it as if it were *mine*." [*Pause.*] "Mine," meaning "his."

ATTENDANT: It was his, though. [*Pause.*] It was his ... wasn't it?

ATTORNEY: Yes.

ATTENDANT: Alright. Yes. Alright. So. I see. He meant "Treat it With the Respect Which It Deserves."

ATTORNEY: Yes.

ATTENDANT: He said that.

ATTORNEY: Yes.

ATTENDANT: ... and you forgot it.

ATTORNEY: No. Not *then*. MMM? I forgot it *subsequently*. I *didn't* forget it. I *suppressed* it. Mmm? As in *hydraulics* where the very act of the *suppression* causes it to rise, with greater *force*. You see? In my subconscious.

ATTENDANT: You, you, you found it profound that he asked you to treat his lawnmower with respect? [*Pause.*]

ATTORNEY: I had mouthed a *platitude* ...

ATTENDANT: ... mmm?

ATTORNEY: And he suggested, through *wit*, that that which, to my infant mind, was *meaningful*, might be discarded in favor of a more mature philosophy.

ATTENDANT: He was suggesting that you treated your own gardening tools with less-than-well? [*Pause.*] Was he?

ATTORNEY: Well, he may have been.

ATTENDANT: How did that make you feel?

ATTORNEY: I don't remember.

ATTENDANT: Can it have made you "proud"?

ATTORNEY: No, I can't think so, though ...

ATTENDANT: ... or "Happy."

ATTORNEY: I ... no, no, no, no, I see your point.

ATTENDANT: Perhaps it enraged you?

ATTORNEY: Yes. Yes. I see where you're ...

ATTENDANT: ... and that is why you suppress it.

ATTORNEY: ... mmm.

ATTENDANT: ... and your whole business life has been the effort to repay that man for your humiliation.

ATTORNEY: Heh heh. [*Pause.*]

ATTENDANT: Maybe you did bury the lawnmower.

ATTORNEY: "Maybe" I did, yes. But I didn't.

ATTENDANT: Why did you, alright, then, why did you say "maybe I did"?

ATTORNEY: I was agreeing with you.

ATTENDANT: Yes, but why ...

ATTORNEY: ... I was agreeing with your ... it's a "debating" device, if you will. To agree to the *lesser* ... Abraham *Lincoln* did it. *Cicero* did it. To grant that which can not be successfully disputed, thereby gaining credibility, for those few objections one *may* make.

ATTENDANT: Why could it not be successfully disputed?

ATTORNEY: Why, why could what not?

ATTENDANT: That you had buried the ...

ATTORNEY: ... is that, now, is that what we were ...

ATTENDANT: ... yes.

ATTORNEY: Refresh me.

ATTENDANT: I said "Maybe you buried the lawnmower," and you said as how you'd grant me that, as it could not be successfully disputed. [*Pause.*]

ATTORNEY: Well. It could not.

ATTENDANT: Why?

ATTORNEY: ... because, because ...
How...

ATTENDANT: You could have said "No, I didn't."

ATTORNEY: How would I prove it?

ATTENDANT: Are you suggesting that that which cannot be documented must be abjured? [*Pause.*]

ATTORNEY: Can't we drop it?

ATTENDANT: If you wish.

ATTORNEY: Thank you.

ATTENDANT: ... though you're the one that brought it up.

ATTORNEY: I'm aware of that.

ATTENDANT: ... n'I must suppose you raised it for a reason.

ATTORNEY: Yes, ah, well, no, there's no such thing as "Randomness," that the thing ... ?

ATTENDANT: How would I know? [*Pause.*] Hm. You were saying?

ATTORNEY: I'm sorry. Is there someone else I could talk to?

ATTENDANT: No.

ATTORNEY: I don't *mind*, do you see? Being treated, in the hackneyed phrase, "just like anybody else," in fact, had it been given me to choose I would have *requested* such treatment ... that I *not* be granted special favors. And I am, in fact, *glad* that this is being conducted on a "level playing field." Mmm? Like the Sons of the Rich, I would hate to feel that my *distinction* was owing to factors not of my control. Do you see, and, so, then, to suffer anxiety about whether my preferment was, in fact, deserved ...

ATTENDANT: ... I'm listening.

ATTORNEY: I do not, as I said—nor is it given me, and, I must say, *nor do I feel that I require* preferment, preferential "treatment," or, or, or "grading on a Curve." Nor do I ask for such. But I must say that I feel that the, the, the, the *components* of the interchange, You and "I," in effect, that, it may be said "Are Not a Good Mix." ... where is the shame in that? And, so, I ask if I might, purely at random, do you see—I don't ask, and I *would* not ask, even if it were given to me, which it is not, and which is a situation I endorse, for the reasons—and think it specious of me, if you will, but I believe I've stated my position on them—I do not ask to, to "speak to your Superior," or any of that, that, "Hogwash." But I would like, at the risk of offending you—though why should I, for neither of us has done anything remotely construable as giving offense—I would like to be returned to the "pool," if you will, if such exists, and if I use the right term, to take my chances, being assigned randomly, as I assume it is done, and if it costs me a ... *seniority* of any sort, so be it—to be assigned to another, well, if I may, to another interviewer. [*Pause.*] Might we ... [*Pause.*] Might we do that? [*Pause.*]

ATTENDANT: No. [*Pause.*]

ATTORNEY: Yes. I expected your response, and I endorse it. But: if I might state my reasons ... mmm? No ... ? "I've Said Them"? Hm. Alright. Good. Fine. Well, fine. I've said it, and it "clears the Air." And one lesson of business, I feel and it is in divergence from most Accepted Belief, and, perhaps, for that *reason* has served me so well—it's founded not on *theory*, but on observation is: It Is Not Necessary To Be Liked. [*Pause.*]

That may be heresy to you, I know it was to many in my field. I presume that it conjures images of disgraceful behavior; of *discourtesy*. Of *"rudeness."* But I put it to you: may not an *antipathy* occur from organic and *legitimately* differentiating interests? Of *course* it can. In business ... —what is business but the bringing together of dissimilar, or of *apparently* dissimilar mmm? What? Goals. Is it essential that two parties ...

ATTENDANT: No, you've lost me.

ATTORNEY: What?

ATTENDANT: You've lost me.

ATTORNEY: I was saying ... [*Pause.*] Where did you ... Where did I lose you... ?

ATTENDANT: At the beginning.

ATTORNEY: ... the beginning.

ATTENDANT: Yes.

ATTORNEY: Of what?

ATTENDANT: Of the whole thing. [*Pause.*]

ATTORNEY: ... I ...

ATTENDANT: Why did you bury the lawnmower?

ATTORNEY: *Fine.* I'd like to... "recast" my remarks. May I do that?

ATTENDANT: I don't know what you mean.

ATTORNEY: I'd like to ... to "recast," to "re-*state*" my, in answer to your question, I would like to ...

ATTENDANT: ... what question ... ?

ATTORNEY: You asked me ... you asked me ... you ... you aren't going to help me.

ATTENDANT: [*Pause.*] No.

ATTORNEY: You asked me, you suggested that I *may* have buried the lawn-mower.

ATTENDANT: Yes.

ATTORNEY: and I agreed.

ATTENDANT: Mm.

ATTORNEY: Now, alright, and Why Would I have Agreed, had I *not*, in fact, done that Heinous Thing?

ATTENDANT: Yes.

ATTORNEY: That's your Question.

ATTENDANT: That's one of them.

ATTORNEY: Heh heh. Then we're going to be here awhile. Is that it? [*Pause.*] Is that it? Is that the thing? We're going to be here a wee while, and can go "nowhere" until we dispose of this point. Is that the thing? I've brought it up, and, so, it, what, we have to, is that the thing?

ATTENDANT: Yes.

ATTORNEY: Thanks for your candor. That's it. Let me ask you: what *weight*, then, does the assertion have?

ATTENDANT: That you buried the lawnmower?

ATTORNEY: Yes.

ATTENDANT: What weight?

ATTORNEY: If it were to be proved.

ATTENDANT: How could one prove it?

ATTORNEY: Mmm. Quite. If I *admitted* it ... ?

ATTENDANT: Is it true?

ATTORNEY: Let's just, for a second, say, that, under certain circumstances, I might *say* that it's true.

ATTENDANT: Why?

ATTORNEY: To "move this Thing Along." Eh?

ATTENDANT: You'd swear to what was false?

ATTORNEY: I'd ...

ATTENDANT: ... you'd ...

ATTORNEY: I'd "fib," alright? I'd "fib." You're going to tell me that you don't know what a "fib" is? It's a "lie," alright ... ? It's a "White Lie" ... a "white Lie is a Lie," yes, alright. Yes, yes, yes, yes, and I'm suggesting that I'd do it. What a Bad Man. What a Bad Bad Man. No. Never seen his like. What a Tale for the Boys at the Club. What a sad reminiscence for the odd Commemorative Banquet. "I cannot discharge from my mind the instance, singular, in all my service, of a man, I can not couch it so's to Spare your Feelings ... but ... He Told a Fib" [*Pause.*] *HA?* [*Pause.*] *HA?* [*Pause.*] ... Oh, the hell with it. I buried the Lawnmower.

ATTENDANT: Next Case.

ATTORNEY: Let me retrace my steps a moment.
We live in a World of Norms.
It may be unfortunate, but it is so.
I feel we always have. That norm once supplied by the Church is gone ... "If you act Otherwise than As God Wills it, you are Lost." That's gone.
But let's examine it a moment, if we might.
... I shun the philosophic argument, and proceed to the social ...
That Person who ignored the dictates of the Church did so at immediate risk of social ostracism—leaving, as I say, the question of perpetual, et cetera—Now: that Norm's Vanished, but, but ...
Mass *Media*, do you see, *supplant* it. We are not *told* of Salvation, but *shown* it, and Not To Live Up To That Norm, brings not *guilt*, no. Not *Guilt*, but *Anxiety*. We strive, therefore, to live up to that Norm. Not to do so so to court Anguish. No, I don't think that's too strong a word ... this *second*, where was I ... ?

ATTENDANT: ... I don't know.

ATTORNEY: ... two norms. Alright? Social Behavior. Standards ... all founded, whether the *Church*, or the Lines of a New Car, on—though they may *contain* truth, on, on an *arbitrary*, for what *is* truth?

ATTENDANT: ... what is truth?

ATTORNEY: Yes.

ATTENDANT: What?

ATTORNEY: "What is truth?"

ATTENDANT: Yes.

ATTORNEY: What?

ATTENDANT: Who knows.

ATTORNEY: "Who knows what 'truth' is?"

ATTENDANT: Yes.

ATTORNEY: Who?

ATTENDANT: Who? I don't know. You brought it up.

ATTORNEY: Alright. Is there such a "thing" as Truth? *If* there is Such a Thing as Truth … you see, I say "If," if there is such a thing. If truth exists, then, in truth, I know the truest thing I know is this: I never buried a lawnmower. [*Pause.*] I may have done *other* things. I'm sure that I did. I did things I *regret*, I will go so far, make of it what you will, as to inform you I did things which I *despise*. Which of us hasn't? Does that excuse them? No. Exonerate me? No. Not at all. I did them, I own up to them, if you would like to know what they are, ask me, and I will enumerate them. Does the urge to excuse myself render me corrupt? I do not *wish* to excuse myself. I wish, being human, to "present" myself, "warts And All." *Both* the good and the bad, and to receive fair, if I may, impartial, what, "enlightened"—if that falls to my lot—consideration. Am I willing to be educated? Yes. Am I willing to fawn, no. [*Pause.*] No. I am not. Ask me why, I can't tell you, save that I'm a man. I confess it. I lived, I sinned, I am not perfect. The list of my sins, if compiled …

ATTENDANT: Why did you bury the lawnmower?

ATTORNEY: I did *not* bury it.

ATTENDANT: Who did?

ATTORNEY: Who did? *No* one.

[*Pause.*]

ATTENDANT: How do you know?

ATTORNEY: Because I was there.

ATTENDANT: You were there. When? [*Pause.*]

ATTORNEY: Alright. [*Pause.*] Alright. Fine. Fine. I buried the lawnmower. How Bad is That? I buried it. I *did* it, I'm *guilty*, put it down to my account. I buried it. I did it. Fine. Fine. "Rot in Here." It can't be worse than this.
I buried the lawnmower. [*Pause.*] I stole. [*Pause.*] I … [*Pause.*] I … I subverted the Judicial.
I misused my client's funds.
Process. [*Pause.*] I suborned perjury. I screwed little Dot Callahan, and left town. I don't even know if she got Pregnant.
That's not the lot, but that's the tone of the thing.
Eh? May I go now.
Whatever the thing is. Fine.
May I go?

ATTENDANT: Yes. [*Scribbles on a pad. hands it to the* ATTORNEY.]

ATTORNEY: [*Reads.*] Eternity in Hell, bathed in burning white phos-
phorous, while listening to a Symphonic Tone Poem.
Because of the Things I Had Done. Such a bad man.
Fine. Just, just for my edification. What *particularly*, mm? Cause it
looks to me like a Kangaroo Court. Mm?
To what do I owe this sentence?
Pray, what are they?

ATTENDANT: Two things. Either in itself, excusable. Both, in conjunction, requiring the punishment of Hell: You passed the Bar, [*Pause.*]
and you neglected to live forever. [*Pause.*]

ATTORNEY: You know, prejudice is a terrible thing.
It can take many forms. Sexual, Racial, or, it seems, professional. I
would not have thought it, but here you are prepared to damn a
man because of supposed attributes of a profession to which he
belongs. That's wrong. That's just wrong.
Are you saying there are no honest lawyers? [*Pause.*]
"No comment?"
Well, I'll tell you what. Are you a sporting man? I'll name you one.
By your own definition. You choose. I will name an honest lawyer.
Mm?
And then you apologize to me. And you set me free.
What do you say to that?

ATTENDANT: Go ahead.

ATTORNEY: How much time do I have?

ATTENDANT: We hope that you'll like it here.

Steve Martin

WASP
A Play in One Act

"*WASP* was originally presented by the Emsemble Studio Theater, Curt Dempster, Artistic Director, Kevin Convey, Executive Producer."

"Presented by New York Stage and Film Company in association with the Weissberger Group, RJK Productions, and the Powerhouse Theater at Vassar, August 3rd, 1994."

Steve Martin

In the fall of 1993, Steve Martin's first play, an original comedy-drama entitled *Picasso at the Lapin Agile*, was presented at Chicago's Steppenwolf Theatre. The play was subsequently produced in Boston and Los Angeles, and will be produced in New York City during the 1995–96 theatre season.

Mr. Martin's dramatic writing career, however, goes back much further than 1993. In the late 1960's, he won an Emmy for his writing on "The Smothers Brothers Comedy House," and by the end of that decade was performing his own material in clubs and television. He continued writing for television by co-writing four highly-rated television specials. His talent was additionally honored with two Grammy Awards for "Let's Get Small," and "A Wild and Crazy Guy," as well as a gold record, "King Tut."

Inevitably Mr. Martin found himself writing for film, where his first film project, "The Absent-Minded Waiter," a short he wrote and starred in, was nominated for an Academy Award. In 1979 he moved into feature films co-writing and starring in *The Jerk*, directed by Carl Reiner. He continued his collaboration with Reiner on two other projects while acting and co-writing for Hollywood. In 1987, his motion picture, *Roxanne*, won for him the Best Actor Award from the Los Angeles Film Critics Association as well as the Award for Best Screenplay from The Writers Guild of America.

The theatre of this nation is happy to welcome Steve Martin among its artists and the Best American Short Plays anthology is especially happy to welcome him to our family of contributors.

CHARACTERS:
   Dad
   Mom
   Son
   Sis
   Female Voice
   Male Voice
   Choirmaster

SCENE 1: **Wasp**

   [*A kitchen in a fifties' house. A dining table is center stage, with four chairs around it. MOM sets the table in silence. Around the table are DAD, SON, and SIS. MOM sits.*]

DAD: Oh God in heaven which is seventeen miles above the earth, bless this food grown on this earth that is 4325 years old. Amen.

   [*They pantomime eating. We hear loud, amplified pre-recorded chewing sounds. A long time goes by.*]

SON: Jim, where's heaven?

DAD: Son, it's seventeen miles above the earth. You enter through clouds. Behind the clouds there are thirteen golden steps leading to a vestibule. Inside the vestibule is St. Peter. Next to the vestibule are gates twenty-seven feet high. They are solid gold but with an off-center hinge for easy opening.

SON: Then heaven's closer than the moon?

DAD: What do you mean?

SON: Well, according to my science teacher, the moon is 250,000 miles away.

   [*There is a moment of silence while they contemplate this. MOM bursts into tears. DAD stares at him and starts to chew. Sounds of loud chewing for a long time.*]

SON: Jim, if Adam and Eve were the first people on earth and they had two sons, where did everybody else come from?

DAD: Huh?

   [MOM *stares at* SON.]

SON: Well, if there were only two sons, then who did they marry and where did everybody else come from?

   [*Another moment of silence. MOM bursts into tears.*]

DAD: *Do you like your science teacher?*

SON: *Yeah.*

DAD: *Well that's too bad because he's going to have his tongue pierced in hell by a hot poker.*

[*The phone rings. SIS looks up in anticipation, grips the table.*]

SIS: Oh my god it's Jeremy!

[MOM *goes to wall phone and answers.*]

MOM: Oh, hi June!

[SIS *dies when she realizes it's not for her.*]

MOM: [*Cont'd.*] ... uh huh ... yeah ... really? ... REALLY? Thanks! Bye. [*Hangs up, then to herself.*] Oh great! Great! [*She looks at everyone in anticipation. No one asks her anything. She sits back down.*]

[*Sounds of loud chewing.*]

SIS: Guess what I learned in home economics.

[*More munching.*]

MOM: I went to a flower show today and I just thought it was beautiful; they have the most beautiful things there ... I was with Mariam and she had been before but there was a new exhibit so ...

[DAD *starts talking louder and over* MOM.]

MOM: ... she wanted to go again and she knew someone there and she got tickets for me so I got in free. Normally it costs three dollars to go in so I used the money I saved and picked up a nice arrangement.

DAD: [*Loud and over* MOM.] I want the lawn raked this weekend. No ball playing until the lawn is raked. There's plenty for you to do around here before you have fun. *And I want to see those grades improving.*

[MOM *dialogue peters out.*]

SON: Okay dad, I mean Jim.

[*The phone rings. SIS looks at the phone in anticipation.*]

SIS: [*Frantic.*] It's Jeremy, it's got to be!

[MOM *answers it.*]

MOM: Hello? Oh. Jim, it's for you. It's Mister Carlyle.

[SIS *collapses again.*]

DAD: I'll take it in the living room.

[DAD *exits. Big relax from the family.*]

DAD: [*Offstage, loud and muffled.*] I don't give a damn what they're talking about if they can't meet us then we've got to reconsider the whole arrangement. There's no sense in doing what we talked about unless we're willing to do it without a contract and I don't want to see the situation turn around unless we want it to turn around ...

[MOM, SIS, *and* SON *begin to quake, rattling dishes and cutlery. MOM starts to clear dishes, shaking her way with cups and saucers to the sink. Phone call is over.*]

SON: [*Relieved, trying to make conversation.*] Where's the dog?

SIS: Yeah, what happened to Coco? I haven't seen her in about two days. And it's not like she comes back at night, the food's always left in the dish.

MOM: She just wouldn't stay off the furniture so I put her to sleep.

[SIS *stares horrified into space.* DAD *returns, sits.*]

DAD: Where's grandmom. We haven't heard from her in about a week.

[*All the kids look horrified at* MOM. MOM *looks guilty, shifts uncomfortably.*]

MOM: [*Then:*] In Europe they eat the salad after the main course and that's what we're doing tonight.

DAD: [*Incredulous.*] Salad *after* the main course?

SON: Weird.

MOM: Here it is ...

[MOM *brings out huge cherry jello ring with fruit bits on it.* DAD *looks into the cherry ring and points to a piece of fruit.*]

DAD: What's that on top?

MOM: Mango.

[SON *stifles a vomit.*]

SIS: Eyew. I don't think I want any salad. May I be excused? I have to go to choir molestation.

MOM: Okay, you run off.

DAD: I'll have a little piece.

[*He takes a piece, carefully cutting around and avoiding the mango.* MOM *starts to cut a piece for* SON.]

SON: I don't think I want any either, Mom.

[DAD *glares at him.*]

SON: [*Cont'd.*] Okay just a little piece. [*Bows his head and utters to himself:*] No Mango, no mango, no mango ...

[MOM *carefully cuts him a piece.* SON'*s eyes widen in terror as she gives him the piece with the Mango in it. He thinks about it for a second and starts rubbing his forehead rapidly back and forth with his hand. He continues to do this during next dialogue.* MOM *takes out a letter and sets it nervously on the table.*]

DAD: What's that?

MOM: [*Nervous.*] It's a letter from the Chamber of Commerce.

SON: [*Finishes rubbing his forehead.*] Mom, can I be excused? I feel like I have a temperature.

[MOM *feels his forehead with the back of her hand.*]

MOM: My, oh my you sure do. You better go straight to bed.

[*He disappears quickly, not having to eat his mango.*]

DAD: What's it about?

MOM: Well, you know our lawn jockey?

DAD: Yeah.

MOM: They want us to paint its face white.

DAD: Why on earth would they want us to do that?

MOM: They feel it's offensive to some of the negros in the community.

DAD: That's like saying there never was such a thing as a negro lawn jockey. It's really a celebration of the great profession of lawn jockeying.

MOM: They think it shows prejudice.

DAD: Well that's ridiculous. Some of my best friends are negro. Jerry at work is a negro and we work side by side without the slightest problem.

MOM: That's true, he is a negro. Well he's a Navajo.

DAD: But, times have changed. I'll make a compromise with them. I'll paint three of them white.

MOM: That sounds fair.

DAD: Oh hey honey, didn't we have some rope? I wanted to take some down to work the other day, couldn't find it. Phil is going show me how to tie a sheepshank.

MOM: Oh I have it here.

[*She opens the cupboard below the kitchen sink. Brings out some rope. It's tied in a noose. She hands it to him.*]

DAD: [*Ignores noose.*] Thanks, baby.

MOM: Jim, I have something to discuss with you. Maybe you can help. Lately, I've been having feelings of ... distance. My heart will start racing and I feel like I'm going to die. I don't like to leave the house because when I get to a supermarket I always start to feel terrified ...

[SIS, *dressed for choir, enters with the evening paper.*]

SIS: Evening paper's here. [*She exits.*]

DAD: Thanks Judy ... uh Sandy.

[*She turns away; it says "Kathy" on the back of her choir robe.*

DAD *takes the paper, opens it spread eagle, covering his face, and starts to read silently.*]

MOM: ... my mouth gets dry ... my palms get moist, and I feel like ... like I'm going to die. [MOM *continues as though nothing is different.*] And when I don't feel that way, I spend most of the day in fear that the feeling is going to come over me. Sometimes I hear things. I don't think I can live like this.

DAD: [*From behind paper.*] Honey, it's sounds to me like you're having symptoms of fear without knowing what it is you're afraid of. I'm not going to pretend to know how to cure something like that, but I want you to know that I will be beside you while we together figure out how to conquer this thing. I appreciate how difficult your job around this house is. You are deeply loved. I admire you as a person as well as a wife. I'm interested in what you say and if there's anytime you need me, I will stop everything to help you.

MOM: Oh my God, Jim.

[*She is moved. He leans over to kiss her, and although he still holds the newspaper in front of his face, he kisses her through it. It's a tender smooch and he's so moved he closes his arms around her head, still holding the newspaper. Her head is completely encircled in it. They break.*]

DAD: [*Still holding newspaper.*] Hmmm. You still get me excited. [*Brings down paper.*] Now why don't you pour us a drink and I'll meet you upstairs?

MOM: Oh! Oh, yes ...

[DAD *exits. She goes to the cupboard, removes a cocktail shaker, throws in some ingredients, shakes it. She takes out two glasses, one a tiny shot glass, the other glass tankard size. She pours the drink in the tiny glass, then in the large one. She picks up the two drinks, starts to exit, then walks center.*]

MOM: [*To the air.*] Voices?

VOICE (FEMALE): Yes?

MOM: Hello.

VOICE: Hello, Diane.

MOM: Would you visit me if things were different?

VOICE: There would be no need.

MOM: Does heaven exist?

VOICE: No.

MOM: Does hell exist?

VOICE: No.

MOM: Well that's something anyway. Do things work out in the end?

VOICE: No.

MOM: Am I still pretty?

VOICE: Happiness will make you beautiful.

MOM: You've made me feel better. [*Starts to go, then:*] Voices ... ?

VOICE: Yes?

MOM: Is there a heartland?

VOICE: Yes.

MOM: Could I go there?

VOICE: You're in it.

MOM: Oh. Does the human heart exist?

VOICE: Listen, you can hear them breaking.

MOM: What is melancholy?

VOICE: Wouldn't you love to dance with him in the moonlight?

MOM: [*She starts to go, then turns back.*] Voices, when he says he loves me, what does he mean?

[*Silence. Lights slowly fade.*]

SCENE 2: **Lepton**

[*Lights up. SON's room. He sits at a desk with a look of horror on his face. We hear MOM's sexual cries coming through the wall. She finishes. Immediately, DAD comes into the room, wearing a robe.*]

DAD: [*Holding a doorknob sign that says "private."*] Private? It's not really private is it?

SON: No.

DAD: Well let's not have the yablons. Der fashion rests particularly well. I hop da balloon fer forest waters. Aged well-brood water babies. In der yablons.

SON: Huh?

DAD: Oh yeah, you're too young to understand now, but one day you'll have response not too fer-well keption.

SON: Jim, do you think I could get a bicycle?

DAD: Sure you could get a bicycle. How would you pay for it?

SON: Well. I don't know. I was hoping …

DAD: You see son, a bicycle is a luxury item. You know what a luxury item is?

SON: No.

DAD: A luxury item is a thing that you have that annoys other people that you have it. Like our very green lawn. That's a luxury item. Oh, it could be less green I suppose, but that's not what it's about. I work on that lawn, maybe more than I should, and I pour a little bit o'money into it, but it's a luxury item for me, out there to annoy the others. And let's be fair, they have their luxury items that annoy me. On the corner, that mail box made out of a ship's chain. Now there's no way I wouldn't like that out in front of our house but I went for the lawn. What I'm getting at, is that you have to work for a luxury item. So if you want that bicycle you're going to have to work for it. Now, I've got a little lot downtown that we've had for several years, and if you wanted to go down there on weekends and after school and put up a building on it, I think we could get you that bicycle.

SON: Gosh.

DAD: Yes, I know, you're pretty excited. It's not easy putting up a building son, but these are the ancient traditions, handed down from the the peoples of the epocian Golwanna who lived on the plains of Golgotha. Based upon the precepts of Hammurabi. Written in cuneiform on the gates of Babylon. Deduced from the cryptograms of the Questioner of the Sphinx, and gleaned from the incunables of Ratdolt. Delivered unto me by the fleet-footed Mercury when the retrograde Mars backed into Gemini, interpreted from the lyrics of "What a Swell Party." Appeared on my living room wall in blood writ there by God himself and incised in the Holy Trowel of the Masons. Son, we don't get to talk that much, in fact, as far as I can remember, we've never talked. But I was wondering several years ago, and unfortunately never really got around to asking you until now, I was wondering what you plan to do with your life.

SON: Well …

DAD: Before you answer, let me just say that I didn't know what I wanted to do with my life until I was twenty-eight. Which is late when you want to be gymnast, which by the way, I gave up when I found out it was considered more an art than a sport. But now, your mother and I have seventeen grand in the bank, at today's prices that's like being a millionaire. See, if, you've got a dollar and you spend twenty-nine cents on a loaf of bread, you've got sixty-one cents left. But if you've got seventeen grand and you spend twenty-nine cents on a loaf of bread, you've still got seventeen grand. There's math lesson for you.

SON: All I know is, it's going to be a great life.

DAD: Well son, I have no idea what you're talking about but I want to suggest that you finish school first and go on to college and get a Ph.D. in Phrenology. But let me just say, that no matter what in life you choose to do, I will be here to shame you, unless of course you pass seventeen thousand mark. Then you will be awarded my college sigma delta phuk-a-lucka pin. Goodbye, and I hope to see you around the house.

[*He shakes the SON's hand, exits. SON stays in the room, takes out a purple pendant which he puts around his neck. He then takes out a small homemade radio with antenna, dials it; we hear glitches and gwarks, then the sound of a solar wind.*]

SON: Premier ... Premier ... come in Premier.

MALE VOICE: Yes?

SON: How are things on Lepton?

MALE VOICE: 385 degrees Fahrenheit. It rained molten steel. Now that's cold.

SON: Tell me again, okay?

MALE VOICE: Again?

SON: I need it now.

MALE VOICE: How long has it been since my first visit?

SON: Ten years.

MALE VOICE: Ah yes. You were four and you were granted the Vision.

SON: Yes.

MALE VOICE: So much is credited to the gene pool these days. But the gene pool is nothing compared to the Vision. It's really what I enjoy doing most. Placing the Vision where it's least expected. Anyway, you need to hear it?

SON: Yes.

MALE VOICE: All right. Her skin will be rose on white. She will come to you, her breath on your mouth. She will speak words voicelessly which you will understand because of the movement of her lips on yours. Her hand will be on the small of your back and her fingers will be blades. Your blood will pool around you. You will receive a transfusion of a clear liquid that has been exactly measured. That liquid will be sadness. And then, whatever her name may be, Carol, Susan, Virgina, then, she will die and you will mourn her. Her death will be complete and final in all respects but this: she will be alive, and with someone else. But time and again you will walk in, always at the same age you are now, with your arms open, your heart as big as the moon, not anticipating the total eclipse. They call you a WASP, *but it's women who have the stingers*. However, you will have a gift. A gift so wonderful that it will take you through the days and nights until the end of your life.

SON: I'm getting a gift? What is it?

MALE VOICE: The desire to work.

[*Fade out.*]

SCENE 3: Choir

[*Lights up. Choir practice. SIS, wearing her choir robe, stands on a riser. A CHOIRMASTER faces upstage, conducting the rest of the invisible choir.*]

SIS: [*Singing.*]

> I saw three ships a sailing
> On Christmas Day.
> On Christmas Day.

> I saw three ships a sailing
> On Christmas Day in the morning.

> And all the bells on Earth
> Shall ring
> On Christmas Day.
> On Christmas Day.

> And all the bells on Earth
> Shall ring
> On Christmas Day in the morning.

[*Pause ... she waits with the count.*]

> On Christmas Day.
> On Christmas Day.

[*Waits another count.*]

> On Christmas Day in the morning.

[*Pause. She waits, then starts to sing on her own. The CHOIRMASTER can't hear this and he keeps on conducting 'Three Ships.'*]

SIS: [*Cont'd.*]
>
> *She was only sixteen ...*
> *Only sixteen*
> *I loved her so.*

[*The* CHOIRMASTER *points at her.*]

SIS: [*Cont'd.*] *On Christmas Day in the morning.*

[*Pause.*]
>
> *But she was too young to fall in love*
> *And I was too young to know.*
> *She was only sixteen ...*

All pink and white and fluffy like a marshmallow. So many desirable qualities. She could have been on a poster in black sunglasses and blond hair. Her pretty ears admired by the choirmaster. All this at sixteen, the weight of the years not yet showing. Entering the stage in a beaded dress that weighed so much she could hardly stand up straight. But she did, this tiny girl from the Southland, her pupils made small from the flashbulbs.
>
> *On Christmas Day.*
> *On Christmas Day.*

I love to sing; I wish I could be a castratti. Boys get all the fun.

CHOIRMASTER: Kathryn ...

SIS: Yes?

CHOIRMASTER: You're not paying attention.

SIS: Sorry ...
>
> *On Christmas Day ...*

I guess pretty pink ears don't count for much. How can I possibly pay attention? How can I possibly focus on this little tune when I am so much more fascinating? Those who pass within the area of my magnetism know what I'm talking about. My power extends not just to the length of my arms but all around me when I pass in the hallways, lockers, to those who hear my voice. I am a flame and I bring myself to the unsuspecting moths. Unnaturally and strangely the power ceases when I'm home. There, my sphere of influence stays within here [*She indicates her head.*], all within. It's all silent in the presence of my mother and father and brother. What they don't realize is that one idea from *this* little mind changes the course of rivers. Not to mention families.

CHOIRMASTER: Kathryn!

SIS: Sorry. [*Pause.*] I know from where my salvation will come. I will give birth to the baby Jesus. The baby Jesus brought to you by Kathryn, the near virgin. I will have to buy swaddling clothes. The sweet baby Jesus, the magician. He will wave his hand and the dishes will wash themselves and he will wave his other hand and the water on the dishes will bead up and rise to the heavens in a reverse dish-drying rain. *I* will put them away. And I will sweetly cradle him. People will come to him for miracles and I will look proudly on. He will grow and become my husband, the true virgin and the near-virgin. Both of us perfectly unspoiled, perfectly true. He couldn't work the miracles without me. I would run the mini-mart and be the inspiration, the wife of Jesus. And at the end of our lives, he would become the baby Jesus again and I would put him in the swaddling clothes and carry him upward, entering heaven in a beaded dress that weighed so much she could hardly stand up straight. But she did, this tiny girl from the Southland, her pupils made small from the flashbulbs.

> *On Christmas Day.*
> *On Christmas Day.*
>
> *I saw three ships a sailing*
> *On Christmas Day in the morning.*

CHOIRMASTER: Kathryn, see me after class.

SIS: Finally.

[*Lights down.*]

SCENE 4: Ye Faithful

[*Lights up. Christmas morning around a tree. Several presents lie under it; a shiny bicycle stands next to it with a small ribbon around the handlebars. SON enters.*]

SON: Yeah!

[DAD *enters in his robe.*]

DAD: Aren't you going to open it?

[SON *unwraps the ribbon.*]

SON: Great bicycle! Thanks Jim!

DAD: Well, that was a nice little seven story building you put up, Son.

SON: Did you really think so?

DAD: Well, you're no Frank Lloyd Wright.

[SIS *enters.*]

SIS: Christmas already? Wasn't it just Christmas?

[*She goes over and casually starts tearing open presents. MOM enters, carrying an elaborate Christmas goose on a tray.*]

MOM: Good Morning!

EVERYBODY: Not really hungry ... I'm full, I had some cereal, etc.

MOM: [*Cheery.*] Fine!

DAD: How would all you kids like to take a trip to Israel? [*They stare at him.*] Well, all that history, going back 4325 years. All the big names: Moses, David, Solomon, Rebecca, Daren, Sasafrass. See the manger, the tablets with the ten commandments.

SON: Wow!

DAD: Not the originals of course, those are put away. Since it's Christmas, what if we went through those commandments? Who can name them? Huh?

SON: Thou shalt not kill? Thou shalt not lie ...

DAD: Right. *Numero uno* and *numero duo*. Don't kill, don't lie. Good advice around the home.

MOM: Don't worship false gods?

DAD: Exactly. Now who can tell me what that means?

SON: Uh ...

MOM: Don't know.

[SIS *shrugs her shoulders.*]

DAD: Well, you know, false gods. Don't worship 'em. What's another?
[*They all think.*]

SON: How about, thou shalt not commit adultery?

[DAD *goes into a coughing fit.*]

DAD: Next.

SIS: Don't change horses in the middle of the stream.

DAD: Good one, peanut. If you start out as one thing, don't end up another thing. People don't like it.

SON: Everything's comin' up roses?

DAD: Good, that's six.

MOM: Honor thy father and thy mother.

[*The children cough violently.*]

DAD: Good. Well, there you go. Ten commandments.

SIS: How come it's ten?

DAD: Ten is just right. Fourteen you got enough already. Eight's not enough, make things too easy. But ten, you can't beat ten. That's why He's God.

We got ten fingers, ten toes, and through His wisdom we don't have ten heads. All thought out before hand. Well this has been a real fun morning. Oh by the way, unhappy childhood, happy life. Bye. [*He exits.*] [MOM, SIS, *and* SON *wait a beat to see if he's gone. They all begin to speak in upper-class English accents.*]

SON: Is he gone?

[*The children gather round* MOM *and kneel.*]

SON: Mummy, this has been the most wonderful Christmas ever.

MOM: Well now off you go to write your thank you notes. When you're done, you bring them down here and we'll take each note and set it next to each present you received and we can make sure you've mentioned each gift in the right way.

SIS: I've already written my thank you notes. I did them last week.

MOM: How could you have written a thank you note before you knew what the gift was?

SIS: I didn't mention the gift.

MOM: Well, we'll have to do them all over again won't we?

SIS: Yes, Mummy.

[DAD *enters. The kids break away from* MOM *and they all revert to American accents.*]

DAD: Where are my keys ...

SON: Over there Jim.

DAD: [*To* SON.] Christmas or no Christmas, I want that lawn mowed today.

SON: [*American accent.*] I don't wanna!

MOM: [*American accent, sharp.*] You do as you're told!

SON: [*Faking.*] Oh Mom!

DAD: Christ! Where are my keys.

SIS: [*American accent.*] In the drawer, Dad.

DAD: [*Picking them up.*] How could they get there?

MOM: The butler must have put them there.

[DAD *starts to exit.*]

DAD: What butler?

MOM: I mean, I must have put them there. Did you remember your clubs? ...

[*But he's gone. The children kneel by* MOM *again.*]

SIS: [*English accent.*] I have never understood golf.

MOM: [*English accent.*] Nor I.

SON: [*English accent.*] Nor I.

MOM: [*English accent.*] Scottish game 'tisn't it?.

SON: [*English accent.*] Oh yes, Scottish.

SIS: [*English accent.*] *Very* Scottish!

[*They all chuckle.*]

MOM: Oh Roger!

[*An English butler enters carrying a tea tray.*]

ROGER: Yes'um?

MOM: Oh Good. Tea. Has he gone?

[ROGER *looks offstage.*]

ROGER: Just driving off now, Ma'am.

MOM: We're so naughty!

SIS: You know what I'd like, a big bowl of Wheat-a-bix!

MOM: On Christmas you can have anything you want. Roger, would you be so kind, one bowl of Wheat-a-bix?

SON: Oh I'll have a bowl too!

MOM: Well, me too.

ROGER: Three bowls of Wheat-a-bix. Clotted cream?

MOM: Of course. Clotted cream and oh just bring a bowl of bacon fat.

ROGER: Mango?

SON: Mango? Oh Mummy pretty please!

MOM: Oh you do love your mango. We'll take it in the garden. [*Afterthought.*] By the Folly.

ROGER: Yes'um.

MOM: Go along then.

[*The children and* ROGER *exit.* MOM *is left alone on stage.* MOM *still speaks with her accent.*]

MOM: [*English accent.*] Voices?

FEMALE VOICE: Yes?

MOM: [*English accent.*] Thank you for these moments.

FEMALE VOICE: Would you like to be Italian?

MOM: Oh no, I'm afraid I would burst. Unless …

FEMALE VOICE: Unless what?

MOM: [*English accent.*] Unless, late at night, when I'm with him, you know, sort of, in bed, well, you know. Maybe just for five minutes.

FEMALE VOICE: You'd like to be Italian for five minutes?

MOM: I was thinking him.

FEMALE VOICE: I see.

MOM: Well, I'll be in the garden by the folly. [*She starts to go.*]

FEMALE VOICE: One moment. I have an answer to your question.

MOM: [*English accent.*] Which one?

FEMALE VOICE: 'When he says he loves me, what does he mean?'

MOM: [*Normal voice.*] Please.

FEMALE VOICE: He means if only, if only. If only he could call to you from across a river bank.

MOM: Like Running Bear.

FEMALE VOICE: Yes, as well as Little White Dove. He would dive into the river, swim to you and drown. He knows this. He cannot come close. He would drown. He knows this. The water has no value like it does to you, it is only trouble. He does not know the meaning of the water like you do. Standing on the bank, calling to his Little White Dove, with her so small in his vision he loves her fully. Swimming toward her, his words skipping across to her like flat rocks, he drowns, afraid of what she wants, not knowing what he should be, realizing his love was in the words that he shouted while on the bank, and not in the small whispers he carries to hand to her.

MOM: Is it ever possible for them not to drown?

FEMALE VOICE: Oh yes.

MOM: What makes the difference?

FEMALE VOICE: When the attraction is chemical.

MOM: Chemical?

FEMALE VOICE: Oh yes. The taste of the skin to the tongue. The touch of the hand to the neck. Can the chemistry of the breath across the lips inhibit the chemistry of bitterness. Oh this is too hard long distance, let me come down to earth. [*The FEMALE VOICE appears from offstage, she wears a conservative Chanel suit and holds a handbag. It doesn't strike MOM as unusual that VOICE walks into her living room.*] Chemistry. The scientific combination of the voice and shade of the hair. The shape of the face on the retina. The way the prepositions strike the eardrum: do his vowels produce pleasure.

MOM: I see. Would you like something?

FEMALE VOICE: Oh no thank you. *I can only stay a few minutes.*

MOM: Coffee?

FEMALE VOICE: Well maybe some coffee.

MOM: Cake?

FEMALE VOICE: No thanks. I'm trying to lose a few pounds. Maybe a small piece. Here let me help. [*She helps set the table.*]

MOM: You were saying about pleasure?

FEMALE VOICE: Oh yeah. Uh, where was I? Oh, what I'm trying to say is, sex is the kicker. It's there to cloud our judgment. Otherwise nobody would pair off. Once I slept with a guy just to get him to quit trying to sleep with me. I knew he just wanted to go to bed with anything that moved, so I laid there like a lump.

MOM: Did it work?

FEMALE VOICE: Not really. I guess I was better than nothing. Although I tried not to be.

MOM: I could never do that.

FEMALE VOICE: You're forty. I'm 4325.

MOM: Any kids?

FEMALE VOICE: I have a girl 1100 and a boy eight hundred thirty-five. The eight-hundred-thirty-five-year-old is a terror.

MOM: So, how did you get to be omniscient?

FEMALE VOICE: I went to class.

MOM: They have a class? What do you study?

FEMALE VOICE: Every teeny weeny little thing. We memorize it. Every little rock; every blade of grass. Everything about people, about men, about cats, every type of gravy, ducks. It's one class where et cetera really means et cetera.

MOM: That must be hard.

FEMALE VOICE: It is one son of a bitch. You know what one of the questions on the final was?

MOM: What?

FEMALE VOICE: Name everything.

MOM: Wow.

FEMALE VOICE: When I read that question, my mind went blank. Which is a terrible thing when you're asked to name everything.

MOM: What happened?

FEMALE VOICE: Oh you know, you get through it; I got an eighty-four. Eighty and above is omniscient. Well, I better be going ...

MOM: [*Stops her, concerned.*] So you know everything.

FEMALE VOICE: Somewhat.

MOM: So ... what would it be like if I left him?

FEMALE VOICE: *You won't believe this but that was one of the questions on the final.* Let's see ... you will live in a small cottage. It will be surrounded by a white fence. In the backyard will be many colored flowers. Inside will be small lace doilies like your mother's. You will stand outside on the green lawn, your face up toward the sun, your hands will be outstretched, palms open, and you will *repeat* these words: "what have I done, what have I done, what have I done."

[*Slow blackout.*]

SCENE 5: The Logic of the Lie

[*The dinner table again, the family of four sitting around. DAD's in the middle of a golf story of which the family feigns enjoyment.*]

DAD: ... Phil tees off; lands midway down the fairway but off to the right. With the three wood, I'm about ten yards shy of him but straight down the middle. I can see the flag damn straight up with a trap off to the right. Phil's gotta fly over the trap.

[MOM *and family emit sounds of delighted interest.*]

DAD: [*Cont'd.*] What happens? Jerry eight irons it and flies the trap; he's on the green, I full swing my nine and land right in the trap!

SON: [*Laughs.*] Oh man!

SIS: Wow.

MOM: [*Laughing.*] Man, you don't need a nine iron, you need a hoe!

DAD: So now Phil on the back of the green putts and rolls right past the hole and it keeps going to the edge of the fringe.

SIS: [*Laughing.*] Did he use a eight iron for that too?

[*The whole family over-laughs.*]

DAD: I pop it out of the trap and ... [*Starts to laugh.*] ... the damn thing ... [*More laughs.*] ... rolls right up about ten inches from the hole!

[*They all really laugh.*]

DAD: [*Cont'd.*] Phil three putts and I drop it in without hardly looking.

[*Really big response from family.*]

MOM: Oh ... ha ha ha.

[*She has to drink water and fan herself. The phone rings.* MOM *answers it.*]

SIS: Oh my god it's Jeremy!

MOM: Hello? Just a minute. [*To* SIS.] It's Jeremy.

SIS: Tell him I'm not in.

MOM: She's not in right now. [*Hangs up.*] I thought you wanted to talk to him.

SIS: [*Practically sinister.*] He'll call back.

[*The table goes to silence as* DAD *is lost in thought. He hears the sound of the solar wind. Suddenly he stands up, but the rest of the family can't see him.*]

DAD: Voice? [*No answer.*] Voice? [*No answer.*] Voices? Voice? Typical, nothing. Left here on my own, with only the images of Washington, Jefferson and Lincoln. Hello? Hello? I'm living the lie, I know it. Nothing but the rules of road, the ethics of the lumberjack, the silence of the forest broken only by the sound of the axe getting the job done, the axe never complaining. Truth handed down through the pages of *Redbook*, and the *Saturday Evening Post*. Becoming leader and hero, onward and stronger to a better life. I know my feelings cannot tolerate illumination under the hard light, but when seen by the flickering light of the campfire surrounded by the covered wagons heading west, I am a God that walks on earth. Must be strong, must be strong and in my silence I am never wrong. The greater the silence the greater the strength. And therein is the logic of the lie.

MOM: Butter? [*She passes the butter to* SON.]

DAD: [*Looks back at* MOM.] Her. Once, with one hand I held her wrists behind her back and kissed her. Once, I entered her like Caesar into Rome. Once, I drank her blood. Now I stand at the foot of her bed and watch her sleep, and silently ask the question, "who are you?" Oh, I know what she goes through. She aches with desire. She reaches out for nothing and nothing comes back. She is bound by walls of feeling. They surround me too; but I must reach through the walls and *provide*. There is no providing on a lingering summer's walk. I have been to the place she wants me to go. [*Bitterly.*] I have seen how the king of feelings, the great god Romance seats us in his giant hand and thrusts us upward and slowly turns us under the sky. But it is given to us only for minutes, and we spend the rest of our lives paying for those few moments. Love moves through three stages: attraction, desire, need. The third stage is the place I cannot go.

SON: Jim, can I be excused?

DAD: Finish your meal. [*Back to his soliloquy.*] If I can't be excused, why should he? The denial of my affection will make him strong like me. I would love to feel the emotions I have heard so much about, but I may as well try to reassemble a dandelion. [*He snaps out of it and speaks to the family, back to his vigorous delivery.*] Ninth hole, dog-leg left, can't see the pin.

[*The family reacts with oohs and ahs. He turns, walks back to the table.*]

DAD: [*Cont'd.*] I decided to go over the trees but I hit a bad shot and it goes straight down the middle of the fairway. I don't say a word! Phil [*He starts chuckling.*] ... just slow turns and stares at me with this look ... !

[*The family laughs ...*

The sound of munching resumes as they fall silent. Slow fade out ...

Curtain.]

Elaine May

HOT LINE

Elaine May

Elaine May was a member of the original Second City troupe and part of the comedy team of Nichols and May. She appeared on Broadway with Mr. Nichols in *An Evening with Nichols and May* and acted in the movies *California Suite*, *A New Leaf*, *Enter Laughing*, *Luv*, and *In the Spirit*. Among her screen credits are *Heaven Can Wait*, *Mikey and Nicky*, *Ishtar*, and *A New Leaf*, the last three of which she directed. She has had three plays produced: *Adaptation*, *Not Enough Rope*, and *Mr. Gogol and Mr. Preen*. She directed *Adaptation/Next* (by Terrence McNally) Off-Broadway and the movie *The Heartbreak Kid* by Neil Simon. She is currently working on her apartment.

CHARACTERS:
Ken Gardner
Marty
Dr. Russell
Dorothy Duval

SCENE:

The stage is divided in half by a diagonal platform that angles off into shadow.

Before the lights rise on stage, we hear assorted phones ringing in the dark and voice-overs, people in distress calling in to the Hot Line.

KEN GARDNER *sits at a table on which there are two phones, bathed in a single light. The sound of muted voices, ringing phones, and moving shadows offstage give the impression that there are others at similar tables, answering similar phones.*

As the voices continue, the light brightens and a middle-aged man in a suit enters and walks up to KEN. *He is* DR. RUSSELL, *the supervising psychologist.*

DR. RUSSELL: How's it going, Ken?

KEN: [*With a start.*] Oh! Dr. Russell. You startled me.

DR. RUSSELL: [*Chuckling.*] Scared the hell out of you is what you mean. Let's say what we mean, Ken. If we're going to help others get in touch with their feelings we have to be honest about our own.

KEN: Right. [*Suddenly.*] And I'll tell you something else that's crazy. My phones haven't rung. And I feel it's because they know it's me. I feel they've *decided* to ring for the others because they know they're better at this than I am. I mean, I *know* it's insane and phones are electronic instruments ...

DR. RUSSELL: That's fine, Ken. Be aware of that feeling. Of course, it's not a feeling you'll want to share with a disturbed person. But there can be a lot of resentment when you're talking to someone bent on self-destruction. Recognize it. [*He claps him on the back.*] Then keep it to yourself.

KEN: [*Calling after him.*] Dr. Russell! Do you think ... would it be possible for someone to sit with me for the first couple of calls! In case I run into something over my head ...

DR. RUSSELL: We're all in over our heads here, Ken. Just remember your Schneidman, your training, your seminars, and then follow your instincts.

KEN: Just ... just for the first call? You see ... I've never actually dealt with another human being in trouble. I mean, the ... simulated situations are close, but these are real people. I mean ... someone may actually live or die because of what I say on the phone.

DR. RUSSELL: If you feel that way, Ken, this is not the job for you.

KEN: [*Quickly.*] Right. I mustn't be arrogant.

DR. RUSSELL: Remember that what these people want most is someone to talk to, they want help, otherwise they wouldn't be calling. I'm not going to tell you that a rebuff or harsh treatment couldn't push someone over the edge.

[MARTY *enters from stage left.*]

DR. RUSSELL: [*Cont'd.*] But they're not going to get that from you, Ken, because you're a trained counselor and an intuitive, intelligent human being. But you're not God.

KEN: Right. Thank you, Dr. Russell.

[DR. RUSSELL *claps him on the shoulder again and, as he turns to exit, he also claps* MARTY *on the shoulder and exits off stage left.*]

MARTY: He's a great guy, isn't he, Russell? Sometimes when I get into something really messy I can hear his voice guiding me.

KEN: Yes ... Were you this nervous before the first call?

MARTY: Oh, sure. Listen, we all were. But half the trick is just answering "Hot Line." I don't know why but it opens them right up, makes them feel safe. I don't know why.

[*One of the phones on* KEN's *desk begins to ring. He jumps up, stares at it, and the answers it.*]

KEN: Hello ... Hot line ... That's right. ... That's what I'm here for. Tell me what's wrong.

[DR. RUSSELL *walks on behind* KEN *and stands quietly listening.*]

KEN: [*Cont'd.*] Where are you now, Eddy? ... I see. Well, if you come in off the ledge I think we'll be able to talk better. ... Well, I'll tell you what, why don't you climb back through the window and I'll keep talking so you'll know I'm still here and you don't have to answer. Okay? ... What would you *like* me to say? ... Anything? ... Put down the phone and let's give it a try. [*Suddenly* KEN *raises his voice.*] My name is Ken Gardner and I'm sitting in a room that's about 14 by 10, and I'm behind a table that's about 3 by 4 and I'm talking to you, and

I'm going to keep on talking to you while you climb back through the window, very carefully, because I'd like to talk to you after you get inside and find out what's troubling you. ... And you don't have to rush, you can go very slowly and carefully back through the window, and don't look down, because I'm going to be here, Eddy, talking to you for as long as it takes, so take your ... [KEN's *voice suddenly drops back to normal.*] ... Hello, to *you.* ... Well, good. I feel much better now too. No, that's alright, you rest. That's a good idea. It's exhausting to do what you just did. ... No, no, you call me back whenever you feel like it. I'll be here all night. And I'm proud of you, Eddy.

[KEN *hangs up.* MARTY *and* DR. RUSSELL *burst into applause. Then* DR. RUSSELL *gives a thumbs up sign to* KEN *and exits off left.*]

MARTY: You did great!

KEN: [*Awed.*] I saved a life.

MARTY: It's a great feeling, isn't it?

KEN: I've never felt anything like this before.

MARTY: There's nothing like it. I've worked in drug centers, I've worked with battered wives ...

KEN: It's a *great* feeling!

MARTY: But these people are so vulnerable. It tears your heart out.

KEN: Yes! That's it. The vulnerability. I loved that guy. I've never felt so close to anyone ... in ... in just that way. He was so lost. And I was all he had. I was *it.*

MARTY: Yes.

KEN: *They're* the ones who are nervous. So scared you'll smash their last little hope.

[*The lights have risen on* DOROTHY *stage right and the stage right slider panels have begun to move off stage.* DOROTHY *is looking at herself in a hand-held mirror.*]

DOROTHY: Oh, what the fuck are you looking at?!

KEN: So timid and ... grateful.

[*The stage left slider panels begin to close and the lights fade on* KEN *and* MARTY. DOROTHY *pours two bottles of pills into an ashtray. She picks radio up off ottoman and turns it on. She searches for a station. When she finds one, she pours water into a glass and gets a thought. She turns the radio off and places it on the table. She crosses to phone and dials 411. The lights rise again on* KEN *stage left and the stage left slider panel opens to medium trim.*]

KEN: [*While* DOROTHY *is dialing.*] What would you *like* to hear me say, Hal?

DOROTHY: I'd like the telephone number of the Suicide Center. ... In Manhattan. ... There's more than one suicide center? In Mahattan? ... Well, which one is actually called The Suicide Center?

KEN: ... I don't think you're a bad person, Hal ...

DOROTHY: I don't understand. You mean there are five suicide centers in Manhattan and none of them is called The Suicide Center? ... No, no listen. I want the main suicide center. It would be an emergency listing, like the Fire Station. ... Right.

KEN: No, I don't think that's evil, Hal. Just human.

DOROTHY: ... Well, are all five of them listed the same way? ... Then you're not checking right. Listen, Operator, this is a very special listing, you follow? This is for *morte*. *Yo morte.* So you go now and look for the number of The Suicide Center, not "a" Suicide Center because "The" is part of the name. *"El." El center por yo morte.*

KEN: ... Well, maybe she was upset, too. You know, small things can look awfully big when they all come at the same time.

DOROTHY: ... No, that's not it, Operator. ... You've checked *every* emergency listing? ... So what you're telling me is that in all of Manhattan the only place officially listed as The Suicide Center is a coffee house. ... Fine. Thank you. Can I speak to someone who isn't Spanish?

KEN: I'll be here all night, Hal, so if you start feeling bad again you just call me. [*Laughter.*] ... My name is Ken. I'll be here for you, Hal.

[KEN *hangs up. He leans back in his chair and rests his hands behind his head as the lights fade on him and the stage left sliders close.*]

DOROTHY: ...Yes, you can. I've been trying to get the telephone number of The Suicide Center from one of your operators who can barely speak English and who has informed me that out of the dozens of suicide centers now lining Manhattan the only one called The Suicide Center is a coffee house. Now, I go through this shit almost every time I call Information but I usually let it pass because I go through so much shit every time I do anything that I hate to single out one special group. But this is an emergency. This is the kind of thing where if you don't get the number, you can die. And I don't think you people should hire Information Operators who will be handling life and death emergency cases unless they have some grasp of the language of your customers. ... Yes you can. I want the telephone number of The Suicide

Center. In Manhattan. ... Hello? ... Oh, sorry. I thought you were gone.

[*There is a knock on the door.*]

DELIVERY MAN: Burger shop!

DOROTHY: Oh, shit. Just a minute. [*Into phone.*] ... It's an emergency listing. Like the Fire Station. ... No, it would be called The Suicide Center. Listen, who is this? Are you the same operator I just talked to pretending not to have an accent? ... Well, I don't believe this. You mean you don't have one listing for The Suicide Center? ...Where is that? ... No, that's the number I just got. That's the coffee house.

DELIVERY MAN: [*Knocking.*] Burger shop!

DOROTHY: Wait a minute, will you. I'm on the phone. [*Into phone.*] ... Well, who would know? Who do you suggest I call now that Information is stumped? ... Is that 911? ... The police emergency number, is that 911?

DELIVERY MAN: Should I come back with this?

DOROTHY: Will you wait a fucking minute! [*Into phone.*] ... 911? ... The police emergency is 911? ... Thank you, you moron.

[DOROTHY *disconnects her line and dials 911. As she dials there is another knock from the* DELIVERY MAN.]

DOROTHY: [*Cont'd.*] Shit! [*Hearing busy signal.*] Fuck! Just a second.

[DOROTHY *disconnects her line again and dials* O *for operator. When she hears it ring, she opens the door. The* DELIVERY MAN *enters.*]

DOROTHY: [*Cont'd.*] How much is it ... [*Into phone.*] Operator, I wonder if you can help me. I just dialed 911 for Police Emergency and I got a busy signal. ... Yes, I know that means it's busy. I wondered if you could break in on the conversation for me. This is an emergency. But they're not all as *much* of an emergency. ... No, we can't know that. Thank you. Your simple wisdom has saved me from doing a very selfish thing. [*She disconnects and dials 911. It rings.*] How much is that?

DELIVERY MAN: Seven-fifty.

DOROTHY: For a hamburger?!

DELIVERY MAN: And fries and coffee.

DOROTHY: [*She has picked up her purse and pulled out her wallet.*] ... That's three ... four ... four-twenty ... four-thirty-five ... [*Into phone.*] Answer, you bastards ... How much did I give you so far?

DELIVERY MAN: Four-thirty-five.

DOROTHY: Four-thirty-five? And I owe you seven-fifty ... so seven-fifty minus four-thirty-five is ...

DELIVERY MAN: Three-fifteen.

DOROTHY: ... and another fifty ... and five ... [*Into phone.*] Oh, hi. Jesus, thank God you fellows have an emergency number otherwise the guy who just killed my husband would have gotten away while I called some ordinary precinct. ... No, he stayed here and waited for you to answer. We're watching the Robin Byrd show. ... Yes, it's an emergency. But I'm only going to talk for a minute because I don't want you to trace this call, so don't try to stall me or I'll hang up. ... I'm going to kill myself and I can't get the number of The Suicide Center from Information. Do you have it?

[*She hands the* DELIVERY MAN *a coin.*]

DOROTHY: [*Cont'd.*] ... You're stalling me. ... Yes, you are. ... What's that clicking noise? You're trying to trace this call, aren't you?

[*She hands the* DELIVERY MAN *some more coins.*]

DOROTHY: [*Cont'd.*] ... I don't want anyone from my precinct to talk to me, I want to talk to someone from The Suicide Center. Look, what's the number of the place you call when you're going to commit suicide and they talk to you on the phone and try to get you to change your mind? There was a movie about it with Sidney Poitier about ten years ago and it played on television last month. And there was an article about it in the *Post* a couple of weeks ago. That's the one. And Poitier played the worker. Right. ... Thank you. Just let me find something to write this on. [*She grabs a pencil and a Kleenex from the upstage wall unit and goes downstage to the armchair.*] Slowly please. ... 6-0066. Thanks. And I'm going to thank you in my note. [*She hangs up.*] How much more do I owe you?

DELIVERY MAN: A dollar eighty-eight.

DOROTHY: Listen, this is all I can find right now. But I've got some money here somewhere, I hide it from myself. What time do you close?

DELIVERY MAN: Eleven.

DOROTHY: Oh, good. Well, I'll find it before then ... and I'll bring the dollar eighty-eight plus a tip down to the burger shop. Okay?

DELIVERY MAN: That's alright. I'll wait.

DOROTHY: I have to look for it. Hey, come on, you know where I live. I'm not going to leave town to get out of paying for a hamburger.

DELIVERY MAN: Yeah, but you're calling the cops and you're calling the Suicide Center ... and I'm taking it for granted that you're not serious, but I made less than two dollars in tips today. I don't want to get stuck for a dollar eighty-eight ...

DOROTHY: I'll find you the fucking dollar eighty-eight. And you can shove the hamburger up your ass for a tip.

DELIVERY MAN: Thank you very much. I appreciate it.

[DOROTHY *exits stage right.* DELIVERY MAN *sits reading* People Magazine *as lights fade stage right. The stage left sliders open as lights rise on* KEN *on the phone.*]

KEN: ... Well, I care, Barbara. ... Yes, very much. ... You call whenever you feel like talking. I'm here all night. My name is Ken. Good night, Barbara.

[KEN *hangs up.* MARTY *has been listening.*]

MARTY: You're really good at this.

KEN: It's because I'm not trying. I really feel what I say. You know, I'm not like this in life. I mean, in everyday life.

MARTY: Well, who is? You can't do this twenty-four hours a day.

KEN: It's not that I don't have compassion for people. I do. But I don't ... I don't know what to say to them in life. Sometimes I feel so sorry for someone I can't look at him. You know what I mean?

MARTY: Sure. Because there's nothing you can do for him.

KEN: Well ... I tend to judge myself ... harshly.

MARTY: That's very arrogant.

KEN: Yes. I know. That's what Russell says.

MARTY: He's a brilliant son-of-a-bitch, isn't he?

KEN: He's a good man. I told him I thought he was a great man, but he said it was transference.

MARTY: That's what's so great about him. He has no vanity. Are you a psychologist?

KEN: No, I have an M.S. I was going to stay in research because I tend to be too ... intense about people. I tend to want to help them too much ... to save them. Russell told me to examine those feelings very carefully. It's amazing how much counseling is like Catholicism. You never know whether you're being a good Samaritan or committing the sin of pride. [KEN'*s phone rings. He goes to answer it.*] Excuse me. I have to save a life. Hot Line.

[*The lights fade on* KEN *and the stage left slider closes as lights rise on* DOROTHY'*s apartment on stage right.* DOROTHY *is entering from stage right with an empty coffee can in her hands.*]

DOROTHY: Okay, a dollar seventy-nine ... that's it.

DELIVERY MAN: You don't have nine cents more?

DOROTHY: Fuck off.

DELIVERY MAN: Okay. I hope I haven't inconvenienced you. You know I saw that movie, the one about the Suicide Center on TV.

DOROTHY: Yeah? It was good, wasn't it?

DELIVERY MAN: Excellent. I thought it was one of the best things Poitier's done.

[DELIVERY MAN *exits stage right.* DOROTHY *turns on the radio. She dances over to the wall unit, puts on lipstick and brushes her hair.*]

DOROTHY: [*Singing with the radio.*] "... Those little town blues ..." [*She turns off the radio, picks up the Kleenex with the number on it and dials.*] ... Hi, is this The Suicide Center? ... Is this The Suicide Center? ... The hot line to what? To The Suicide Center? ... Look, just tell me if this is The Suicide Center. I'm not interested in the branch. Yes, but I didn't ask you that. I wasn't interested in that. I just wanted to know if this was The Suicide Center. ... Don't say it again. I don't want you to say "hot" or "line" during this phone call, alright? ... Listen, I just called to tell you that you're not listed. Did you know that? Some asshole Puerto Rican Information Operator told me that there were five suicide centers listed and none of them was you. I had to call the police to get your number. ... I didn't say she was an asshole because she was Puerto Rican. I said she was an asshole *and* she was Puerto Rican. Just like *you're* an asshole and you're not Puerto Rican. See how that works? ... Oh, this is stupid. You're not going to be able to save me. You can't even get the point of a simple story. How are you going to know what to say to make me feel better? ... What would I *like* you to say? ... Are you seriously asking me to tell you what you should say to make me feel better? ... What would be the point? The only reason it would make me feel better is because you knew enough to say it. ... No, I can't explain. Look, let's drop this now. Ask me something else. ... My name is Dorothy. What's yours? ... Ken? [*A pause.*] You're going to have to keep going, Ken. ... I'm fine. That's why I called The Suicide Center. Just called to say that I'm fine. Now I'm going to call the morgue and spread the good news. ... Yes that was a dumb question but we're used to that now, aren't we? ... What are you, a shrink? ... Because shrinks are always doing that. They're always admitting to you how they don't always know the right thing to say, and how sometimes they're wrong, and they make mistakes. They think it gives you confidence to know that even though your

shrink is an asshole, at least he won't lie. ... Oh, do you think that's
an interesting thought? That's interesting. I think it's a dumb
thought. ... Okay, let's drop that now. We're finished with that now.
So what are you if you're not a shrink? ... A para-professional what? ...
Yeah, but there must be an end to that sentence. A para-professional
dentist, a para-professional carrot? What kind of para-professional? ...
Oh yeah? You do this for your whole living? You don't have another
job in the daytime? ... Well, don't get pissed. I thought you guys all
worked on a volunteer basis like firemen. ... You're kidding me.
Firemen don't work on a volunteer basis? ... Oh, yeah, of course. ...
No, no you're right. The minute you said it I realized you were right.
They're civil service employees. Of course. They're like cops. It's just
that I had this idea in my head ... from the movies ... some movie I
saw when I was a kid ... that they were volunteers. Isn't that something? That's really something. Well ... I just learned something
from you, didn't I? [*There is a brief pause.*] So, what do you make at
this job? ... That's pretty good if you're only a para-professional. What
is a para-professional, exactly? Does that mean you know all about psy-
chology and suicide but they only let you answer the phone? ... Oh
what the fuck are you laughing at with that dumb phony laugh. That
wasn't funny and I didn't mean it to be funny so don't try and make
me feel cute. Because I'm not. ... I don't know what's wrong. I just
don't feel like getting up anymore. ... In the morning. In the morning, schmuck. When do people get up? ... Well, isn't that enough? I
don't feel like getting up anymore and death seems like a good way
out of it. ... Nothing happened. Again today nothing happened. ... I
don't know, I guess if everything that happens is just the same as everything else that happens it's the same as nothing happening. ... Well,
then it isn't the same. But it feels the same. ... Yes, it's possible that
it only feels the same to me. I was who I had in mind. ... Look, don't
keep correcting my sentences. I'm not trying to get into college. Do
you want to know how I feel or do you want to know how I think I
feel from your point of view. ... I feel like shit. ... Because nothing
happens. And after nothing happens for long enough you know that
this is the nothing that's going to happen to you for the rest of your
life so why stay around and watch it. Especially when you feel as bad
as I do all the time. ... No I don't think it's sophisticated. I think it's
true. ... Sophistical? Sorry. Hey, are you really this dumb or is this
some new kind of technique to see how fast I'll crack. ... Yes I sound
angry. I went through hell to get this number and every time you open
your mouth you say something so dumb I'm embarrassed to be talk-

ing to you. And I waited until the last minute to call you too because I didn't want to use up my last chance. So naturally, now that you turn out to be this half-wit, I'm angry. ... Well, don't apologize. You're doing the best you can. I didn't believe that for the first ten minutes but you've finally convinced me. ... Well I'm sorry, too. ... No, I'm not. I'm a hooker, sort of. I'm kind of a para-professional. ... Don't do it. I know it sounds like the perfect opening but if you give me that hot line chuckle again I swear to God I'll strangle myself with the phone cord. ... Thank you. [*Suddenly, nervously.*] Hey, am I keeping you on the phone? You must have a lot of other calls. Is it alright to go on this long? ... Oh, okay. ... Well, I'm just too disorganized. If someone gives me a number where I can contact them I write it on a napkin or a Kleenex and then throw it out. Or I write it on the wall and forget to put the name next to it. And I can't set a price. I just can't decide what a good price is. I want something high enough to be classy but not so high it's discouraging. And I let some guy I picked up in a bar the other night give me a check. I didn't even ask to see his identification. And when I looked at it it was no good. ... I didn't look at it until two days later. ... Because I couldn't make it to the dresser. Sometimes I don't have enough to pay my rent and it's all because I don't have any system. ... Yeah, I'm happy with what I do. It's better than answering the phone all night in a suicide center. It's just that I can't handle the paperwork. I have practically no records. That's a catastrophe in a business like this. ... They're all okay. I don't remember them well enough to have a favorite. ... Oh, I guess I'm good enough. But I know I'll never be great. And I'm very bad at small talk and that's a drawback. ... I say as little as possible. "Hello" maybe when they come in and "so long" when they leave. ... No, I don't have that problem with my friends. I don't have any friends. ... Because I'm unpleasant. Surely you must have noticed that during the course of this conversation. Why should anyone want to be my friend? Would you want to be my friend? How would you like to spend an evening like this if you weren't on the hot line. Can you see yourself picking up the phone and saying "I guess I'll call Dorothy just for the fun of it." ... Bullshit. Why should you? Who in their right mind would put up with this crap if it wasn't their job. ... See past what? ... This *is* what I'm like. ... Yes. Always. I'm a little nicer tonight because I need you but that could change in a second if you say the wrong thing. ... Yes, I've "sought help." ... It didn't do any good. He was okay. He never said anything much. Maybe "hello" when I came in and "so long" when I left. Sometimes he would say "See you next week" but then I wouldn't show up. ... Why should he be fucking sure I was going to show up next week? I was the one who was paying. ... You see? You see what? ...You're full of shit. I don't mean anything and you don't see anything. I haven't told you the truth in ten minutes. And even that's a lie. And what do you care? You know no matter what I tell you, when I hang up you'll tell the guy sitting next to you that I hate men. ... Because that's what all you guys say. And you're not smart enough to be different. Christ, how smart can you be if you do night work in a suicide center. Listen, I'm not having as good a time as I was when we first started talking. Maybe seeing you would help. Could you come over? ... Well, I'm an emergency. ... No, I don't want to see someone else. I want to see you. If there's somebody else free to come over, let him answer the phone. I'm sure he can master the technique. [*A pause.*] So are you coming over? ... Not even to save my life? ... Yeah but all those other calls are speculation. I'm *telling* you you can save me. ... No later won't count. I want to see you now. It won't mean anything to me to see you if you don't drop your hot line and come over now. ... Okay, listen, forget it. ... Really. Don't get upset. I know you can't come over. I just asked you out of politeness. I'm not going to kill myself over it. No, I don't want to keep talking to you. Because you can't help me and there's nothing to say. You just want to keep talking because that's what they teach you at Suicide Center Phone School. Just keep them talking. It doesn't matter what they say as long as they don't hang up. Right? Have I got it? ... What are you doing? Thinking about whether or not to tell me if I'm right? Don't bother, I know just how it works. I saw it in a movie with Sidney Poitier. I know the whole training manual. And I know that when you hang up on a failure you tell those you feel closest to that you screwed up. "I kept her on the phone for forty minutes but I couldn't get her name and address." How dare you discuss me with anyone else.

[*Lights have risen on* KEN *stage left and the stage left slider panel has opened.*]

KEN: I won't. I won't.

DOROTHY: Yes you will. And you'll talk it over with your immediate superior, the actual professional, and ask him what you said wrong. And he'll tell you that there's never a right and a wrong thing to say. You just have to feel your way and hope for the best. Your job is to save lives. But you can't be arrogant enough to think you can save them all.

KEN: Dorothy ...

DOROTHY: How dare you think of me as a life you didn't save. I just called to tell you that the movie stank and Sidney Poitier was no better than you are and I think your whole organization is impersonal and full of shit. And I lied to you.

KEN: Just now?

DOROTHY: No, the last lie. I *am* going to kill myself when I hang up and if you'd have said you'd come over I wouldn't have done it. It would have changed everything. You could have surprised me. I would have stayed alive for another ten or twenty years because, after all, if there's one surprise maybe there's another. And you wouldn't even have had to come over. If you'd have said you wanted to I would have let you off the hook.

KEN: Dorothy, please won't you let me keep talking to you?

DOROTHY: No, you can't keep talking to me. You're not interested in me. You're just interested in keeping me alive. Who the fuck are you to keep anyone alive? Who the fuck are you anyway? You're a para-person working in a para-suicide center. And you have just personally cost me my life. You have failed not because you couldn't succeed, but because you weren't on your toes. Another cup of coffee, a few hours more sleep and I could've gone to the movies tomorrow. So think about that tonight, killer. [*She hangs up.*]

KEN: [*On phone.*] Dorothy? Dorothy?

[*Without hanging up he quickly picks up the second phone and dials O. DOROTHY has placed her phone on the ottoman and then she takes four pills in quick succession. She then continues taking pills throughout.*]

KEN: Operator, this is an emergency. Get me the police! ... No, no, don't give me the number! Connect me with the police! ... I don't know my precinct. ... Operator, I'm reporting a murder! ... I know it's 911 but can't you ... fuck it, I'll dial it myself. [*He slams down the second phone.*] You idiot!

[*He picks up the second phone again and dials 911. MARTY enters and sees him holding both phones.*]

MARTY: Got two? I'll take one. Never take two calls at the same time.

[*He reaches for the first phone. KEN leaps back.*]

KEN: No! I ... a suicidal woman just hung up on me. I'm trying to trace the call. I don't want to break the connection.

MARTY: Well, if she hung up on you the connection's broken.

KEN: Yes, but ... it might be easier to trace if ... if both of us haven't hung up. ... Oh, *God!* ...

MARTY: I can hear the dial tone from here.

KEN: I don't believe this. The Police Emergency number has been ringing for three minutes. I could be dead by now. I could have killed someone by now. I probably *have* killed someone by now.

MARTY: Ken, hang up the other phone. You're tying up a line.

KEN: [*He slams the first phone down.*] Oh, shit! That's right. What if she
calls back and my line is busy! It will ring at another table.

MARTY: Right.

KEN: Will you please inform everyone out there that if a woman calls they're
to find out if her name is Dorothy and then notify me immediately.

MARTY: Doesn't she know your name?

KEN: Yes, but she may not ask for me. She may not want to talk to me.

MARTY: Well, then ... what's the problem? Whoever gets her will handle it ...

KEN: [*Grabbing him by the shirt.*] She's going to kill herself, don't you understand? I'm the only one who knows how to prevent it. I don't care who
else she talks to. *I'm* the only one who knows what to say to her to
keep her alive.

[*The phone rings. KEN releases* MARTY *and snatches it up.*]

KEN: Hot ... Suicide Center. ... Dorothy? ... Hold on. [*To* MARTY.]
How do I switch this call to another table?

MARTY: You can't once you pick up.

KEN: [*Into phone.*] I'm sorry, Miss. I'm expecting an emergency call on this
number. Can you call back?

[DOROTHY *has finished taking all the pills.*]

MARTY: Are you crazy? [*He snatches the phone away.*] Hot line.

KEN: [*Trying to grab the phone back.*] No! You've got to clear that line.
Dorothy will call on that line.

MARTY: [*Fending him off; into phone.*] ... What's wrong, Glenda?

KEN: [*Raising his voice.*] If anyone here receives a call from Dorothy,
please notify me at once. Do you hear? [*Suddenly speaking into the phone
he is holding.*] Well, it's about time! Do you realize I've been ringing
this number for five minutes to report a police emergency and no-
one ...

MARTY: Oh, that's terrible Glenda ...

KEN: My name is Kenneth Gardner. I'm a counselor at the Downtown
Suicide Center—666-0066. I need immediate help with a case. Please

call as soon as someone is available. [*He slams the phone down.*] This is
unbelievable. They have an answer phone at police emergency.

MARTY: [*Into phone.*] ... You must feel very helpless, Glenda. ...

[*The second phone rings. KEN snatches it up.*]

KEN: [*Into phone.*] Downtown Suicide Center.

MARTY: [*Into phone.*] ... Well, maybe he was upset, too, Glenda ...

KEN: [*Into phone.*] Sir, can you call back ...

MARTY: [*Covering his mouthpiece; to KEN.*] No! You can't!

KEN: [*Covering his mouthpiece.*] Please! I have to keep this phone free ...

MARTY: You can *not* ask a potential suicide to call back later. How many
people do you want to kill tonight?

KEN: [*After a moment; into phone.*] Hello? ... Sorry, sir. We're ... we were
having a little trouble with this line, but it's alright now. ... Yes, I want
very much to talk to you, Mark. What seems to be the trouble?
[*Covering mouthpiece; to MARTY.*] Get off that line. Free that line.
That's my line. Take that call on your own line. [*Into phone.*] ... I see.
That must have been very painful ...

MARTY: [*Into phone.*] ... Yes, that's a very bad feeling ...

KEN: [*Covering mouthpiece; to MARTY.*] Get off that line before I disconnect
you. [*He tries to disconnect MARTY's phone.*]

MARTY: [*Into phone.*] What's your number, Glenda? ... Alright, Glenda;
you hang in there. I'm going to call you back in one minute. [*He hangs
up; to KEN.*] You're psychotic. And I'm reporting you to Russell
now! [MARTY *exits stage left.*]

KEN: ... Uh-huh. I see. ... Do you have a family, Mark? [*He stares at the
second phone in agony.*] ... I see. How many children?

[*The second phone rings. KEN presses the receiver he is holding against his
chest and answers it.*]

KEN: [*Softly.*] Hello? [*He glances around.*] Uh ... what number are you calling? ... Oh, well, you've got the wrong number. This is a private residence. Try again. You probably misdialed. [*He hangs up; into first phone:*]
... Yes, a depressed person can be a burden, but have you considered
how painful it will be for them if you commit suicide, Mark? They'll
blame themselves perhaps for the rest of their lives. ... I don't think
you *can* take care of it in a note. [*Staring at second phone; under his breath.*]
Oh, please. Dorothy, please! [*Into first phone.*] ... What is it that seems
so hopeless? ... I see. How sick? ... Terminally. ... I see. ... Well, Sloan
Kettering is an excellent hospital. ... Really? How long a waiting
list? ... That long? ... No, I don't know of any oncologists attached

to freestanding clinics in this city, but I believe there may be some in other states. ... Well, why don't I check into this for you? I could call you back or you could call me back. ... My name is Ken. Absolutely. ... Give me until tomorrow. ... Good, because fine work is being done in that field. No, no. Crying is not a bad thing. You go ahead and cry. ... No, I'll wait. I'll be right here on the other end of the line for as long as you cry.

[*He puts his hand over his face and sits listening ... glancing constantly at the silent second phone.*

DR. RUSSELL *comes up behind him, sees he is on the phone and stands watching.*

Downstage DOROTHY *drops the now empty pill bottle, picks up the phone and dials.*]

DOROTHY: [*Into phone.*] This is Miss Duval ... box 72 ... 5. Are there any messages for me?

KEN: [*Into phone.*] Oh! my. Oh! my, my, my. You must feel so bad.

DOROTHY: [*Into phone.*] Nothing? Oh. Okay ... [DOROTHY's *head droops. She hangs up.*]

KEN: [*Into phone.*] ... Yes, I'm here, Mark. ... Good. Now you hold on to that feeling and I'm going to get to work on this right away. ... You bet there's hope. I'll talk to you tomorrow night, Mark.

[*He hangs up.* DR. RUSSELL *steps forward.*]

DR. RUSSELL: I hear you've been having some trouble, Ken.

KEN: Yes. I have a cancer patient, no money, three children, he's on the waiting list for Sloan Kettering but, of course, since they've only given him six months to live he's nervous about time. Can we do anything for him?

DR. RUSSELL: Well, that's out of our province, Ken. But what we *can* do is get him in touch with Cancer Patients Anonymous which gives free counseling to terminal cancer patients.

KEN: I think he was hoping for something more ... positive. He seems to want to live.

DR. RUSSELL: Well, in that case, there's nothing we can do for him. Is this the caller Marty told me about ... who hung up on you?

KEN: No. She called earlier and asked me to come over and save her and I said I couldn't because I had to man the phones. When she hung up she called me killer.

DR. RUSSELL: [*Gently.*] You must feel enraged, Ken.

KEN: Yes.

DR. RUSSELL: And helpless.

KEN: Yes.

DR. RUSSELL: I think you have to remember, Ken, that potential suicides are potential killers. They're powerless and impotent and if you let them they'll make you as powerless and impotent as they are.

KEN: I wasn't powerless. I had a choice. I could have gone over.

DR. RUSSELL: And saved her.

KEN: Yes.

DR. RUSSELL: Ken, that is so arrogant ...

KEN: Please don't say that to me again, Dr. Russell. I don't want to hear that anymore. Either we're answering these phones because we think it makes a difference, in which case we're arrogant, or we're answering these phones because it makes us feel nice and that's really arrogant.

DR. RUSSELL: Don't tell me my motives! I'm not the villain here.

[DOROTHY *gasps and sits up.*]

KEN: I know that ...

DR. RUSSELL: So don't make me one.

DOROTHY: My note. [DOROTHY *grabs a notepad and pencil and begins laboriously printing a note.*]

KEN: I won't. I just want you to help me. Help me find out if a woman named Dorothy ever called here before ... she's a hooker ...

DR. RUSSELL: We get hundreds of calls ...

KEN: Whoever talked to her will remember her. She's got a vicious tongue and she aims for the balls.

DR. RUSSELL: Look, I understand why you're so frantic. You must have felt so angry when you talked to her that, somewhere, you wanted her ...

KEN: I didn't want her to die. I still don't want her to die. That's why I'm frantic. Why is that so hard to understand for people who work in a suicide center.

DR. RUSSELL: All I can tell you, Ken, is that you're over-reacting to this. This is way beyond ...

[*The phone rings.* KEN *grabs it.*]

KEN: [*Into phone.*] Hello?

DR. RUSSELL: Always answer with "Hot Line," Ken.

KEN: [*To* RUSSELL.] Shut up. [*Into phone*.] ... Yes, this is Mr. Gardner. The emergency is a potential suicide victim named Dorothy. ... No. No last name. ... Yes, I understand you can't ... please let me finish. She informed me that she got the number of this particular suicide center from Police Emergency. She called Police Emergency specifically for that purpose. So will you please ask everyone who was on the board or taking messages off the answer phone if they spoke to a woman asking for that information. ... Yes, and please hurry. This is urgent.

[*Downstage* DOROTHY *stops printing her note, picks up the phone again, dials 911, and sits waiting as it rings.*]

DR. RUSSELL: Ken, I'm going to allow you to finish this, but I don't want you to take any new calls.

KEN: [*Into phone*.] ... Yes? ... I just spoke to someone regarding the nature of my emergency. ... May I ask who I'm speaking to now? ... Sergeant Dryer? Sergeant, I'm a little unnerved by your asking me the nature of my emergency after I've just spent five minutes explaining it to another officer. Is this just confusion about which calls have been answered, or is it possible that whoever I spoke to has just forgotten about me. ... Thank you. I'm very relieved. It's about a bomb that's been allegedly planted at Police Emergency. ... No, that's alright. I've already given the details to the officer who called me back so, as you just said, why worry.

DR. RUSSELL: You didn't tell me this, Ken. My God, I didn't know ...

KEN: Yes, I'll hold. That's what I was doing when you got on the line.

DR. RUSSELL: Ken, I ... didn't understand the nature of this call. You didn't tell me this woman was psychotic ...

KEN: [*To* RUSSELL.] Well, now that you understand, I would appreciate it if you'd try and get the information I asked for. Dorothy. Hooker. Vicious tongue.

DR. RUSSELL: Right.

[DR. RUSSELL *exits stage left.* KEN *sits waiting.* DOROTHY *sits holding the phone. Her eyelids droop, then snap open.*]

DOROTHY: [*Into the phone; thickly*.] Hi, I'm calling to find out the name of the officer I spoke to earlier who gave me the name of a Sidney Poitier movie. ... It *is* an emergency.

KEN: [*Into phone*.] Yes. Still holding.

DOROTHY: [*Into phone*.] I promised to thank him in my note and I don't know his name. [*She begins to cry*.] I didn't even ask him his name.

KEN: [*Into phone.*] ...I'm holding for Sergeant Dryer. ...

DOROTHY: ... No I don't want to give you my name. I want his name. He's the only name I have in my note and I don't know it.

KEN: [*Into phone.*] ... Hello, Sergeant Dryer. Yes? ...

DOROTHY: [*Into phone.*] ... Yes, but I'll only hold for 30 seconds because I don't want you to trace this call. Hello? One-one thousand ...

KEN: [*Into phone.*] ... That's why I'm trying to find her, Sergeant. She's a potential suicide who claims she's planted several bombs around the city, some at Police Emergency and others in the private homes of specific policemen.

DOROTHY: [*Counting the seconds.*] ... Five-one thousand, six-one thousand, seven-one thousand ...

KEN: [*Into phone.*] ... From my experience as a Hot Line Counselor I don't think it was idle boasting. ... Yes, if we can locate her I'm pretty sure I can get it out of her, but not if she commits suicide first.

DOROTHY: ... Ten-one thousand ...

KEN: Right.

DOROTHY: ... Eleven-one thousand ...

KEN: Good.

DOROTHY: Twelve-one thousand.

KEN: Keep checking.

[MARTY *enters from stage left.*]

MARTY: Ken, I'm really sorry. I didn't know ...

[DR. RUSSELL *enters from stage left.*]

DR. RUSSELL: No luck! No one remembers her.

KEN: [*Into phone.*] ... Yes, Sergeant. ... Let's hear it. ... What time was that? ... Yes, that would be about the right time. ... Yes! That's her! ... Definitely. She mentioned the Poitier movie to me too.

DR. RUSSELL: They should start evacuating the emergency center ...

DOROTHY: ... Sixteen-one thousand, eighteen-one ... seventeen-one thousand ...

KEN: ... Now? Is he talking to her now? ... Well, put him the fuck on with her before the thirty seconds are up. ... No, don't mention the bombs. I'll handle the bombs. Just get him on before she hangs up. ... Are you tracing it now? ... How long does it take? ... That long? ... Tell him to talk to her about ... anything. Tell him to spell out his name, tell him to make up a middle name, tell him to spell out his rank and precinct. ... Is there some way you can tie me into the line so I can talk to her? I think I can get her name and address. I know what to say now. ... Yes, but it's my specialty. I've been doing it for years. ... Right. [*Without hanging up, he picks up the second phone and dials; then speaks into the first phone.*] Okay, it's ringing. [*Into second phone.*] Operator, the Police have told me ... Oh. Okay. [*Into first phone.*] The operator says she's talking to you. ... Right.

DR. RUSSELL: What's happening? Have they tied you into her line yet?

KEN: Not yet.

MARTY: What are they doing?

KEN: I don't know. Hello? Hello? Hello! Goddamit!

DOROTHY: ... Twenty-five-one thousand, twenty-seven-one thousand ...

KEN and DOROTHY: Twenty-eight-one thousand.

KEN: Hello!

DOROTHY: Hello?

KEN: Hello? Dorothy? This is Ken. *Surprise!*

DOROTHY: Ken ...

KEN: Tell me where you live, Dorothy. I'm coming over.

DOROTHY: I can't ...

KEN: You fucking tell me where you live! I found you. You owe me another twenty years of your life, because if there's one surprise, maybe there's another. Now tell me where you live.

DOROTHY: 120 ... 26th street ...

KEN: East or West? Dorothy? East or West?

DOROTHY: East ... [*Her head droops.*]

KEN: Alright now listen to me. [*He shouts.*] Listen to me!

DOROTHY: [*Her head jerks up.*] East ...

KEN: Do you have coffee? Dorothy?

DOROTHY: [*She looks over at the cardboard container from the Burger Shop.*] S'too far ...

KEN: You can reach it.

DOROTHY: S'too far ...

KEN: Do it, Dorothy. Just *do* it. And I'll keep talking. I'll talk very loud so you can hear me.

[*She looks over at the cardboard container on the table as* KEN *continues speaking.*]

KEN: [*Very loud.*] My name is Ken Gardner and I'm sitting here talking
   to you, and I'm going to keep on talking to you for as long as it takes
   because I found you, I found you, I found you ...
   [*As he speaks* DOROTHY's *hand struggles to reach the coffee container,
   the lights begin to fade and the voices of the other counselors come up over*
   KEN's.]

1ST VOICE: "You sound very upset, Paul. What's wrong?"

2ND VOICE: "Hot line. ... I see. Why don't you tell me what's wrong?"

3RD VOICE: "Hot line. ... Yes, I am. ... Well, that's what I'm here for.
   Tell me about it. ..."

Max Mitchell

LIFE SUPPORT

Max Mitchell

Max Mitchell left his native Canada to study acting with Uta Hagen and got hooked on the Big Apple. Performing on stage for many years before turning to writing, he is the winner of the 1988 Ann White Play Contest, a 1989 Edward Albee Fellowship and was a finalist in the 1991 and 1994 Writers Film Project. His stage plays have been performed in New York, Florida, and Los Angeles. He lives in West Hollywood.

Life Support was first produced at West Coast Ensemble in Hollywood, Les Hansen, Artistic Director. It starred Forrest Witt and was directed by Fred Gorelick.

This play is dedicated to the memory of David G. Marriage who said it was possible.

CHARACTERS:
  David
  Patrick

AT RISE:
  A hospital room. A man lies on a bed with tubes sticking in his arms and a machine connected. He is unconscious, his eyes closed.

MAN'S VOICE: [*O.s.*] I'll bring it back!

[*PATRICK, late thirties, enters pushing a wheel chair full of bags. He wears a silk shirt and tie.*]

PATRICK: ... later.

[*He looks at the man in the bed and nods his head. He crosses to the man in the bed and kisses him on the forehead.*]

PATRICK: Today's the big day. [*He lifts the blankets to look under.*] Just as I thought. You're not even dressed. Typical. I go to a lot of trouble to organize a party and you don't even care. Typical. Well, I brought some of your friends. [*He takes an urn out of one of his bags.*] Since his untimely death, Michael's been to London, Palm Springs, Fire Island, and twice to Barney's half price sale. [*To the urn.*] Haven't you, Michael? More than when you were living. Say, hello to David. Hello. Hello. Hello. Here, you sit over here. [*He puts the urn on the bedside table and takes another urn out of another bag.*] And, of course, your friend, Bruce. Hello. Hello. They won't travel in the same bag. You sit over here and try to get along. [*He places Bruce's urn on the bedside table on the opposite side of the bed. He takes some decorations out of the bag.*] I spoke to your doctor. She said nothing's changed. We thought maybe you ... well. Typical. [*He holds up some streamers and balloons.*] Do you like these colors? Knowing you, I should've hired a decorator but on what I make I'd have to ... but then, I never met a decorator I'd wanna' ... Oh, I brought your favorite flowers. [*He takes some fresia out of one of the bags, smells them.*] They smell like heaven. [*He places them in a vase and then goes about tacking up streamers.*] I went to that Course in Miracles and they said death is just another part of life. Well, what have we all been so upset about? Right? Doesn't really matter one way or the other. Dead, alive, just as good. Well, look at Michael and Bruce. They travel, get to the important sales, don't have to work, I suppose it's not a bad ... death at all. I do all the work. Course, you don't either, but still, you're ... [*He stops and speaks directly to* DAVID.] I mean they don't even listen, they're above it all ... but you ... are you listening,

Sweetheart? [*He begins to blow up a couple of balloons. He speaks between puffs.*] No ... of course not ... typical ... we have to be out by one ... it's like the damn Best Western. Speaking of Best Western, I'm taking the towels ... I know ... but with what your insurance pays for the room, the towels should be included ... and thicker ... soon be fourth of July ... would you like to go to the island ... we're going ... can't miss an invasion ... there ... starting to look festive, huh? ... oh, your favorite ... [*He takes a bottle of champagne and four champagne flutes out of a bag and puts them on the table, one by each urn.*] ...champagne ... I didn't get the cheap stuff, so shutup ... they can't hold their booze anymore, but if I don't give them a glass, they act like two-year-olds. You know how it is. Bruce has a stemware fetish. [*He attempts to pop the cork. When it's corked, he pours four shots.*] I didn't know what to wear, so I put on your clothes. The tie I gave you for Christmas. And your silk shirt. I've never done this before. It's not something anybody gets to do ... much. They say it's an act of love. I don't know how they got to that. Do you? Those course in miracles people ... they've probably reframed it ... reconceptualized it ... so it's like a christening or something ... What, Michael? Oh, you're right. Toast. Toast. [*He raises his glass. Party time.*] To a wonderful man who used to be ... [*Pause. He puts his glass down.*] I called your parents. Three times. Last time your father wouldn't come to the phone. I told them to come. I told them this was their last chance. They just don't wanna' hear anything. Anything. I told your father if he didn't come and visit you that I'd move to Alberta and rent the house across the street. And tell everyone I was their son-in-law. They didn't think it was funny. Well, fuck 'em. Right? It's beyond me. If they hadn't given birth to you, I wouldn't believe they were humans. I forgot ... the President ... the President sent a telegram. [*He takes a piece of paper from his pocket.*] "Dear David, on this momentous occasion, the First Lady and I hope that you party hard." That's just the White House. What did I do with Buckingham Palace? It's ... never mind. [*He raises his glass once more.*] To you. To a sweet beautiful guy who ... I miss. I can't sleep, you know. Can't decide which side of the bed to stay on. I take them ... [*Points at urns.*] ... to bed with me ... and I wear your ... I wear your t-shirts to bed ... [*Breaks down.*] ... so I can feel close to you ... so I can sleep. [*He pulls himself up.*] But soon you'll be home and we'll sleep together every night, just like before, and I'll hold you against my cheek the whole night just like before, and we'll be happy. [*He takes a new urn out of the bag. He places it beside the bed. Beat.*] I suppose it might be construed as bad taste to show you your urn before you ... but I saw this one, I liked it, it was … okay, it was on sale … and if I didn't buy it this week, I'd have to pay thirty-five dollars more. I know, typical. You like it? It's Limoges. You love Limoges. I hope it fits. I'd hate to have to put the overflow in a drawer or something. [*He examines the machine.*] The doctor told me how it's done, I guess this is the … [*He touches one of the buttons. Beat. Seriously. He looks up.*] God? Can't you make a miracle? Just this once? Why him? What did he ever do to anybody? He signalled all his turns and gave money to the homeless and … God? Are you sure I'm supposed to do this? God? I can't hear you. Okay. Okay. I know. [*He walks to* DAVID *and speaks into his ear.*] Are you ready? [*Nothing. He takes a party hat from a bag and puts it on* DAVID's *head. He puts a hat on each of Michael and Bruce's urns. He puts one on himself.*] I forgot the hats. Aren't they horrible? Oh, well. We're going for that cheap frivolité. Make it fun. Right? Right. There. Out with a bang. You'll like it on the other side. No muss, no fuss, they say. Right, Guys? You'll all be together. I'll be the one alone. Typical. [*Beat.*] But none of me. It's your party. The music! I'm such a mess. I can't remember anything. [*He takes a cassette tape from his pocket and puts it in a ghetto blaster that sits on the table. He sits on the bed, takes another drink of champagne, finishes it, and drinks from one of the other glasses.*] Excuse me. [*He looks at* DAVID.] I won't say goodbye. I hate goodbyes. You're just changing shape. You'll just be easier to carry. But if there was anything I could do to bring you back to the way you were five years ago … when we were happy just to sit on the couch holding hands and watch the news … [*He loses control.*] … I would. But I'm not that strong. I'm sorry. I'm not that strong. [*Regaining it.*] Let's just get on with it. Okay? Okay. [*He goes to the machine. He reaches for a switch and hesitates.*] No. No. No. [*Beat. He looks at* DAVID.] I don't think I can do this. Can't you just … do it yourself? [*Beat.*] Where is an incompetent nurse when you need one? Maybe I shouldn't. Maybe I … [*Beat. He sits on the bed and strokes* DAVID's *forehead.*] You're right. There's nothing left but fuss. "Fuss, fuss, fuss. Nothing but fuss," said the King. Nothing but pain and fuss. When your whole existence is pain … [*Beat. He thinks. He looks at the machine.*] I can't. I … just can't. You understand. You'll just be done when you're done. It's not for me to say. [*Beat. He picks up his drink. He walks to the door. He takes a drink. Thinks. Puts the drink down. He walks over to the machine, takes a deep breath, closes his eyes, shudders, and solemnly and deliberately flicks a switch. Nothing happens. The machine is supposed to shut off but doesn't.*] Oh, my God. Shit. I'm sorry. It's … [*He starts to laugh.*] Aw shit. It doesn't work. Typical. [*He laughs. It's ridiculous. He looks around to see if anyone is nearby.*] Candid Camera?

Look, I'll just ... [*Flying into a rage he kicks the machine. Nothing happens again. He kicks it again. Nothing.*] Shit! Fuck! [*He starts to laugh.*] I'm ... really sorry. I ... typical. [*Beat. He absent-mindedly reaches over and simply pulls the plug out of the wall. The machine dies. David's body spasms.*] What was that? Oh. Right. It's off? It's off. It's off. Okay. Goodbye. Goodbye. Goodbye. [*Beat. Quiet. He places his hand on DAVID's forehead.*] Peace. No more fuss. [*To Bruce and Michael's urns.*] Right guys? Peace and quiet.

[*He hits the tape player and Edith Piaf's voice rises singing "Milord." He tops off the other glasses and raises his glass, sits on the bed, strokes David's forehead, and sings along.*]

PATRICK: [*Cont'd.*] [*Quietly.*] "*Allez, venez, Milord, vous assoira Milord ...*"
[*Etc.*]

[*Slow fade to black.*]

Rich Orloff

THE WHOLE SHEBANG

Rich Orloff

Rich Orloff has written four full-length plays, three of which received their professional premiere during the 1994–95 theatrical season: *Damaged Goods*, a romantic comedy, at Flat Rock Playhouse in North Carolina; *Someone's Knocking*, an absurdist comedy, at Saint Michael's Playhouse in Vermont; and *Veronica's Position*, a comedy about art, love and politics, at Florida Studio Theatre in Sarasota.

Rich's fourth full-length play, *Days of Possibilities*, adapted from true stories of Vietnam era college students, premiered at his alma mater Oberlin College in 1989 and has since been produced throughout the country.

The Whole Shebang, winner of the Little Theatre of Alexandria National One-Act Play Contest, was produced at Theatre Forty in Beverly Hills, and then televised on General Motors Playwrights Theatre on A&E cable in a production starring Mark-Linn Baker, Teri Garr, and Martin Mull. Rich's other one-act plays have been produced at the Manhattan Punch Line, Circle Repertory Theatre Lab, National Theatre Workshop of the Handicapped, and elsewhere.

A native of Chicago, Rich currently lives in New York City with his wife Amy. He's a member of the Dramatists Guild.

CHARACTERS:

> The Student, *mid-20's, earnest, enthusiastic, and currently rather anxious*
> The Dean, *wise, patient, experienced, balanced*
> Professor A, *skeptical, critical, cool**
> Professor B, *instinctual, passionate, warm**
> A Man, *near 40, average, unexceptional, human*
> A Woman, *the man's wife, same age, also average, unexceptional, human*

> **The "A" and "B" connotation is for script purposes only. In the program, the professors should be listed in some other manner, such as "The Professor on the Left" and "The Professor on the Right," or "The Tall Professor" and "The Short Professor," or something like that.*

SCENE:

> *A college classroom. The present.*
> *Before the play begins, we hear the following announcement:*

VOICE: The following is a true story. Some minor changes have been made because the actual event took place in a dimension beyond human comprehension.

> [*Lights up on a college classroom, arranged for an oral exam. PROFESSORS A and B and THE DEAN sit behind a large table. On the table are strewn all sorts of papers, photographs, charts and such. Each professor has a legal-sized note pad. Across from where the professors sit is an area where students give their presentations. In this area could be some visual aids, such as the periodic table of the chemical elements, Leonardo da Vinci's diagrams of man and woman, etc. At the side are a few chairs.*
> *As the scene begins, THE DEAN and both PROFESSORS are chatting amiably.*]

DEAN: … and all in all, it was one of the best presentations I've seen this semester. 'A' plus work from start to finish. I'm sure that's one student who's going to go far.

PROFESSOR B: I'm glad to hear it.

DEAN: [*Checking his, or her, watch.*] We might as well start.

PROFESSOR A: No reason to make the poor boy more nervous than he already is.* [**Or "girl" and "she," if the Student is played by a woman.*]

[THE DEAN *crosses to the door, opens it and calls out.*]

DEAN: Are you ready?

STUDENT: [*O.s.*] [*A bundle of nerves.*] Yeah ... I'm ... I'm, uh ...

DEAN: It's time to start.

STUDENT: [*O.s.*] I'm coming.

[THE STUDENT *enters. He carries a globe, a briefcase, and some papers, etc. He appears very anxious and pressured.*]

STUDENT: [*Cont'd.*] [*To* THE DEAN.] I'm, uh, there is—there's just one part of my presentation I don't have with me yet.

DEAN: Do you want us to wait?

STUDENT: Oh, no. My roommate is getting it. It should be here any second now ... I hope.

DEAN: Please relax. This is just an informal review.

STUDENT: You told me my grade depended on this.

DEAN: [*Comforting.*] Try not to think about it.

PROFESSOR B: We've all read your thesis and supporting material ...

[PROFESSOR A *places a hand on a tall stack of material.*]

PROFESSOR A: [*Wishing there had been less.*] *All* of it ...

DEAN: Actually, I must confess I haven't gotten to all of it. I'm sure you can fill me in on anything I missed.

STUDENT: I'll try my best.

DEAN: Why don't we begin with a brief summary of your project?

STUDENT: All right. For my master's thesis, I elected to devise a self-sustaining and self-evolving, matter-based ecosystem in a universe of three dimensions. And so I created the heavens and the earth.

DEAN: Now that you've devised this planetary ecosystem, how do you feel about it?

STUDENT: Well, to be honest ... I think it's good.

PROFESSOR B: Could you be a little more specific?

STUDENT: Certainly. I think the Earth has succeeded in every way I hoped it would. The amount of gravity is sufficient to keep things on the planet and yet light enough to let trees grow tall and animals run and jump. The weather cycle, given its complexity, is quite efficient. Photosynthesis and oxidation balance each other effectively. All in all, the Earth is fundamentally capable of sustaining itself.

PROFESSOR A: Unless, of course, the human being blows it all up.

DEAN: The human being?

PROFESSOR A: Those are the two-legged creatures with the smelly armpits.

DEAN: Oh, yes. We'll get to them later. [*To* THE STUDENT.] Go on.

STUDENT: In designing the Earth, I considered aesthetics an essential aspect. I'm fully aware I could have simplified the ecological chain; there's no vital need for zebras or kidney beans. But I wanted to create a planetary ecosystem that was not only efficient but also beautiful and wondrous.

PROFESSOR A: Kidney beans are beautiful and wondrous?

STUDENT: Maybe not in themselves, but without them, there'd only be two-bean salad.

DEAN: [*Pointing to the element chart.*] It is very impressive how much diversity you created from so few elements.

STUDENT: Thank you. It was the only way I could create a whole universe and stay within budget.

DEAN: I'm most impressed with your creation of water.

PROFESSOR A: I must admit, so am I. It may be one of the most efficient liquids any student has designed.

PROFESSOR B: I like how when the temperature drops below freezing, you've designed it so that water falls as snowflakes instead of ice cubes.

STUDENT: Thanks. That took a lot of work.

DEAN: [*Reviewing a paper.*] *Here's* a most impressive statistic: Over 453 zillion snowflakes so far, and only 12 have been alike.

STUDENT: Thanks.

PROFESSOR A: By the way, why did you have an ice age?

STUDENT: I ... I ... Well, to be honest, I screwed up.

DEAN: Well, that happens. It was early in the term.

PROFESSOR B: I think one of your major aesthetic accomplishments is the fish. I never thought there could be one type of creature with so many colorful variations. Why you even bothered with creatures that slither, crawl and fly, I'm not sure.

STUDENT: Well, you have to understand that—

PROFESSOR B: They're just adorable.

STUDENT: Thank you.

PROFESSOR B: Of course, I could do without catfish.

STUDENT: They're good scavengers.

PROFESSOR B: They're ugly. Couldn't you give them a little silver stripe down their side, or *something*?

PROFESSOR A: Can we begin discussing the human being? It seems to me that everything else is insignificant in compar—

PROFESSOR B: Fish are not insignificant.

PROFESSOR A: Granted. Nevertheless, the human being does seem to be *the* determining factor in the eventual success or failure of the planet.

DEAN: Good point. Let's examine the human being.

STUDENT: I consider the human being the crowning achievement of my universe.

PROFESSOR B: [*Looking at some photos.*] You know what I like best about human beings?

PROFESSOR A: What?

PROFESSOR B: Their feet. Not only are feet durable and sophisticated in their design, they're—well, they're very cute.

STUDENT: Thank you.

PROFESSOR B: [*Referring to the photos.*] Can I save these?

STUDENT: Sure.

PROFESSOR A: I have *one* question regarding the human being.

STUDENT: Yes?

PROFESSOR A: Why did you make them so stupid?

DEAN: That's a biased question.

PROFESSOR A: All right, I'll rephrase it: Why didn't you make them smart?

STUDENT: I think they're smart. They've created great civilizations. They've developed magnificent tools and brilliant works of art. Their awareness of the universe is increasing exponentially.

PROFESSOR A: Stop exaggerating. It took them centuries just to come up with the concept of the sandwich. How smart do you have to be to think of putting a piece of meat between two pieces of bread?

STUDENT: But look at what else they've done. Look at what they've done with their languages. Look at English. With only 26 letters, they've built a body of literature with great power, feeling and insight.

PROFESSOR A: So? The creatures on one of the other students' planets created a body of literature that's twice as profound, and with only 17 letters. No wasted, inefficient letters like X or Q. Imagine inventing a letter you can only use if it's followed by a U. What was going on in their heads?

STUDENT: Still, any species that has produced William Shakespeare ...

PROFESSOR A: Isn't he the one who wrote, "What a piece of work is man! How noble in reason, how infinite in faculty."

STUDENT: Yes.

PROFESSOR A: What a bunch of self-serving rubbish.

DEAN: You don't expect a good grade just because you created *one* genius, do you?

STUDENT: Of course not. The species has also produced Socrates, Freud, Madame Curie, Gandhi, Darwin—

PROFESSOR A: All of whom were resented, misunderstood, ostracized or killed. This is how human beings treat their geniuses.

PROFESSOR B: And what type of organism would let the Marx Brothers make only thirteen movies? They were easily good for another dozen.

DEAN: What I don't understand is, why are human beings so arrogant? They act as if they own the planet just because they're one step up from apes.

STUDENT: The humans do have much to be proud of.

PROFESSOR B: If any creature has a reason to be arrogant, it's the cow.

DEAN: I missed the section on cows.

PROFESSOR B: This one animal spends all day doing nothing but eating grass, and at the end of the day, she secretes a liquid that is not only nutritious, but it can also become cheese and yogurt and butter and over three dozen flavors of ice cream. Now if cows aren't arrogant, why are humans? Granted some of them secrete milk, too, but you can't even make cottage cheese from it.

STUDENT: May I remind you the human being is the sole creature capable of transforming milk into all those other products. Without the human being, the earth would have been a mass of raw material with unrealized potential.

PROFESSOR A: Are you saying it's a better planet because of cheese doodles?

STUDENT: There's more to the picture than that.

PROFESSOR A: From what I see, the rest of the planet would be just as well off if the human being didn't exist.

STUDENT: Yes, but—

DEAN: It appears they can barely manage their own lives, let alone the life of the planet.

PROFESSOR A: Most of them, to quote one of their own, live "lives of quiet desperation."

PROFESSOR B: Except for New Yorkers, who seem quite vocal about it.

DEAN: Why did you give these creatures domain over the planet?!

STUDENT: Well, you see …

[THE STUDENT *sighs and checks his watch.*]

DEAN: Yes?

STUDENT: My roommate was supposed to transport a couple of human beings here so I could … It's very hard to understand them unless you meet them up close. They really are wondrous creatures.

PROFESSOR B: Wondrous they may be, but do you honestly think they can run the planet as well as cows? You would never see holsteins enslaving guernseys because of "the white cow's burden."

STUDENT: Look, I'll admit it. I did make one major error in designing the human being.

PROFESSOR A: Their capacity for cruelty?

STUDENT: No.

PROFESSOR B: Their proclivity towards prejudice?

STUDENT: No.

DEAN: Their desire to destroy that which they can't control?

STUDENT: No, no, no.

DEAN: What then?

STUDENT: None of them seem to do sex right.

PROFESSOR A: They certainly try hard enough.

STUDENT: When the universe was still in draft form, I realized I had to create some mechanism to compensate for the brutalizing aspects of life, something sweet and inspiring that would ensure a peaceful planet. And so I created sex.

PROFESSOR A: [*Wanting more information.*] And?

STUDENT: And I saw it was good.

PROFESSOR B: Are you saying the world would be a safer place if people had more sex?

STUDENT: Oh, no. I'm not talking about quantity; I'm talking about quality. It is psychologically impossible to detonate a nuclear device if you've just had a satisfying intimate experience.

DEAN: [*Skeptical.*] Really.

STUDENT: Oh, yes. But I don't mean just physical sex. Physical sex is good only for procreation and curing acne. But when humans are willing to reveal their souls during the sexual act, they're reunited with all of the energy flowing through the universe. This spiritual/sexual union was designed to cleanse fear from the soul, so that the human's capacity for goodness would rise to the surface and transform into enlightened action ... [*Responding to the professors' disbelief.*] It worked great in test cases.

[*From the hallway, we hear voices.*]

MAN: [*O.s.*] What do you mean "Go in there"?! Maybe I don't want to go in there!

WOMAN: [*O.s., to* THE MAN.] Don't cause a scene!

MAN: [*O.s.*] This jerk's causing the scene! Look, buddy, I don't know who you are, but I'll go in there when I'm good and ready!

[A MAN *comes flying into the room, as if thrown in by someone else. A* WOMAN *follows quickly. Both are dressed for bed. They look around, quite bewildered about what's going on.*]

MAN: What the—

STUDENT: Oh, good. Just in time. I'm so glad you're finally here.

MAN: What the hell's going—

[THE STUDENT *pulls up a couple of chairs.*]

STUDENT: Make yourselves at home.

WOMAN: [*Frightened.*] Where are we?

STUDENT: Just sit. You're late.

WOMAN: Late for what?

STUDENT: Relax. This won't take long ... Please.

[*The humans look at each other and hesitantly sit down.*]

STUDENT: [*Cont'd., to* THE PROFESSORS.] I'd like to introduce two typical human beings: John and Mary Doe. They're not extraordinary in any way, which is exactly why I chose them. John and Mary live with their two children in Dayton, Ohio. John works as an urban planner, helping to prepare Dayton for the next century. Mary is a doctor, specializing in internal medicine.

Although their jobs show their dedication to their fellow humans, it is as parents that John and Mary feel their greatest responsibility. Their two children are sensitive and alive, and also excellent students.

John and Mary have many hobbies. Mary plays the dulcimer, and John recycles aluminum. I am proud to put the destiny of Earth in the hands of average people like these: John and Mary Doe.

MAN: We're not them.

STUDENT: You're not John and Mary Doe?

MAN: No, I'm John's brother, Harvey Doe, and this is my wife, Edna Doe.

WOMAN (EDNA): Hi.

STUDENT: But I told my roommate to bring up—

EDNA: They're on vacation. We're house-sitting for them.

STUDENT: Really? [*To* THE PROFESSORS.] See how caring the human being is?

EDNA: Well, John and Mary have cable. We don't.

MAN: Uh, can I ask a question?

STUDENT: Yes?

HARVEY: Who the hell are you, and why are we here?

STUDENT: Well, since you asked, my roommate teleported through a warp in dimensional barriers to Dayton, Ohio, where he realigned your molecules into a pure energetic code. Then he teleported you here and, having analyzed your cellular structure and DNA, reatomized you into this dimension.

HARVEY: Yeah, I figured it was something like that.

EDNA: You don't hope to gain information so you can destroy our planet, do you?

STUDENT: Oh, no.

EDNA: 'Cause we don't know a thing. Honest.

PROFESSOR A: [*Whispering to* B.] I believe them.

STUDENT: [*To* THE HUMANS.] Don't worry. This is just what, in our dimension, is the equivalent of one of your universities. These are professors in my department, and I'm a student. You're just here as part of my project.

HARVEY: Oh, yeah? And what's your project?

STUDENT: I created the heavens and the earth.

[*It takes a moment for this to fully sink in on* THE HUMANS.]

HARVEY: Wait a second. Are you telling us that *you* are—

STUDENT: I am who I am.

EDNA: Sounds like him.

HARVEY: You mean to tell us that, like the entire universe is just like ... a science fair project?

STUDENT: More or less.

HARVEY: Suddenly, I feel so cheap.

STUDENT: So if my professors could just ask you some questions, it would really help my grade.

HARVEY: I work my fingers to the bone, and all I am is part of some nerd's-science project?!

EDNA: Harvey, please. [*Whispering.*] You'll go to Hell.

STUDENT: Oh, don't worry. Nothing you say here will be held against you.

HARVEY: Eh, I don't care. With my luck, I could give the Pope CPR and I'd still go to hell.

STUDENT: [*Beginning to have intelligent doubts about these folks; to* THE PRO-FESSORS.] Maybe this wasn't such a good idea. These aren't the ones I planned—

DEAN: But they are average human beings, aren't they?

STUDENT: I'm not sure they're as common as John and Mary.

EDNA: The other day my hair stylist called me one of the most commonpeople she knew.

DEAN: Well, then.

STUDENT: I really don't think these people are in any condition to be questioned.

PROFESSOR A: That's too bad. I've got *so* many questions I'd like to ask them.

HARVEY: Go ahead. Waste your time. Ask about my life.

STUDENT: Actually, I think we've bothered them enough—

PROFESSOR B: I think this is a wonderful opportunity to gain some insight-into the human condition.

STUDENT: But these aren't the ones I wanted to—

DEAN: Why don't you just sit and be quiet for awhile?

STUDENT: But I don't think you'll—

DEAN: *Very* quiet.

STUDENT: But if—

DEAN: *Sit.*

[THE STUDENT *sits.*]

DEAN: Now then, Harvey and Edna, why don't you tell us a little about yourselves?

EDNA: Not much to say. We're just people. Ordinary people.

PROFESSOR B: Harvey, what is your occupation?

HARVEY: You mean, what did I *use* to do, before a bunch of pea-brained assholes laid me off?

[THE STUDENT *sighs.*]

DEAN: Yes.

HARVEY: For fourteen years, I worked on an assembly line. I got up every morning, drove twenty miles and spent eight hours tightening nuts.

PROFESSOR A: Why were you laid off?

HARVEY: My entire division was replaced by a silicon chip.

PROFESSOR A: I see.

HARVEY: Apparently, sand can do my job better than I can.

PROFESSOR B: Have you tried to get help from your union?

HARVEY: Not yet. But I do plan to talk to my local union official, as soon as he's paroled.

EDNA: The guy was framed.

HARVEY: It's her brother.

EDNA: He was doing a friend a little favor. If the government hadn't wire-tapped that prostitute, nobody would have ever known.

PROFESSOR A: Have you considered changing careers, Harvey?

HARVEY: Well, I've thought about becoming a truck driver, but amphetamines give me headaches.

PROFESSOR A: I see.

HARVEY: I do have an interview next week at the toxic waste dump. They tell me garbage is a growth industry.

DEAN: Edna, do you work?

EDNA: Oh, yeah. I'm a directory assistance operator.

DEAN: What's that?

EDNA: Well, when people are too lazy or stupid to use their phone book, they call me up, and I say: [In her operator's voice.] "Directory assistance." Then they tell me who they want to call, I push a button and this computer says: [In the computer's voice.] "The number is 465-3912." or whatever the number is.

PROFESSOR B: And how often each day do you do this?

EDNA: Eight, nine hundred times.

PROFESSOR B: Are you concerned that this might eventually become boring?

EDNA: Oh, it got boring after the fourth call.

PROFESSOR A: Then why don't you change jobs?

EDNA: Gee, I don't know. Most of life is boring, isn't it?

STUDENT: If I can just put this into the proper perspective—

DEAN: Later. You'll get a chance.

STUDENT: But —

DEAN: Sit.

[THE STUDENT sits.]

PROFESSOR A: Do the two of you have children?

EDNA: Oh, yes. Michael, who's sixteen, and Wendy, who's just about thirteen.

PROFESSOR B: Can you describe them?

EDNA: They're just wonderful.

PROFESSOR A: Harvey?

HARVEY: They're pips.

PROFESSOR B: Are they good students?

EDNA: They're okay.   HARVEY: Hah.

PROFESSOR A: What do they excel at?

[HARVEY *and* EDNA *think about this. Nothing comes to mind.*]

PROFESSOR A: [*Cont'd.*] Anything?

EDNA: Michael was just made group leader at his drug rehabilitation center.

PROFESSOR B: Does Wendy take drugs?

EDNA: Oh, no. Never.

HARVEY: She just spends all day in the bathroom, dyeing her hair unnatural colors.

EDNA: [*Trying to put things in a good light.*] Some of which are *very* creative.

HARVEY: Yeah, like one day her head's going to end up in an art gallery.

EDNA: She's going through a rough time. She still hasn't gotten over the shock of menstruation.

HARVEY: [*To* THE STUDENT.] Not to question your ways or nothing, but couldn't you think of anything better than *puberty*?

STUDENT: No, not really. I tried.

EDNA: Harvey, please.

HARVEY: Well, he's supposed to be all-knowing and all-powerful, and he can't even make their teeth grow in straight. [*To* THE STUDENT.] Do you know how much that cost me?

EDNA: Harvey, please. We're supposed to be representing the entire human race.

PROFESSOR A: I think you're doing a *splendid* job.

PROFESSOR B: How's your sex life?

EDNA: Pardon me?   HARVEY: Hey!

DEAN: We really could use the information.

EDNA: [*A bit defensive.*] It's fine.

PROFESSOR B: Harvey?

HARVEY: [*Unconvincingly.*] Yeah, it's fine.

PROFESSOR A: So you're both completely satisfied with your sex lives?]

EDNA: Completely.   **HARVEY:** More or less.

PROFESSOR B: More or less?

HARVEY: [*Seeing* EDNA's *look.*] It's fine. It's just fine.

DEAN: Is it?

HARVEY: [*To* THE STUDENT.] Well, you designed women. You know how it is.

PROFESSOR A: How is it?

HARVEY: They just don't seem to like it as much as men.

EDNA: I like it.

HARVEY: [*A bit surly.*] Yeah, I know you like it.

EDNA: I like it just fine.

HARVEY: You don't always like it.

EDNA: I always fulfill my obligations, don't I?

HARVEY: I can't tell you what a turn-on that attitude is.

EDNA: Maybe it's because I get tired of hearing you yell out Vanna White's name when you get excited.* [**Or any current female television star.*]

HARVEY: I did that *once*, and you've brought it up fifteen million—

EDNA: I swear there isn't one actress on television he hasn't slept with. In his mind, that is.

HARVEY: This isn't the place to discuss this.

EDNA: They want to know what we're like!

HARVEY: [*Overlapping with the above; to* THE STUDENT.] Hey, I've got a question!

STUDENT: Yes?

HARVEY: When you designed women, why did you make it take 'em so long to have an orgasm?

STUDENT: Actually, if their response cycle hasn't been repressed, it shouldn't take long at all.

HARVEY: [*To* EDNA.] See! I told you it wasn't *his* fault.

EDNA: Well, it wasn't mine.

PROFESSOR A: [*Mimicking* THE STUDENT.] Excuse me. Has either of you ever had a spiritual/sexual union where you feel reunited with the energy flowing through the universe, so that all of your goodness rises to the surface and transforms into enlightened action?

HARVEY: Hey, what do you think we are—perverts?

EDNA: We have read many of the manuals. Harvey lasts up to six minutes sometimes.

HARVEY: [*Under his breath.*] Those are six minutes *you'll* never see again.

PROFESSOR B: Do you believe that intimacy is important in a relationship?

HARVEY: You mean sex?

PROFESSOR B: No, I mean intimacy ... being open and vulnerable.

EDNA: I think intimacy is the keystone of a healthy relationship.

PROFESSOR B: And what makes you say that?

EDNA: I read it in last month's *Cosmo.*

DEAN: *Cos*—

HARVEY: It's a "woman's" magazine.

EDNA: But I do think it's important. After all, without real intimacy, sex would be nothing but, uh ...

HARVEY: Fun.

STUDENT: [*Standing.*] If I can ... [*Sensing what* THE DEAN *is about to say.*] I know—"Sit."

PROFESSOR A: Harvey and Edna, what would you say has been the best moment of your lives?

EDNA: Oh, that's easy. It was the day Harvey proposed to me. It was the first nice day of spring, and we were having a picnic in the park. I had made chicken salad sandwiches and potato salad and carrot-raisin salad and macaroni salad ...

PROFESSOR B: Did Harvey make anything?

HARVEY: I think I picked up a six-pack.

EDNA: No, you were going to, but since I had to go back to the store to pick up more mayonnaise, you decided to let me get it.

DEAN: Why couldn't Harvey purchase the mayonnaise when *he* went to buy the six-pack?

[HARVEY *and* EDNA *look at each other. Apparently, this idea never occurred to them.*]

EDNA: Anyway, so we were having this picnic, and when we finished eating, I wiped Harvey's mouth with my napkin, and he wiped my mouth with his—

HARVEY: It's this thing we do.

EDNA: And, and I remember, I remember Harvey looking right in my eyes and saying ... "Let's make it legal." And I thought, this man knows what I want.

PROFESSOR A: And was that day the best moment of your life, too, Harvey?

HARVEY: Uh, yeah, yeah, of course, yeah.

EDNA: You don't have to lie to them. You told me what you thought was the best.

HARVEY: Well, the day I proposed was one of the best.

PROFESSOR B: What was the best?

HARVEY: Well, okay, um, it was last summer, and well, I was having this really lousy day, I mean, 100% sucko lousy.

DEAN: "Sucko"?

PROFESSOR B: A colloquial adjective derived from the verb "suck".

HARVEY: The important thing is, the day stunk. It was like maybe a hundred degrees out, and maybe a hundred per cent humidity, and it was even worse in the house because all of our air conditioners had just been repossessed. And then the mail came, and it was all bills, big bills, and I got so upset I didn't know what to do, and so I turned on the TV. But we always get lousy reception, and this day there were so many ghosts on the tube I couldn't tell what was going on, and I got so mad I threw a shoe at the TV. It didn't break, thank uh— [*Glimpses at* THE STUDENT.] —whatever and then I just left the house and went into the backyard.

PROFESSOR A: And that was the best moment of your life?

HARVEY: I'm getting to it. So on my way to—you know, I hate being interrupted—on my way to the back yard, I stopped in the kitchen and got myself a beer. Now I don't know if any of you guys are beer drinkers ... I guess not. Usually, when you drink beer, it's either too cold, or not cold enough, or it's got too much foam, or it's just a lousy brand. And you still drink it, because that's what life's about, accepting the beer you're given, but it's nothing that, nothing you'd ever get *enthused* about. But this beer, it was delicious. Just right. I can still remember sitting in my backyard, thinking, "I'm broke, I'm unemployed, and I have lousy reception. But this moment, this moment, is perfect."

STUDENT: I really must interrupt—

DEAN: I told you—

STUDENT: But I don't think it's fair to judge the whole human race based on such a limited sample.

HARVEY: Hey, take a little responsibility for your own actions, why don't you?

EDNA: We're going to Hell, I know it.

HARVEY: He said we could say what we want.

EDNA: [*Whispering to* HARVEY.] Yes, but we don't know if he's going to be loving and forgiving or righteous and vindictive.

STUDENT: Why do you insist upon giving me human qualities? It's quite a projection.

HARVEY: Hey, you created us.

STUDENT: But I gave you free will!

HARVEY: That's it. Pass the buck.

STUDENT: I am not passing the buck.

HARVEY: You and your "free will." What good is it, huh? I exert my free will all over the place, and all it does is get me thrown out of bars.

STUDENT: You don't understand the concept. I gave you choices—

HARVEY: Yeah, like being able to vote for a president and then making all the candidates jerks?

STUDENT: There's more to it than that.

HARVEY: Hey, if I really had free will, do you think this is the life I would have free-willed?

STUDENT: Maybe it is!

HARVEY: Yeah, well, let me tell you, if you designed me so that I'd make the free will choice of *this* life, then you're *really* sick.

EDNA: Harvey!

STUDENT: You could have made better choices.

HARVEY: I can't afford better choices! My credit cards are already up to the limit!

DEAN: Excuse me—

EDNA: Harvey—

HARVEY: It's like everything that's great about life, he's supposed to get credit for, and everything that's lousy is supposed to be our fault. Well, it's not fair!

EDNA: Harvey, please.

HARVEY: It's just not fair!

DEAN: Excuse me! … I'm sorry, but our time is almost over.

PROFESSOR B: If I may, I have one final question.

DEAN: Go ahead, Professor.

PROFESSOR B: [*To* THE HUMANS.] Do you think the world is getting-better or worse?

HARVEY: Oh, worse.

EDNA: Much worse. Everyone knows that.

PROFESSOR A: Then why do you keep living?

HARVEY: Whaddaya mean?

PROFESSOR A: Your lives vary in quality from boring to dismal. Your future holds no promise. Why do you keep living?

[HARVEY *and* EDNA *think for a moment, look at each other.*]

EDNA: I just dropped ten pounds. I'm not going to die now.

HARVEY: Yeah.

PROFESSOR A: And this is why you keep on living?

EDNA: Well, well, we also have to stick around for our kids.

HARVEY: Yeah!

EDNA: After all, if it weren't for us, who'd be their role models?

[THE PROFESSORS *exchange looks with each other.*]

HARVEY: [*To* EDNA.] I think you just blew it.

EDNA: They're good kids.

HARVEY: I know, I know, they're great kids. But you can't tell that by looking at 'em.

EDNA: They're going to be fine, eventually. They're just going through a difficult phase.

HARVEY: Yeah, it's called life.

PROFESSOR A: I still don't understand. With your attitudes, why do you two keep living?

HARVEY: Hey, if you're suggesting I drop dead, *forget* it. It'd make too many people happy.

EDNA: There are things in life to look forward to, you know. Special things, things that make life worth living.

PROFESSOR A: Name three.

EDNA: Well ... every Thursday the paper has double-discount coupons ... and on weekends, I get to sleep in late ... oh, and about every six months, I'll give out a phone number and somebody'll say "thank you" like they really mean it.

PROFESSOR A: Don't you think those are rather trivial things?

EDNA: So? I lead a rather trivial life. I know it.

HARVEY: I don't think you guys realize how hard it is being a human being.

PROFESSOR B: Is it difficult?

HARVEY: You bet it is.

EDNA: You never feel like you have enough brains.

HARVEY: And you're always getting these impulses—these urges—that make no sense whatsoever.

EDNA: Your kids look to you for answers, and you can't think of anything. So you end up giving them the same stupid answers your parents gave you.

HARVEY: When I think there are people dumber than I am, I get scared. [*To* THE STUDENT.] So why'd you do it?

STUDENT: Do what?

HARVEY: Why'd you make us so messed up?

STUDENT: You're missing the point! I didn't create the human being so that each one would work perfectly. I created the human being so that humanity as a whole would work perfectly.

HARVEY: But humanity as a whole doesn't work perfectly!

EDNA: It doesn't work perfectly at all. And we have it better than most people.

DEAN: Do you?

EDNA: Oh, yes. Most people, if they get through childhood without dying of hunger or disease, all they got left is a life of misery, pain and injustice.

STUDENT: But I gave human beings all the resources they need. Why, I've given you the ingredients for paradise.

EDNA: Ohh ... You're a real tease, you know that?

STUDENT: What do you mean?

EDNA: You made the world so wonderful, and our lives so difficult. I mean, maybe we're not the best examples of human beings, but, well, we're trying as hard as we can, and, and we want to be decent people and we want our kids to turn out right and we want to have happy lives, and, and we're trying so hard, but ... [*Breaks into tears.*] You know what it's like to know you're doing your best and that your life still stinks?

HARVEY: [*To* THE STUDENT.] Good work, buddy. [*Comforting* EDNA.] Hey, come on. Don't cry. You do okay.

EDNA: I do not.

HARVEY: You do, too. You're a good mother, you're a good wife, and you're one of the best damn directory assistance operators in Dayton.

EDNA: You really think so?

HARVEY: Hey, as far as I'm concerned, anyone who needs a phone number and who calls you is a lucky man.

EDNA: Thanks.

HARVEY: And if our kids turn out okay—

EDNA: If?

HARVEY: And *when* our kids turn out okay, it'll be all because of you.

EDNA: Well, you had a lot to do with—

HARVEY: I hope they don't end up like me at all. That's *my* hope for the future.

DEAN: I think we're ready to decide your grade.

STUDENT: But all humans aren't like this. If only you had met John and Mary.

HARVEY: Of course. Show off a couple of bozos you've made life easy for.

STUDENT: I gave them the exact same universe I gave you.

HARVEY: You sound just like my dad sometimes, you know that?

STUDENT: [*To* THE PROFESSORS.] John and Mary have done so much with their lives.

HARVEY: John's the biggest kiss-ass in Dayton.

STUDENT: He is not!

HARVEY: Oh, yes he is. Even when he goes to church, it's not to pray. He just wants to suck up to you.

PROFESSOR A: I see.

HARVEY: And Mary's worse.

PROFESSOR B: Is she, Edna?

EDNA: Do I have to be honest?

DEAN: We'd appreciate it.

EDNA: Well then, Mary—who, for the record, no longer has the nose you gave her—I mean, she may spend all day curing people, but have you ever tried to just sit down and have a nice conversation with her? "I healed so many people today, Edna. Of course, not as many as you gave phone numbers to."

HARVEY: They're great human beings, all right. I'm sure they would have given you all the answers you wanted.

EDNA: And for the rest of our lives, they would have bored us at dinner-parties saying, "We helped the Almighty get an A."

STUDENT: Can I just say one thing on my behalf?

DEAN: Go ahead. This is your chance.

HARVEY: Yeah, go ahead.

EDNA: Yeah.

PROFESSOR B: Please.

PROFESSOR A: We're listening.

STUDENT: I … Um … [*Sighs, then.*] They looked so good on paper.

DEAN: Thank you. We'll caucus now to decide your final grade.

[*The teachers gather together and start to whisper. We occasionally hear some arguing tones.*]

EDNA: They decide right on the spot?

STUDENT: Yes.

HARVEY: What degree are you going for, anyway?

STUDENT: My M.U.

HARVEY: M.U.?

STUDENT: Master of the Universe.

[*We hear some heated mumbling.*]

PROFESSOR B: You have to consider the exquisite beauty of their design.

PROFESSOR A: But they're not practical.

HARVEY: [*To* THE STUDENT.] Can I ask you a question about the universe that has troubled me since I was a kid?

STUDENT: Sure.

HARVEY: How come there's maple walnut ice cream and butter pecan ice cream, instead of maple pecan and butter walnut?

STUDENT: I don't think I can answer that one.

HARVEY: Nobody can.

DEAN: Despite all their flaws, they have survived for thousands and thousands of years.

PROFESSOR B: And they have such nice feet.

PROFESSOR A: Their feet are indeed nice. It's from the ankles up that they make me nervous.

PROFESSOR B: Still, their genetic engineering is most advanced.

DEAN: And they're also biodegradable.

HARVEY: [*To* EDNA.] This is going to make some story to tell our friends.

STUDENT: Oh, I'm afraid once you're teleported back to Earth, you won't remember a thing.

HARVEY: [*To* EDNA.] Oh, well. There goes the movie sale.

EDNA: And I had already decided what I was going to wear on the talk shows.

HARVEY: Let's face it. We're going to have to spend the rest of our lives as average people.

EDNA: [*Softly.*] Damn.

DEAN: Yes, yes, yes. There is much wrong with the project. I still don't think it's fair to call the student an underachiever.

PROFESSOR A: I don't know why he created them; they serve no useful purpose.

PROFESSOR B: Maybe they're not perfect, but there is something so beautiful and special about them.

EDNA: [*To* THE STUDENT.] Is it, is it okay if I take off my slippers?

STUDENT: Go right ahead.

EDNA: Thanks.

[EDNA *takes off her slippers and rubs her feet. Without* THE STUDENT *noticing, this gets* PROFESSOR B's *attention.*]

HARVEY: Your bunions acting up again?

EDNA: [*Defensively.*] Yes.

HARVEY: You gotta stop buying those teeny shoes. You don't got teeny feet.

EDNA: I buy shoes the right size.

HARVEY: No, you don't. You keep insisting your feet are smaller than they are. That's why your feet are always in such lousy shape.

[PROFESSOR B *walks over to* EDNA *and examines her foot.*]

PROFESSOR B: I'm changing my grade.

[PROFESSOR B *returns to the other teachers.*]

EDNA: What did I do?

STUDENT: Nothing.

[THE TEACHERS *end their conference.*]

DEAN: We've decided your grade.

[THE TEACHERS *resume their previous positions.* THE STUDENT *and* THE HUMANS *face them.*]

DEAN: [*Cont'd.*] There is much that is commendable about your project, both in Earth'sevolutionary ability and its astonishing variety of beauty. The human being is wondrous and fascinating. Nevertheless—

HARVEY: [*To* EDNA.] Uh, oh.

EDNA: Shhh.

DEAN: The three of us agree that the human being's design is tragically flawed. Look at them. They're so scared and confused by their own drives. What good are all their noble qualities when by adulthood, most of them have developed a grudge against life itself? I'm afraid we're going to have to give you a C plus.

STUDENT: C plus?!!!

EDNA AND HARVEY: [*Simultaneously.*] C plus?!!!

DEAN: I'm sorry.

HARVEY: Wait a second. We do not live in a C plus universe.

EDNA: It's at least a B.

STUDENT: I created fruits and vegetables and birds that fly and fish that swim and artists and athletes and thinkers and leaders, and all I get is a C plus?! I gave this project everything I had. Everything!

PROFESSOR A: Some of us felt the grade was generous.

HARVEY: [*To the* PROFESSORS.] All I can say is—it's easy to sit back and judge. Real easy. How do you guys know you're not just somebody else's science project? Huh? Huh?! I bet right now some higher being is giving your entire dimension a D.

PROFESSOR B: I don't understand. After all of your complaints—

HARVEY: So I was in a bad mood! You got us at a bad time.

EDNA: It was just before bedtime.

HARVEY: And on Saturday night, if you get my drift.

EDNA: Those six minutes mean a lot to us.

HARVEY: [*To* EDNA, *surprised.*] They do?

EDNA: You know they do.

HARVEY: Well, I sorta hoped, but, uh, I never assumed ...

EDNA: Well, of course.

HARVEY: I keep worrying one day they'll come up with a silicon chip—

EDNA: No ... Never.

PROFESSOR A: [*Getting ready to go.*] I don't see why they go on living. I really don't.

EDNA: [*Fed up.*] *I'll tell you why!*

DEAN: Why?

EDNA: [*Straining hard to think of a reply.*] Well ... Because ... [*Suddenly inspired.*] Because things could get better, that's why!

HARVEY: That's right. Things could always get better.

PROFESSOR B: And what makes you think that?

HARVEY: [*To* EDNA.] Tell 'em.

EDNA: I haven't the slightest idea. I guess we were just designed that way. When push comes to shove, I guess we were designed to have ... faith.

[*Everyone looks at* THE STUDENT. *He smiles and nods.*]

HARVEY: [*To* THE PROFESSORS.] See? He's not as big a jerk as you think he is.

DEAN: I'm sorry. The grade is final.

PROFESSOR A: [*To* THE STUDENT.] You want my advice? Next time, don't design them in your own image. It's very narcissistic.

[PROFESSOR A *exits*.]

PROFESSOR B: [*To* THE HUMANS.] Take care of your feet, and always treat cows with respect.

[PROFESSOR B *exits*.]

DEAN: [*To* THE STUDENT.] Now don't be too hard on yourself. You did your best.

STUDENT: That makes it even more depressing.

DEAN: It's only a universe. It'll pass.

[THE DEAN *exits*. THE STUDENT *starts to clean up*.]

EDNA: Uh ... I'm sorry if we blew your grade.

STUDENT: It's my fault. I should've never goofed off on the seventh day.

EDNA: Well, if it means anything, we *are* glad you created us.

STUDENT: Are you? ... Are you, Harvey?

HARVEY: Well, all in all, when I think about it, I mean, life's not that bad, once you get over the disappointment that it stinks.

STUDENT: I'll remember that.

HARVEY: So you want to grab a brew?

STUDENT: I better have you teleported back to Earth.

HARVEY: Oh, yeah, well, sure.

EDNA: By the way, if there is such a thing as reincarnation—

STUDENT: I really can't discuss such things—

EDNA: You don't have to tell me, but if it does exist, could you bring me back as a bunny rabbit? Everybody likes bunny rabbits.

HARVEY: And could you bring me back as an eagle?

EDNA: An eagle?

HARVEY: Yeah. Just once I'd like to fly real high on my own power, real high, so I could look down and get a clear view of the whole shebang.

STUDENT: That's a very nice desire, Harvey.

HARVEY: Yeah, well, I got my moments.

STUDENT: Shall we go?

HARVEY: Okay.

STUDENT: After you.

[HARVEY *and* EDNA *exit.* THE STUDENT *is about to go, but then he turns around and picks up the globe.*]

STUDENT: [*Shrugs to himself.*] I think it's good.

[THE STUDENT *sighs, puts the globe under his arm, and exits. The lights fade.*]

Jacquelyn Reingold

DEAR KENNETH BLAKE

Jacquelyn Reingold

Dear Kenneth Blake was produced by the Ensemble Studio Theatre in 1994, directed by Brian Mertes, and acted by Jodi Long and Matthew Cowles. It had been workshopped at Manhattan Class Company, directed by Arnold Mungioli, acted by Larry Bryggman and Jodi Long; and at EST, with actors Dawn Saito and Matthew Cowles. Jacquelyn's other plays, which include *Girl Gone, Tunnel of Love, A.M.L., Lost and Found,* and *Freeze Tag* have been seen in New York at MCC, EST, Naked Angels, the Circle Rep Lab, and at theatres across the country. Jacqueline received the 1994 Kennedy Center's Fund for New American Plays Roger Stevens Award, and was a finalist for the 1994–95 Susan Smith Blackburn Prize. Her work has been published in *Women Playwrites: The Best of 1994,* by Dramatist Play Service and Samuel French. She is a member of New Dramatists.

This play is for Brian.

CHARACTERS:
> **Tina,** *30s. From Cambodia. She has great dignity and strength. She has a sense of humor, and knows how to be blunt. She wears a blouse and a skirt.*
> **Kenneth,** *40s. He has great dignity and strength. Gruff. Blunt. Used to solitude. He wears work clothes and work boots, no socks.*

PLACE:
> *The apartment where* TINA *works and the farm where* KENNETH *works.*

TIME:
> *The present. Late spring.*

SCENE ONE
> [*Two separate areas.* TINA *is in the apartment where she works. She sits behind a window box that rests on a small bench, a watering can beside her.* KENNETH *is on the farm where he works. He stands behind a makeshift barbed-wire fence he is building. He talks to an unseen person.*]

TINA: Dear Kenneth Blake,
> I saw you this afternoon on the television talk show, and I want to say I wish you best of luck in your new home. You seem like a nice man.

KENNETH: If this is the best I can do then this is the best I can do, but I tell you, I'm not sleeping with that bunch of beggars and drug addicts!

TINA: [*She starts to make small holes in the soil.*] I hope you stop drinking and smoking, and learn to breathe fresh air and have a new start.

KENNETH: [*He starts cutting "barbs" out of a wire hanger.*] Telling me when to sleep and how to comb my hair and wash my asshole, and when to snore, and who the hell are they, huh? Bunch of panhandlers trying to steal my cigarettes?

TINA: You say you are looking to meet a wife in the country and maybe a pretty one with blonde hair.

KENNETH: Well, I never begged for nothin' in my whole life, you hear?

TINA: Maybe we can write letters and be friends.

KENNETH: And I'll tell you another thing, I'm not a slave, and the only time anyone ever wants something from me around here is when they want something from me!

TINA: Dear Kenneth Blake,
I hope you are doing well. I did not hear from you, and I wonder if you got my last letter.

KENNETH: You expect me to get up at the crack of dawn after sleeping with this bunch of losers and work all day, and pay me next to nothin'—

TINA: Maybe you did not. I hope you are learning to plant, and getting along with the other people that have no homes and are also learning to plant. Have you met any nice friends?

KENNETH: —to grow these organic damn vegetables, like they're a religion 'cause they have no damn chemicals on them—

TINA: [*She puts seeds into the soil.*] Dear Kenneth Blake,

KENNETH: —and you charge a fortune of money by selling 'em to a bunch of long hairs and yuppies who pay quintuple price for 'em 'cause they don't want any toxins in their food—

TINA: My letters don't get returned, so I hope you are reading them, and are too busy to write.

KENNETH: —while they go out into the street and breathe in more toxins than could fit on all the organic tomatoes they could eat in twenty years. And you do all this 'cause you say you have a pact with Mother Earth.

TINA: In the house where I work they have a terrace with plants and flowers, and I think about you. I watched you on that show while I ironed, and was sad you had to live in a train tunnel for so many years, and then they made you leave. When I was a girl we had a house, and they made us leave. I am glad they have a good program to teach you to be a farmer.

KENNETH: And now you tell me I can't keep my pet rabbit in the damn "communal sleeping room" 'cause those stinky bums don't like the smell?! 'Cause I won't give the rabbit a shower!?

TINA: How does your rabbit like it there?

KENNETH: Well, I ain't gonna just dump her! Where I goes, she goes!

TINA: P.S. When I saw your face I think you have a look in your eyes I understand.

KENNETH: I would leave here if I could, but I can't 'cause you don't pay enough money. Even Mr. Greenjeans made enough money!

TINA: Dear Kenneth Blake,
Do you like being on a farm? Do you work too hard maybe?

KENNETH: I got nowhere to go and no way to get there.

TINA: Do your eyes look different now that you live in the country? Is it hard to get along with people after being alone for so long? Is it different to have a home after not having one?

KENNETH: Working like a dog for a do-good-for-the-homeless organic hippie—

TINA: Do you wish you had a family? Have you found a wife?

KENNETH: —think you take a bunch of drug addict drunks and put 'em on a farm—

TINA: [*She waters the soil.*] Is it lonely to be in a far away place?

KENNETH: —and they'll turn into a do-good organic hippie like you.

TINA: I think about your face, and I wonder if you wonder about me. Maybe we will never meet, but at least there is someone who knows how I feel.

KENNETH: I may not be able to leave here, but me and my rabbit will not sleep with those smelly animal hating bums! You say you got a pact with Mother Earth, well she gave birth to my rabbit, and she don't mind the smell!

TINA: Dear Kenneth Blake,
You have a look in your eyes I know.
[*Pause, as they both change their focus.*]

KENNETH: Dear Tina,
Uh. Thanks for your letters. Things here stink. I don't know how to keep doing this, and I don't know what else to do. They got me planting these guru tomatoes all day. My feet are so tired they're gonna drop off. Keep writing, if you like. It's nice to get to know you. They want me to give up my rabbit, and I won't. Maybe someday we could meet.

TINA: Kenneth, Kenneth, Kenneth, we can.
[*Scene transition. Lights dim. Music.*]

SCENE TWO

[*Lights up.* KENNETH *is working on the barbed wire fence.* TINA *enters, carrying a tote bag. She carefully looks to see if it is him. He doesn't see her.*]

TINA: Kenneth.

KENNETH: [*He doesn't look up.*] Yeah?

TINA: Tina Sen.

KENNETH: [*Gruff.*] Your what?

TINA: Tina Sen.

KENNETH: [*He looks at her, he stands.*] Oh.

TINA: You remember?

KENNETH: Uh.

TINA: I come to see with you.

KENNETH: What?

TINA: I come to see you.

KENNETH: Oh. Well, uh. I'm, uh, not much to look at at and—

TINA: You said maybe we could meet, and I thought maybe we could. I brought you some shoes for your feet and some food for the rabbit.

KENNETH: You work for a charity, is that it? Some kind of pen pal United Way? Well, I don't take no charity.

TINA: No. From me. A present from me.

KENNETH: Huh?

TINA: A gift. Like, uh, birthday.

KENNETH: Oh. Well, you got the wrong guy, I ain't got no birthday. [*He crosses away from her to his tool box.*]

[*She takes a new pair of shoes out of her bag, puts them on the ground.*]

TINA: See?

KENNETH: Look, uh, I, uh, don't know what to say.

TINA: You can say thank you.

KENNETH: Yeah, right. Thank you.

TINA: And you can say, "please let's talk," or you say, "I don't wish to see you," and I can go.

KENNETH: Now, now, how—how did you get here?

TINA: I walked.

KENNETH: You walked all the way from New York?

TINA: No. I take the bus.

KENNETH: And from the bus stop you—

TINA: —Walked.

KENNETH: How long it take you?

TINA: Ten hours.

KENNETH: Jesus. I. Look, um, I'm a little, I mean, what made you come here, I, uh, don't imagine you were just in the neighborhood, I mean you didn't just come to get some fresh organic air.

TINA: No.

KENNETH: No.

TINA: Kenneth.

KENNETH: Listen, I'm uh. I'm doing something here. And it's important. I mean. I wrote you that—, but. I didn't. You shouldn't. See. I'm ... busy. [*He crosses to the window box.*]

TINA: I give myself to you, and I wonder if you give yourself to me.

KENNETH: What?

TINA: There is no one to choose for me, and I saw you and you say you wanted a wife, and I want to be your wife, but I don't have blonde hair.

KENNETH: What?

TINA: If you want me. Do you think you might want me?

KENNETH: Well, I mean—

TINA: I would be a good wife.

KENNETH: Well, we just, we just don't do it like that, I mean, you don't just take a bus and, that's not how we do it, maybe that's how you do it from—where are you from?

TINA: Cambodia.

KENNETH: Well, that's very far from here, and this isn't. I mean, we take our time here.

TINA: How old are you?

KENNETH: Forty-five.

TINA: That's time enough, don't you think?

KENNETH: Well, well, I uh—what about your mother and your—

TINA: Dead.

KENNETH: [*He picks up window box, crosses back to the fence, puts it down.*] Well, I'm sorry, but that still—

TINA: At home it would be different. I would never be so bold. I would always be modest, but this is America, and they say on the talk show if a horse gallops by your house you must jump on or it will gallop by without you.

KENNETH: What?

TINA: Maybe we can go inside to your house and talk more.

KENNETH: This is my house.

TINA: [*She looks around.*] This?

KENNETH: This is where I sleep.

TINA: Outside?

KENNETH: It's a lot better than with those creeps, and I can keep Bugs with me. Suits me fine. I don't need much. Plenty of fresh air out here.

TINA: Oh.

KENNETH: You wouldn't believe some of the things that go on around here. You just wouldn't believe it.

TINA: I would believe.

KENNETH: Well, I guess that's it. Maybe you were looking for a nice home in the country, I mean, maybe that's what this was. Well, I ain't got that, and I ain't got a white picket fence or a dog named Spot, and there ain't no galloping horses around here, just me and a rabbit, and a barbed wire fence to keep out the creeps, so I'm not your ticket to a better life. I guess you can get the next bus.

TINA: [*She leans over the fence to him.*] It's private here?

KENNETH: Believe me, no one comes out to where I am. Popular, I ain't, and I guess you can see why.

[*She puts her scarf on the ground, and sits.*]

KENNETH: What are you doing?

TINA: I think that you sit down now, and we sit here together in your house ... Your feet hurt?

KENNETH: Does a rabbit shit on a farm? ... Yeah.

TINA: Then you sit here, and maybe we eat something for lunch and—

KENNETH: Boy oh boy, I don't, I mean, I don't, what you just, who said you could—

TINA: If your feet hurt, it's good to sit and take off your shoes.

KENNETH: Well—

TINA: I see you don't want to. You think what is this crazy—a crazy lady—why would I do that? I am afraid of this crazy lady I do not even know. But what can be bad, huh? What is there for you to lose? You don't have to want to get married. I am just asking you to come here, and we say words to each other, and we see which words come out.

[*He is looking away.*]

TINA: [*Cont'd.*] I see you look around. Sometimes you can look around so much you don't see what's next to you.

[*He almost looks at her.*]

TINA: [*Cont'd.*] I see you almost look at me. You can look at me. I understand hurting feet.

KENNETH: Oh yeah?

TINA: Yeah. You ask why I came here, well, I learn that life is short, and in this country you have to go for it, or it's gone. But first you have to sit, and you have to take off your shoes, and then we see.

KENNETH: Lady, if I sit next to you and take off these shoes, you'll want to get away so fast you won't need a bus to get to New York. I mean, they stink. I mean, we're talking about stink.

TINA: I decide that.

KENNETH: My feet, well, see my feet are like a hot foot, you know what that is? It's like on a cartoon, you ever see that? They put a match on your feet and it burns, and I got one on each toe that won't go out and, well, it's kinda like rotting burning foot flesh. Not too nice. So, I don't think so. [*He crosses to the tool box.*]

TINA: [*She takes handfuls of dirt from the window box, and puts them on the ground.*] Maybe if you put them in the ground, it's cooler.

KENNETH: No amount of organic dirt is gonna help me.

TINA: Maybe not, but you do it anyway.

KENNETH: Oh?

TINA: Maybe if we think things aren't going to work sometimes we do it anyway. Maybe we are just afraid. Maybe we think it cannot be different. You say Cambodia is far from here, but they write about it in *The New York Times*. And do you know what they write about now? They had elections this year. And this country is trying to help make peace there. How do they think they can do that—now? How can they think they can do that?

[*He looks at her.*]

TINA: [*Cont'd.*] I lose my family, my home, my country. I come here and see a man on TV, and he has the eyes of my father when they took him away. I watch him, and I feel a love for this man, this man I don't know, this man I am afraid will think I'm crazy if I tell him. I write him many letters, he writes me one back, I take a bus and I find him, and I see he does have those eyes, and I see—I can see—he has a soul like my family, and he doesn't smile when he looks at me, and he does not want the gifts I bring him, and he says he has no home, and I am afraid, and I do it anyway. I ask him to take off his shoes, and when he says "no" I am again afraid, and I think it will not work, but I know, I know what I see, even if he doesn't, even if he will never know, I know, and I say, Dear Kenneth Blake, I say it anyway, if your feet hurt you take off your shoes and put them in the dirt. I ask for nothing else. Just that.

[*He crosses to her, sits, and takes off his shoes. He puts his feet in the dirt. He feels relief as his feet feel better.*]

KENNETH: I'm not talking about marrying you, I'm just—. I'm not good at talking. I don't get along with people when I talk. How about you? How about your feet?

TINA: No. My eyes. My eyes.

KENNETH: What?

TINA: They cry and sometimes I can barely see. Look, see they cry.

KENNETH: Oh.

TINA: Look, I cry. [*She laughs.*] Even if I am happy, I cry.

KENNETH: Oh ... Tina.

[*She wipes the tears from her eyes, then drips them onto the dirt covering his feet.*]

TINA: My tears water your feet.

KENNETH: Yeah. Huh.

TINA: Is it OK if we just sit here? We just sit here in your house. I like your house.

KENNETH: Uh, sure.

TINA: I like the view. And the furniture.

KENNETH: Sure ...

TINA: I've come a long way to get to your house.

KENNETH: Uh huh.

TINA: I brought food.

KENNETH: Oh.

TINA: We can sit here. My tears drip onto your feet and we can see what will grow.

[*They sit. She leans over to cry onto the dirt that covers his feet.*]

Ronald Ribman

THE CANNIBAL MASQUE

Ronald Ribman

Born in New York City in 1932, Ronald Ribman was educated at the University of Pittsburgh, where he earned a Ph.D. in English Literature. He is the author of *Cold Storage*, winner of the 1976–77 Hull-Warriner Award of the Dramatists Guild, and the Obie Award-winning *Journey of the Fifth Horse*. Both plays, as well as *Harry, Noon, and Night*, *The Ceremony of Innocence*, *Fingernails Blue as Flowers*, and *Buck* were originally presented at the American Place Theatre in New York. Ribman's other plays include *Passing Through from Exotic Places*, produced at the Sheridan Square Playhouse, *A Break In the Skin*, staged by Yale Repertory Theater, and *The Poison Tree*, produced on Broadway at the Ambassador Theater. *Sweet Table At the Richelieu* was produced by the American Repertory Theater in Cambridge, Massachusetts, and subsequently published in *American Theater*; *The Rug Merchant of Chaos* was produced by the Pasadena Playhouse; and *The Dream of the Red Spider* was produced by the American Repertory Theater. His latest play, *Turkish Favors* is scheduled for presentation by the American Place Theatre during the 1995–96 season.

Avon Books published *Five Plays by Ronald Ribman* in 1978. The winner of one of the first "Playwrights USA Awards," *Buck* was included in TCG's *New Plays USA 2 Anthology* in 1984. *Journey of the Fifth Horse*, *The Ceremony of Innocence*, and *Cold Storage* have all been televised; in 1967 Ribman's teleplay *The Final War of Olly Winter* was seen on CBS, receiving five Emmy nominations. Ribman's adaptation of Saul Bellow's *Seize the Day* was shown on PBS in May, 1987. In 1991 he did a three hour miniseries for PBS entitled *The Sunset Gang*. His one major screenplay was a collaboration with Bill Gunn in 1970 of *The Angel Levine*.

Ribman has been a fellow of the Rockefeller Foundation, the Guggenheim Foundation, and the National Endowment for the Arts. In 1975 he received a Rockefeller Foundation award "in recognition of his sustained contribution to American Theater."

The Cannibal Masque was first produced by the American Repertory Theatre in Cambridge, MA. David Wheeler directed. The cast was as follows: Diner, John Bottoms; Workman, Richard Grusin; Waiter, Ed Schloth; Pianist, Jane Loranger.

For Joyce and Edwin Starr.

CHARACTERS:
Diner
Workman
Waiter
Pianist [Woman]

SETTING:

The action takes place in Bavaria at the Alley Cat Cafe one winter day 1923. Upstage a black piano against a wall tiled halfway up with black and white checkered linoleum tile. Downstage, a row of pedestal tables, art deco style, with round colored glass tops.

A WOMAN, skeletal thin, her spangled evening gown hanging by its straps from her bony shoulders, plays the piano and sings a German love song to her amour, the WAITER. The WAITER, a bloodless rakehandle with slicked-down, receding hair and a soiled tuxedo, rests his arm against the piano and gazes back into her soulful eyes. Seated at one of the tables, playing with a piece of looped string, winding it about his fingers, is a slight, non-descript and unimposing DINER whose body seems sucked inside his tired overcoat. In his lap he holds a well-worn leather briefcase. After some moments a burly WORKMAN, wrist-length underwear sticking out of his rolled-up shirt-sleeves, thick suspenders holding up his pants, enters. He glances about the cafe, a stranger taking his bearings in an unknown place, and then he sits down, facing the DINER with the string at an adjacent table. For a few seconds he looks sourly at him, as if daring the DINER to meet his gaze, but the DINER with the string keeps his eyes lowered to the table. A visible sneer of contempt crosses the WORKMAN's lips. He stares over toward the PIANIST and the WAITER, but they seem unaware of his presence. When he glances back at the DINER with the string, the DINER has formed a cat's cradle, and, although his eyes still appear lowered to the table, the cradle seems thrust forward, as if inviting the WORKMAN to play. When the WORKMAN turns from him to call the WAITER, the cat's cradle suddenly disintegrates in the DINER's hands as swiftly as a crushed spider's web.

WORKMAN: You! Hey, you! [*Gesturing with his finger at the* WAITER.] Come over here. I want to talk to you.

[*The* WOMAN *stops playing as the* WAITER *walks over to the* WORKMAN.]

WORKMAN: [*Cont'd.*] I heard this place got good eats. That right?

WAITER: Yes.

WORKMAN: That's good, because I'm hungry. I haven't had anything to eat since I got in my truck this morning. I want you to bring me some pork. You got pork here? Fresh pork?

WAITER: Yes.

WORKMAN: You sure? A lot of places say they got fresh pork and then when they get you inside they got nothing but blood sausage and worm meat.

WAITER: We have fresh pork.

WORKMAN: Okay. Some nice thick slices ... eight, nine, ten of them. No la de da slices you can see through like they was wax paper ... thick ones with the fat still dripping on the ends. Something that's gonna satisfy a man's hunger. You understand what I'm saying?

WAITER: Yes.

WORKMAN: I came a long way out of my way to get to this part of the city because I heard you had good eats here, that you served a decent portion, that you didn't stick your customers next to a plate glass window with a lot of faces staring in at them, bothering them while they ate.

WAITER: Nobody will bother you here while you're eating.

WORKMAN: I don't want to be annoyed while I eat. I don't want to look up and see half a dozen drooling faces hovering over my table with their tongues hanging out. You understand?

WAITER: Of course. Every man has the right to devour his meal in peace.

WORKMAN: A man works, does an honest day's labor, he's entitled to be left alone to enjoy his food.

WAITER: Absolutely, as long as he has the money to pay.

WORKMAN: I've got the money. Don't worry about that.

WAITER: You would find it incredible to see the number of people who come in here, just as you do, demanding this and demanding that. "Give me sautéed calf's liver with Pommery mustard sauce! Give me noisettes of lamb glazed with shallots and green pepper reduction! Give me filets and sweetbreads, mandelkirch with sour cherries and ground almonds, elefantenkopf with marzipan and butter cream! Give me everything my stomach cries for!" And what do they intend to pay for all this with?

WORKMAN: You don't have to worry about that with me. I pay up front.

WAITER: Wallets filled with counterfeit currency! Shopping bags bulging with make-believe fabrications: French francs, British pounds, American dollars! Bogus illusions printed up by themselves in futile attempts to ward off starvation by deceit! Wretched green and yellow ink smeared on newsprint and cardboard, packing paper and rice paper! Forged yen from China, false rupees from India, ersatz pesos from the back-waters of South America!

WORKMAN: [*Reaching for his wallet.*] There's nothing ersatz about what I got! I got the old mazuma! The old moolah!

WAITER: No one eats here who cannot pay for his food.

WORKMAN: [*Opening his wallet.*] Feast your eyes on that wad. Is that the real cabbage, or isn't it? The real lettuce, the real spinach, the real scratch?

[*Allowing the* WAITER *to remove some bills and examine them.*]

WORKMAN: [*Cont'd.*] None of your crummy billion dollar marks in there. You won't rub any color off that.

[*As the* WAITER *carefully finishes examining the bills.*]

WORKMAN: [*Cont'd.*] Well, what do you say? Is it good enough for you, or do you want me to pick myself up and walk out of here? Plenty of other restaurants I could go to.

WAITER: No need to raise your voice, sir. I can tell the genuine from the fraud.

WORKMAN: Then get me what I want to eat! I'm hungry and I want to eat!

WAITER: [*Clicking his heels.*] Of course. I am at your service.

WORKMAN: I've been driving all morning in from the border, and my stom-ach is empty.

WAITER: I understand. You have the money to pay and I am at your ser-vice.

WORKMAN: You tell the cook I want a double order of mashed potatoes with brown gravy. Tell him I want him to scoop out a lake on top of the potatoes and pour the gravy into it. Tell him I want the gravy poured over the pork, too. I want to be able to sop my bread in it ... a whole loaf, nice and fresh, big thick three-inch slices. You understand what I'm saying? The best of everything you got!

WAITER: [*As he reaches over and plucks some additional bills out of the man's wallet.*] Of course. You're hungry, you have the money to be fed, and only the best will do under the circumstances.

WORKMAN: And bring me a bottle of schnapps. The best in the house.

WAITER: Excellent choice. I'm sure you will be completely satisfied with our best schnapps. [*Reaching into the man's open wallet again and start ing to pluck out one bill after the next.*] Not every customer is one for whom money is no object.

WORKMAN: Wait a minute. Not so fast. Just give me a bottle of your moderate priced schnapps. Save your so-called best for some poor sap who doesn't know what's what.

WAITER: [*Relinquishing the last bill.*] Of course. [*Turning and starting to exit.*]

WORKMAN: And make sure everything's hot! I wanna see steam coming out of it!

[*The* WAITER *turns to look at him.*]

WORKMAN: [*Cont'd.*] I get cold pork with slimy brown gravy congealed all over it, you know what you'll get for a tip?

[*Raising his rear end and noisily passing gas. The* WAITER *continues to stare at him for a few seconds more.*]

WORKMAN: [*Cont'd.*] Well, get going! I don't have all day. I've got deliveries to make east over the mountains.

[*The* WAITER *exits, and the* WORKMAN *notices the* WOMAN *at the piano is looking at him.*]

WORKMAN: [*Cont'd.*] What are you looking at?

WOMAN: I was just wondering if the handsome gentleman had any favorite song he'd care to have me play.

WORKMAN: Why? Is it for free?

WOMAN: [*Gesturing toward a small plate on top of the piano before she begins to play.*] Whatever you care to leave. A few francs, a few lira.

WORKMAN: Forget it. I don't need music while I eat. All I want to do is eat.

[*The* WOMAN *smiles slightly, strikes a few more notes, and then exits. The* WORKMAN *notices the other customer is glancing at him.*]

WORKMAN: [*Cont'd.*] What's your problem?

[*The* DINER *looks behind him as if someone else might be being addressed.*]

WORKMAN: [*Cont'd.*] Yeah, you. I'm talking to you, Krautface. You got a problem?

DINER: No. Not at all.

WORKMAN: Then what are you giving me the fish eye for? Ever since I drove into this city everybody's been staring at me, giving me the fish eye. You all gone nuts, or what?

DINER: I was merely admiring the way you put the two of them in their place. Yes. Good for you. Good for you, indeed.

WORKMAN: [*Starting to rise menacingly out of his chair.*] That supposed to be some kind of smart ass remark?

DINER: No. No. I assure you. I was simply admiring the way you handled yourself with that woman and the waiter. Quite extraordinary. Really. It's too bad there aren't more people like you to put people like that in their place.

WORKMAN: [*Sitting down again.*] All I did was order my lunch.

DINER: Oh, no, no … if you don't mind my disagreeing. You did quite a bit more than that. You brought back a sense of proportion into things. The way you handled that woman who's notorious for her ability to extort money out of everyone, shaming and wheedling hungry diners into tipping her for music they don't want, was marvelous. "I was just wondering if the handsome gentleman had any favorite song he'd care to hear me play." You don't know how many poor fish she's drawn into her net with that line. God knows what sort of romantic dalliance they imagine she's offering them. Dreams of passion. Nights of amore.

WORKMAN: Who? Her?

DINER: La Belle Dame Sans Merci. Jezebel. Sorceress.

WORKMAN: That bag of bones? You talking about that rag bag of bones?

DINER: You don't find her attractive? Perhaps even alluring?

WORKMAN: I've hung up wash with better looking clothespins than that.

DINER: Yet she excites men. They come in at night and fight for her. The way her shawl caresses the tightened flesh of her shoulders, the succulent movement of her breasts nibbling below the fabric, the slender length of the kneecap bone when the dress parts open just so at the slit … excites … inflames.

WORKMAN: She doesn't do anything to me.

DINER: It is the hunger produced by the famine. It has made the merest sight of flesh on bones irresistible. But you see through all these illusions. Coming from outside this city, you see into the heart of everything in an instant. "I don't need music while I eat. All I want to do is eat." That set her back on her heels I can tell you. That told her what she could do with her music and her lewd undercurrents. And the waiter, the way you handled that waiter who's known for his insolence and bad manners was extraordinary. Believe me there wasn't any doubt in anyone's mind what was what as soon as you called him over. He wouldn't have dared say anything out of the way to you.

WORKMAN: A greasy little creep like that says something out of the way to me, I'd squash him like a bug.

DINER: I'm sure you would, and he knows it. Just one look at your fists and there wouldn't be any doubt in his mind he'd better watch what he's saying. I dare say you could snap his spine with no more thought than you would crack the back of a garden snail with your foot.

WORKMAN: You can believe that.

DINER: Oh, yes, I do. I certainly do.

WORKMAN: Then what makes you think he'd even think about saying something out of the way to me.

DINER: Oh, it's not just you. It's everyone. He's absolutely insolent to everyone he thinks he can insult with impunity. Perhaps you noticed when you came in I was already seated and waiting to be served, but yet he chose to wait on you first. I usually don't complain about things like that, or even allow myself to notice it—things being what they are in this world—but the truth is, even when this place is empty, people such as myself have trouble getting anything to eat. Indeed we have to be very careful about what we do if we are not to lose our dinner altogether.

WORKMAN: What's he got to be so damn uppity about? He don't look like much.

DINER: Oh, he isn't much. He isn't much at all. It's just his delusion, you see. If it wasn't for his delusion, I doubt if he'd dare raise his voice to a kitchen rat.

WORKMAN: What delusion's that?

DINER: He thinks he is a blood relation to Von Hindenburg.

WORKMAN: General Von Hindenburg? The war hero?

DINER: Yes.

WORKMAN: But how could that be?

DINER: It can't. It's absolutely ridiculous, but there you have it. That skinny swayback of a scarecrow with black hollow eyes and hair slicked down with the cheapest of Italian pomades actually believes himself to be related to the greatest war hero in modern German history—his son or nephew—and because he believes it, he has assumed the insolence of the entire military class, behaving in whatever beastly fashion he chooses.

WORKMAN: Anybody ever ask him if he's Von Hindenburg's relative what's he doing working in a place like this?

DINER: He claims to be temporarily on the outs with the old man. Says as soon as the argument is cleared up, he'll be back in the old man's good graces. In the meantime the rest of those high society muckity mucks won't touch him for fear of offending the old man, so he's forced to do this—at least according to him. It's all ridiculous.

WORKMAN: I don't know. Maybe he is who he says he is. Lots of funny things in this world.

DINER: Not that! Germany's greatest military leader, the man who routed the Russians at Tannenberg and occupied Poland, the man who single-handedly saved the fatherland from revolutionists and radicals, could not have a dyspeptic, sunken chested thing like that for a son!

WORKMAN: Okay! Take it easy! I just said there are lots of funny things in this world, that's all.

DINER: You could as soon believe the moon fell out of the sky as he was General Von Hindenburg's son!

WORKMAN: Have it your way. It don't mean spit to me.

DINER: [*Standing up, as if grown bolder by the* WORKMAN'*s mollifying replies.*] When you insult our national leaders, you insult our country!

WORKMAN: [*Standing up as well.*] Nobody's insulting your country! You got some kind of burr up your ass, I've got a thirteen inch boot'll take care of it!

DINER: [*Sitting down.*] Quite right. I apologize.

WORKMAN: Just watch your mouth before you bite off more than you can chew!

DINER: A thousand pardons.

WORKMAN: I kicked you guys' ass in at the Argonne, and you stick it out again I'll do it again!

DINER: Quite right. Quite right. A thousand more apologies. There is no excuse for bad behavior. It's just that the two of them anger me so deeply with their posing, their arrogance, their constant mooneyes at each other, and she ... flaunting herself, exciting the men who come in here, leading them on ... it's disgusting!

WORKMAN: [*Mollified enough to sit down.*] Maybe she thinks she's the Queen of Sheba.

DINER: No. No such simple impertinence for her. Her delusions are as brazen as his. She claims to be a famous concert pianist, reduced to her present state when the General found out about their relationship. He not only refused to permit their marriage, but fixed it, according to her, that she would never be allowed to play again in a German concert hall.

WORKMAN: Well, at least she knows how to play.

DINER: Play? She knows how to play?

WORKMAN: I've heard worse.

DINER: Where have you heard worse? [*Gradually rising to his feet again.*] I'm not talking about playing in some third rate cafe off Bahnhof Strasse! I'm talking about a German concert hall! A concert hall that is the repository of our great German musical culture! Our great symphonies! Our great concertos! Our great ... [*Suddenly stopping, standing still, resting against the table for support.*] Forgive me. I ... [*Sitting down.*] I am sorry. I apologize. I don't know what's the matter with me anymore. My head seems to be floating off my shoulders.

WORKMAN: Maybe you ought to float it into the kitchen and give it something to eat. You don't look so hot.

DINER: No one is allowed into the kitchen but the waiter.

WORKMAN: Suit yourself.

DINER: The cook is vicious. They say he once killed a man who went back into the kitchen. The man got into an argument with the waiter about a piece of sausage in the soup. One thing led to another. The man went back into the kitchen with the soup and never came out again. They said the cook put a six-inch bone trimming knife into him. Supposed to have been in self-defense, but without witnesses, who knows?

WORKMAN: What the hell kind of an argument can you get into over a piece of sausage that you end up killing somebody?

DINER: I can't say. The piece of sausage was no bigger than a woman's pinkie finger. In this time of famine one must do whatever one can to get in the good graces of the cook.

WORKMAN: Well, this is all nothing to me. Like I said, I'm just driving through. People end up getting fed the way they deserve.

DINER: Some eat by bushels, others must be content with spoonfuls.

WORKMAN: A man feels he got better coming than what he gets, he can always eat someplace else.

DINER: Yes, of course, but that's easier said than done. The famine being what it is there's scarcely an icebox left in the city with as much as a carrot in it, and as for the restaurants, most of them are in even worse shape. There isn't a beef tongue to be had for a billion marks. God knows by what miracle of fate it is that this place alone should always seem to be well stocked with food. There have been rumors, of course. Perhaps, in time, the police will investigate.

WORKMAN: Investigate what? What are you talking about?

DINER: [*Taking a cigarette butt out of the ashtray and walking over to the* WORKMAN, *still clutching his briefcase.*] You have a light?

[*Holding the* WORKMAN'*s hand briefly as the* WORKMAN *lights the butt.*]

DINER: [*Cont'd.*] Interesting.

WORKMAN: What is?

DINER: The way calluses tend to form on those little puffy pink pads of skin just below the bottom creases of the fingers—crispy almost as the fried skin of a potato. [*Letting go his hand as he sits down.*] May I?

WORKMAN: What were you saying before about the rumors?

DINER: Gossip, whispers ... how these things start, God knows ... it is all so silly. Still, perhaps you would find it amusing, a slight divertissement in the banal tedium of these gray days.

WORKMAN: A what?

DINER: Pardon my French. There have been a number of disappearances ... people enter restaurants ... order their meal ... poof ... nothing left of them ... a suit is later found floating down the river, complete but for a missing cravat ... a dress strewn on the garbage, shoes, stockings, complete but for a single missing glove. It is almost as if the body had been sucked out of it, a casual souvenir taken ... a cravat, a glove. Though God knows what madman would collect such things.

WORKMAN: Sounds crazy to me.

DINER: Yes, crazy, absolutely.

WORKMAN: [*After a few seconds of silence.*] Well, like I said, I'm just driving through to the east. What you people do to yourselves in this city is your business.

DINER: Yes, of course. It's all nonsense, anyway. If anything happened to these so-called vanished diners, there would be more to it than mere clothing turning up in the snow. There would be the corpus delicti, as the police say. After all a body is not constructed out of thin air, n'est pas? It has weight and substance: a skeleton, a framework, flesh, bones, fluids. Such things cannot simply vanish into the air, melt away like fat in a frying pan. To think so would be to believe that someone as substantial as yourself could go ... poof ... leaving nothing behind perhaps but a vanished set of suspenders and a pair of pants flapping on an icy clothesline. [*Pause.*] But it is too grotesque to even imagine such a thing. [*Pause.*] Poof! Silly stuff.

WORKMAN: Someone try something like that with me, like as not he'd get his neck twisted into a knot before he moved an inch.

DINER: Half an inch, I suppose.

WORKMAN: [*Taking out a fresh pack of cigarettes and opening them up.*] No supposing about it.

DINER: You certainly have the hands for it. [*Pause.*] But as you say you are merely here for your lunch, passing through to the east.

[*Watching the* WORKMAN *tap out a cigarette.*]

DINER: [*Cont'd.*] That is an American cigarette you are about to smoke?

WORKMAN: That's right.

DINER: I used to smoke American cigarettes ... before the war.

WORKMAN: That a fact?

DINER: Yes. [*Pause.*] The American cigarettes are much better than the ones we have here these days.

WORKMAN: I wouldn't know about that. I don't smoke German cigarettes.

DINER: My comrades in the trenches used to say that was the one bad thing about fighting the Americans ... you couldn't get their cigarettes anymore. [*Managing a feeble laugh.*]

WORKMAN: [*Lighting up and exhaling smoke.*] That what they said?

DINER: Yes. [*Pause.*] This is your last pack?

WORKMAN: No. I got lots more of them in the truck. Cartons of them: Camels, Philip Morris, Chesterfield.

DINER: So many of them?

WORKMAN: That's right. All kinds. You name it.

DINER: So many cigarettes. You must be a heavy smoker.

WORKMAN: Could be I smoke a lot ... could be I give some of them away to my friends.

DINER: It is possible to become your friend?

WORKMAN: Sure. I make them all the time. What good's your marks if you can't buy anything with them. Now with cigarettes a good smoke is always a good smoke, and with people who gotta have them—who can tell? [*Turning the cigarette pack over and over on the table.*] Made a nice friend for myself up in Hamburg last week ... shopgirl, wedding ring on her finger. She sees me smoking one of my cigarettes in a bakery and comes over and wants to buy them. When I tell her I ain't interested in selling them for money, she gets the drift of what I want and starts offering me certain favors in exchange for a carton. That's when I hit her with it. "I ain't got a carton, lady, all I got's a pack." Now you may think that was a pretty good deal, her for a lousy carton of cigarettes, but I could see she was a real smoker and I could tell she was really hurting. You know how some people get when they're really hurting for a cigarette. [*Deeply inhaling and blowing the smoke out.*] I figured the longer I dragged things out, the more I could cut the price down. So I just sat there at the table with her, talking, drinking my coffee, eating a stack of those Linzertortes they make up there with the raspberry jam coming out, and all the time pushing around the pack so she could keep her eyes on it.

DINER: [*Watching the* WORKMAN *push around the cigarette pack.*] With so many cartons of cigarettes you could have afforded to be generous.

WORKMAN: Sure I could of, but that would've been missing the beauty part of it, you see, seeing her squirm. That's just the way I am. So now she's down to a pack, so I say, "Fifteen." For five minutes she's laughing in my face about how she ain't gonna go with me for no fifteen cigarettes, so now I tell her I ain't offering fifteen cigarettes no more, now I'm offering five, on account of her wasting my time and making me late on my deliveries. She just sits there looking at me like I was crazy, and I'm taking my hi-ho time sucking in smoke, enjoying myself, watching the expression on her face, knowing I got all the cards in the deck because she's hurting for a smoke and I don't really give a shit. Hell, why should I, with those black circles under her eyes, her lips all cracked, and her nails discolored and broken by the famine? Well, the long and the short of it is ... and this is the real beauty part of it ... you wanna know what I got her for? A cigarette. One lousy cigarette! After we finished, she's sitting there on the edge of the bed with her hands hanging down between her legs and the smoke coming up from the cigarette, telling me how I've degraded her by buying her for a single cigarette, and how it wouldn't have been so degrading if I had just given her a carton, or at least a pack. What the hell? Why should anybody give more than they have to? Besides, if you're gonna sell yourself for smoke, how's a carton less degrading than one? People sure got crazy ideas about what it takes to humiliate themselves. [*Shouting toward the kitchen.*] Let's go with that pork! I don't have all day! [*Turning back to the* DINER.] Now you take a guy like you. Soon as we started talking, I could tell you had too much class to humiliate yourself over anything, no matter how bad you wanted it. Guys like you would rather croak than come out and ask for it ... not that asking would do you any good, if you get my drift, because that's just the way I am. [*Putting away the pack of cigarettes.*] I heard the famine's getting so bad in this city a man can't hardly leave the food on his plate, go to the bathroom and expect to find it there when he gets back.

DINER: Some say that.

WORKMAN: Well, I never leave my plate until it's licked clean.

DINER: One man's licked clean can be another man's supper if some fat is left on, if every bone isn't cracked to the marrow.

WORKMAN: Not with me. I leave a plate cleaned so's an ant couldn't eat off it, and what's left, if anything, I stick my cigarette into. That's just the way I am. So if someone was waiting for my leftovers, he'd do better licking his last meal off his fingers.

DINER: They say the hungrier people get the cleverer they become finding ways to get your food.

WORKMAN: If someone was interested in my food, I would tell him nobody's clever enough to steal it off my plate without suffering a few bad bruises for it.

DINER: They say that out of the famine has evolved an entire new species of flesh-eaters, anthropophagi that walk like men, creatures of terror and camouflage who feast on the wind, enveloping their victims unaware until it is too late for escape.

WORKMAN: Anyone tries to reach out and envelop my food, I'd take his wrist and give it a little snap just to show him what's what. That's just the way I am.

DINER: It's not only the men you have to watch out for. It's the women and children. They come in from the street and snatch the food right off your plate. And then try and catch them. The children don't have an ounce of fat left on them so they run fast as the wind.

WORKMAN: I'd catch them if they blew themselves up to the North Pole.

DINER: Those that can't run because of congenital defects or bone malformations brought on by the famine go to schools that teach them how to swindle honest diners out of their food. Teach them how to stand next to someone who is trying to swallow a piece of sausage or a tiny bite of bread pudding and just make them so ashamed of themselves eating while they're starving, they just turn the whole pudding or sausage over to them. Can't swallow a bite, they're so good at what they do.

WORKMAN: Professional starvers don't bother me none. Nobody's starving ever gave me any trouble swallowing my food.

DINER: I can see you'd give them some run for their money before you gave in.

WORKMAN: Gave in? Put a thousand of them out there in front of my window and I wouldn't let one of them make off with a single raisin out of a pound of bread pudding! I'd swallow a stuffed intestine long as a boa constrictor and not let one inch of skin fall into their mouths!

DINER: That's easy enough for you to say now, but when it actually happens to you, you'll sing a different tune. You'll relent. Everybody always does.

WORKMAN: Not me! That's just the way I am.

DINER: Just such a thing happened to me not so long ago. Took my wife and children out to eat and three of them came up to the window, bold as brass. Couldn't have been more than twelve or thirteen years old, though when the famine has pinched your face so that you look all cheekbones and sockets it's hard to tell. There they were staring through the glass, rolling their tongues around on their lips, making little smacking sounds and what not. It was a pitiful sight. Inside a minute or two the wife had to push her plate away. She couldn't bear to take another bite. I kept telling her it was all an act, that they were using make-up to make their faces even more gaunt and hollow than they naturally were because of the famine, but it wasn't any use. They got our whole dinner. Lamb stew just the way I like it with the fat floating up in little golden globules on the surface, and the spongy marrow bones poking soft and tender out of the meat … bread, sweet butter, everything down to the confectioner's powdered sugar on the candied apricots. A week's trolley fare to the university spent just so I could add the confectioner's sugar to the dessert, and there it all went in an instant like sprinkles of snow melting on their arid lips.

WORKMAN: Just let them try something like that with me and see how far they get.

DINER: You don't know how pitiful children can be.

WORKMAN: Wouldn't matter. Wouldn't have any effect on me.

DINER: They could bring tears to stone.

WORKMAN: Wouldn't matter. Wouldn't let go of what I had.

DINER: Their hollow sunken faces could tear your heart out.

WORKMAN: Wouldn't make me miss a mouthful.

DINER: Not a mouthful?

WORKMAN: Not a sliver. Can't be giving your dinner away to everyone who says he's hungry without going hungry yourself.

DINER: Not a scrap?

WORKMAN: Not a shred. The thinner others become, the fatter the rest. [*Shouting out to the kitchen.*] Let's go with that pork in the kitchen! I'm starving! I don't have all day!

[*The* WAITER *enters with a bottle of schnapps and a glass on a tray. He puts the schnapps and the glass down on the table.*]

WORKMAN: [*Cont'd.*] Where the hell's the pork?

WAITER: Your pork will be out in a moment, sir. The cook has to prepare it properly, otherwise there's always the danger of trichinosis. [*Starts back to the kitchen.*]

WORKMAN: Hey, just a minute! Don't I know you from someplace?

WAITER: I don't think so.

WORKMAN: Sure, I do. You're Von Hindenburg's son, aren't you?

WAITER: How did you know that?

WORKMAN: Don't you recognize me?

WAITER: [*Studying him for some moments.*] No. I'm sorry. I don't believe I have had the honor ...

WORKMAN: I'm Von Hindenburg. [*Pause.*] I'm your father.

[*Starting to laugh as the* WAITER *turns and exits toward the kitchen.*]

WORKMAN: [*Cont'd.*] What 's the matter? Don't you recognize me? [*To the* DINER.] Did you see the expression on his face when I told him I was Von Hindenburg? "I'm your father. Don't you recognize me?" [*Continuing to laugh as he pours himself a glass of schnapps.*] Nothing like a good glass of schnapps to take the chill out of a winter's day. [*Swallowing the drink.*] That's good. Good schnapps.

DINER: What a fortunate man you are.

WORKMAN: I'm not a fool.

DINER: You seem to have everything you want: a good job when so many others are out of work, American cigarettes, a decent schnapps, food coming to fill your belly.

WORKMAN: Some have to eat, some have to watch. [*Pouring out another drink of schnapps for himself and sipping it.*]

DINER: While all this is given to you, another man might have had a wife home sick with two small children in an unheated apartment ... no money, no food to eat, no prospects for anything but starvation.

WORKMAN: He might have.

DINER: One can imagine how difficult it would have been for that man to sit here and watch another man devour such a huge meal by himself.

WORKMAN: I imagine it would be.

DINER: He would want to point out to the man that what he ordered for lunch would be enough to feed them for two whole days.

WORKMAN: At least. Appetites such as that are large enough to feed a woman and two children for an entire week.

DINER: Nine, ten slices of pork thick as a man's thumb, a whole loaf of brown bread cut in three-inch slices.

WORKMAN: Potatoes as well, sweet fresh farm butter.

DINER: For the sake of his family, every instinct in his body would cry out to him to ask the other man if he would share part of his meal with him.

WORKMAN: And the other man would feel obliged to tell him to save his breath and not humiliate himself by asking for a single crumb. He would point out to him that he is not responsible for the condition of his family, and has not the slightest intention of losing a good meal.

DINER: Realizing the embarrassment of turning himself into a common beggar, the demeaning possibility, almost certainty, of being refused, the man might never have asked at all.

WORKMAN: That's the way it is with real gents, professor. Just too much class to humiliate themselves over anything.

DINER: Yes.

WORKMAN: Just thinking of soiling themselves lowering themselves beneath themselves is too unpleasant for them.

DINER: Repugnant.

WORKMAN: It gives them a bad taste in the mouth.

DINER: Foul beyond belief.

WORKMAN: Educated gentlemen as soon see themselves and their family starve to death as do anything that might reduce themselves in their own eyes. You can always count on the educated gentlemen doing the decent thing, those of us who know life's cheap as dirt.

DINER: So hunger turns to weakness, weakness to chills and fever, fever to finality. So a man returns home to find a piece of string wound in the cold palm of a child's hand, a thousand games stored away against a day that will not come. [*Opening his hand to reveal a wound piece of string.*] Perhaps at that moment even delusions set in.

WORKMAN: Oh, yeah? Like what?

DINER: It is impossible to say what might go through a man's mind at a moment like that. [*Pulling the string taut and casually winding it about his fingers.*] Standing there, turning the loops of string tighter and tighter around in his hand, perhaps he might even conceive of himself as already being a murderer, as capable as any other. In a city where every heart is as cold as ice, and every limping dog must run to flee the butcher's knife, how stunning it would be just to warm the senses over life again, to slip a piece of string about another's plump and pulsing neck, to feel it tightening upon trembling fingers, to see his victim's hands reaching up, clutching at the coils of string constricting remorselessly about his throat, the bright ring of blood circling like piquant drops of scarlet sauce where the cord cuts in, the bouquet of gasping breath, the final bulge of eyes that float like grapes in the darkest of sweet liquors ... Such is amusement, such is divertissement when one lives in a city where every steaming restaurant window drips scalding tears of shame.

[*The* WOMAN *enters and sits down at the piano.*]

WORKMAN: Milquetoasts got no stomach for that kind of stuff.

DINER: It would be ridiculous.

WORKMAN: Impossible.

DINER: Entirely out of the question. One might as well believe that dyspeptic swayback of a waiter is Hindenburg's son, or that scarecrow of a woman is a concert pianist.

[*The* WOMAN *suddenly plays with absolute brilliance a classical passage for perhaps thirty seconds and then abruptly stops. The* WORKMAN *is visibly startled by the* WOMAN's *performance.*]

WORKMAN: What do you have in that bag?

[*When the* DINER *doesn't answer right away, he reaches out and snaps the briefcase open himself. The* DINER *makes no movement to stop him.*]

DINER: Nothing of importance.

[*The* WORKMAN *sticks his hand into the briefcase and pulls out three items, one at a time.*]

DINER: [*Cont'd.*] A hat that once wore a head. [*Pause.*] A glove that once put on a hand. [*Pause.*] A scarf that once dressed up in a neck. [*Pause.*] Nothing I admire as much as the French suspenders you are now wearing.

[*As the* DINER *reaches forward to touch the* WORKMAN's *suspenders, the* WORKMAN *moves back so suddenly his chair knocks into the one behind*] *it. The* WAITER *enters, carrying a tray containing the pork. He rather stiffly crosses the room, ceremoniously placing the steaming hot plate on the table. Stepping back a step or two, he takes an elegant silver case out of his jacket pocket, removes a cigarette, taps it on the case a few times, and then lights it. Standing there, puffing on the cigarette held between his fingers in cultivated continental manner, he is the portrait of polished gentility.*]

WAITER: I hope the pork is done to your liking, sir. It was only killed last night.

[*The* WORKMAN *stares from the* WAITER *hovering over him, to the plate of food, to the* DINER *seated in front of him who has formed a cat's cradle out of the string and is slowly extending it toward him as if inviting him to play.*]

DINER: The irony is, of course, as in all of life's buffoonery, that after countless meals, the eater at last must become the eaten.

[*The* WORKMAN *suddenly leaps to his feet.*]

DINER: [*Cont'd.*] I myself prefer the Toulouse style in suspenders, but the Parisian style is not without merit.

[*The* WORKMAN *backs away a few feet, and then turns and flees. The* PIANIST *and the* WAITER *converge on the table, the* WAITER *reaching out for a thick slice of bread to butter, the* PIANIST, *with her hands, for a thick slice of pork. The* DINER *watches them for a moment, and then collapsing the cat's cradle in his hands, pulls the plate closer. Lights fade on the* DINER *eating, the* WAITER *biting into his buttered bread, the* PIANIST *raising the pork above her head to let the meat and juice drop into her upturned mouth.*]

Murray Schisgal

THE ARTIST AND THE MODEL

Murray Schisgal

Murray Schisgal was born in New York City in 1926, attended Thomas Jefferson High School and then continued his education at the Brooklyn Conservatory of Music, Long Island University, Brooklyn Law School, and the New School for Social Research. He served in the United States Navy, played saxophone and clarinet in a small jazz band in New York City, practiced law from 1953 to 1956 and taught English in private and public schools. His initial experience in the professional theater came in 1960 when three of his one-act plays were presented abroad, soon followed by the very successful Off-Broadway production in 1963 of *The Typist and The Tiger*. This production won for Schisgal considerable recognition with both the Vernon Rice and the Outer Critics Circle Awards, but the next production won for him everlasting fame. In November, 1964, *Luv*, directed by Mike Nichols and starring Anne Jackson, Eli Wallach, and Alan Arkin, opened at the Booth Theater on Broadway. His subsequent Broadway productions have been: *Twice Around the Park*, *Jimmy Shine* (starring Dustin Hoffman), *All Over Town* (directed by Dustin Hoffman), *An American Millionaire*, *The Chinese*, and *Dr. Fish*. Off-Broadway he also had produced *Fragments and the Basement* (starring Gene Hackman), the musical of *Luv*, and *Road Show*. Off-Off-Broadway a number of his plays were produced, including *The Pushcart Peddlers*, *The Flatulist*, *Walter*, and *The Old Jew*.

Mr. Schisgal was nominated for an Academy Award and won the N.Y. Film Critics Award, the L.A. Film Critics Award, and the Writers Guild Award for his screenplay of *Tootsie*, starring Dustin Hoffman. His novel *Days and Nights of a French Horn Player* was optioned by Marvin Worth Productions for a feature film. His teleplay *The Love Song of Barney Kempiniski* was nominated for Outstanding Dramatic Program by the National Academy of Television Arts and Sciences. Recently his musical play *The Songs of War* was produced at the Gem Theatre in Garden Grove, California, and at the National Jewish Theater in Illinois; his play *Popkins* was presented in Paris and Rome; *74 Georgia Avenue* at the Jewish Ensemble Theatre in Michigan; and staged readings around the country of *Play Time*, *The Japanese Foreign Trade Minister*, and *Circus Life*. Nine of his short plays have appeared in the Best Plays anthologies over the years. The latest was *The Cowboy, the Indian, and the Fervent Feminist*, published in the 1992-93 collection. His play *Circus Life* was presented Off-Broadway in 1995.

Mr. Schisgal lives with his wife, Renee, and his two children, Jane and Zachary, in New York City and Easthampton.

CHARACTERS:
Bromberg
Angelica

SCENE:
Bromberg's studio in Tribeca.

TIME:
1994. Winter. Twenty-two minutes after eight o'clock in the morning.
LIGHTS.

BROMBERG *is seated on a paint-encrusted, white, straight-backed kitchen chair of the forties, downstage, right; his large, veined hands rest on his knees; between his knees is a darkly varnished cane. A rectangular sketchpad leans against the downstage leg of the chair.*

Further to the right, upstage, is a plant stand on which there is a potted plant, leafy and vibrantly green. A tin watering can is on the floor beside it.

On the left, mid-stage, is a model's platform covered with a worn, faded, Oriental carpet.

If there is any discernible expression on BROMBERG's *face, it is one of displeasure, if not anger. He wears slightly paint-splattered, baggy, white housepainter's pants; heavily paint-splattered, ankle-high work shoes; a bleached, clean, pressed denim shirt with sleeves rolled above his elbows; sticks of charcoal, pens, and pencils protrude from his shirt's breast pocket.*

BROMBERG *is in his late sixties. But he is a vigorous man, with little slackness; his eyes burn with a fierce, truculent intensity. And yet he is old; his hair is in need of a haircut, his face a shave, his nails a brushing. Oddly, he seems to be in a great hurry, poised for movement; still he sits on the chair, hands on knees, immobile, staring relentlessly at the entrance door, offstage, left.*

Shortly ANGELICA *enters. She is late. She has been running. She tries to repress the sound of her breathlessness.*

She removes, quickly, her coat, scarf, knitted cap. It is cold out, although a bright sun shines through the unseen skylight.

BROMBERG's *eyes hold fast to her. He clenches his jaw to prevent himself from speaking.*

ANGELICA *throws her things on an ancient, brown, wicker armchair that is left, angled towards platform. A vintage, paisley shawl lies across the armchair.*

Without a pause, ANGELICA *removes her street shoes, skirt, cardigan sweater, blouse, white athletic socks, pantyhose, bra, and panties; all are thrown on the armchair or, inadvertently, on the floor. A salvaged wooden box with a dozen or so art books on it is at the side of the armchair, downstage.*

ANGELICA *is not particularly attractive. Nor unattractive. She is Latino or Mediterranean. She is in her twenties or early thirties, with a strong, solid, full-breasted body. Her abundant flesh fairly bursts with her naked womanhood. The role requires a professional model.*

Her actions are prompted by three considerations: 1) she needs the job; 2) she is acutely aware of BROMBERG's *age and isolation; 3) she is in awe of his talent, his ability to create beautiful things.*

As soon as she's undressed, she steps up on the platform, waits to receive instructions. She is unable to return BROMBERG's *fixed, obtrusive stare. She invariably turns away from him to look down at the carpet or across at a wall or at whatever object affords her refuge.*

Initially BROMBERG's *voice is a low-spoken growl, a mumble, a muttering of words.*

BROMBERG: If you remember ... when I first retained you to model for me ... months ago ... I asked if it was possible for you to be here at six o'clock in the morning ... since I get up at five o'clock in the morning and by six o'clock in the morning I am anxious to start my work. [*A pause.*] You answered by saying it would be impossible for you to arrive before eight o'clock in the morning because ... you had to take the subway from your apartment in the Bronx ... down to my studio. You said you were afraid to ride the subway so early in the morning. [*A pause.*]

[ANGELICA *stands on the platform. Shortly she will instinctively lower her hands in front of her pubic hair.*]

BROMBERG: [*Cont'd.*] I said you could work for me if you arrived here promptly at eight o'clock in the morning; no later; promptly at eight o'clock in the morning. On those days I required ... your services. You agreed. You agreed knowing full well that when I'm scheduled to work with you ... I am incapable of doing any other work until you arrive. That means from the hour of six o'clock in the morning until ... eight o'clock in the morning ... I am waiting ... I am waiting for you to arrive. [*A pause. He breathes audibly, as if he has exhausted himself; yet his voice becomes more didactic, firm, angry.*] I don't imagine you have any idea what that's like. To wait ... two hours ... two whole hours. Substantive.

Time. When the body and mind are ... energized ... poised to grapple and do battle with the ... the illusive. In-val-u-able hours that can never be ... captured, recycled, like soda bottles, beer cans ... yesterday's garbage. [*A pause.*]

[ANGELICA *folds her arms across her chest; she is cold.*]

BROMBERG: [*Cont'd.*] I imagine that at six o'clock in the morning you're still wrapped in your boyfriend's arms ... without a care or frustrated bone in your body. While I wait ... to work ... to fill my lungs with mouthfuls of fresh air, oxygen, to be able to ... to breathe. [*A pause.*] I believe I told you on more than one occasion that when I am not working ... I have difficulty ... breathing. This difficulty increases the longer I am unable to work. Tension builds. My heart ... palpitates, a-rhyth-mic-a-lly. My abdominal muscles ... cramp. My lungs feel like they're ... co-llap-sing. I have to work so I can breathe. So I won't die ... of suff-o-ca-tion. [*A pause.*]

[*He rises, walks to the rear, right, leaning on his cane; his disabled leg is stiff, as if tied to a board; he moves it along, not with pain or excessive effort.*

He stands at rear and looks through an unseen wall window.

During the above, ANGELICA *runs to armchair, grabs her thigh-length cardigan sweater, puts it on, buttons it, and returns to stand on platform.*]

BROMBERG: [*Cont'd.*] Two hours and twenty-two minutes I waited for you this morning. An intolerable amount of time. For someone who is ... suffocating. I would send you home, right now! this minute! if I could replace you, find someone else, anyone else, immediately, without delay, so I could work. Finally. [*A pause.*] But since I can't on such short notice ... and since I refuse to waste any more time with this ... this rubbish! Be advised that this is the last day of your employment with me. Be so advised. When you leave these premises at the end of the day, I do not wish to see you again. [*A pause.*]

[*He walks to plant stand, picks up watering can and waters plant.*

His voice is a soft, controlled drone, with specified pauses, words frequently spoken reflectively, to himself.]

BROMBERG: [*Cont'd.*] I want you out of my life. Once and for all. I have no need of this ... agitation. I'll get someone in here who's prompt and appreciative and who is a little more fastidious in her *toilette*. A woman of some class, sophistication. I won't have to listen to your endless whining, the endless gossip I've been subjected to. Relentlessly. Relentlessly. No more late-night horror stories about your ... liaisons, your ... debaucheries, your Peter, Peter, Richie, Richie, your hordes of former employers! That ... That grubby second-rate *poseur*

Ostrovski, that no talent, minusculist *pissoir*, Magenetta, your pathetic pap-art *petomane*, Wilberquist. Work for them, why don't you? [*He turns to her.*] They're begging you to go back to them, aren't they? How many times have they phoned you, written to you, waited on your doorstep for you to come home at two, three in the morning! [*Mimics sarcastically.*] Oh, please, my sweet, dear Angelica, please, come back and pose for me! Leave that monster Bromberg, that old, demented, loathsome, egomaniacal cripple! I beg you, Angelica. I can't paint without you, Angelica. I can't create without you, Angelica. You're the best, the most beautiful, the most desirable model in the whole ... [*Suddenly explodes, wagging cane.*] Go! Get out of here! To hell with you! I can't work today. You've made it impossible! Out! Out! I want you out of here!

[ANGELICA *moves to armchair, finds her panties amidst pile of clothes. As she's about to put them on,* BROMBERG *shakes his head, eyes tightly closed; quietly.*]

BROMBERG: [*Cont'd.*] No. [*A pause.*] No. No. [*Anguished.*] I ... I can't afford to ... waste ... anymore ... time. [*Shakes his head.*] I can't.

[ANGELICA *stares at him.*

BROMBERG *opens his eyes. A breath. Firmly.*]

BROMBERG: [*Cont'd.*] Stay. I have to get something done, something ... started. For today. Just today. Finish your work. You'll be paid.

[ANGELICA *places her panties in cardigan sweater's pocket, takes off sweater, steps on platform and assumes POSE # 1: one that says I have no ill will towards you; I want to help you draw something beautiful.*

BROMBERG *sits on kitchen chair, lays cane on floor; he picks up sketchpad, places it on his lap, turns pages, examining previous drawings—none of them pleases him. He finds a clean page, takes charcoal from shirt pocket and begins sketching* ANGELICA.

Now and then we hear the stick of charcoal scratching across the sheet of paper.

BROMBERG *is content. His breathing comes naturally. In a moment he appraises his sketch. He is dissatisfied with it. He turns the page and starts again.*

A smile breaks on his face.]

BROMBERG: [*Cont'd.*] So, who is it this week? Peter or Richie? Did your mother convince you that an unemployed gas-station attendant is preferable to an apprentice butcher? No gossip today? No little tidbits of blue-collar erotica? How about your girlfriend Gloria? Is she having the baby or has the notorious gigolo, Alphonso the Barber, persuaded her that an aborted fetus is next to Godliness? What about your cousin, the disco king? Did he test positive? Did he ever discover the culprit of his concern? [*He sketches a bit.*] You poor young people nowadays. You don't know how pathetic you all are. Scrounging in the garbage dumps for momentary pleasures. In a rotting city. A rotting country. Second-rate. Sliding inexorably into mediocrity. The land of no-more opportunity. Shrinking horizons. Guns and condoms hanging from the gnarled, yellow beak of a bald-headed eagle. America, America, thou hast seen thy day of glory and now lie barren and desiccated under the cold, barren sun. [*Concentrates on sketch for a bit.*] I don't imagine in your vast reading of American history you learned that there was such a thing in the early forties as a World War designated *numero duo.* It was thanks to that effort of moralistic futility that I'm compelled to drag this warped leg about like a superfluous erection. Oh, don't tax your fragile psyche and try to make sense of this. It was an event of no consequence. An irony. A glitch. God, to have lived to see how it all turned out. Where it ended. Where we are today and what it was like then. Poor bastards. Lambs led to the slaughter. Parades and Dole pineapple juice. Poor, poor bastards. [*A pause.*] Now here we are, in the cesspool of the nineties, remembering ... nothing. An event of no consequence. [*Sharply.*] Change pose!

[*Angelica assumes POSE # 2: she's annoyed, doesn't understand why Bromberg's talking so much this morning. Her stance is provocative, seductive, an attempt to get him to concentrate on his work.*]

BROMBERG *turns page, sketches for a while; we hear the charcoal scratching the page; speaks softly, almost to himself.*]

BROMBERG: [*Cont'd.*] I remember, once, during the war, I was standing alone ... in a bar in Tijuana ... drinking a Four Roses and ginger ale. [*He laughs, amused by his sophomoric choice of drink.*] I was all of eighteen years. I don't know where my friends were, probably in a whore house. I don't know why I wasn't with them. I usually was. I remember ... looking up from my drink and I saw, sitting beside me, a young woman, no older than myself. We started talking. I said something funny and she laughed. We exchanged stories, experiences, revealed intimate secrets. We had, along the way, a few drinks. We were high but not drunk. Lifted to that height of reality where we were slightly off the ground ... and sight and sound were ... brilliantly vivid ... Incandescent. [*A pause.*] What was her name, that young woman in a bar in Tijuana, during the Second World War? I don't know. Her hair was ocher, amber, topaz. Her eyes were made of bits of mica, glittering specks of turquoise. Her mouth ... Pale. Pink. Full. Her teeth, her cheeks ... I can see her now. I can taste and smell the soft scent of her.

The closeness of her. [*A pause.*] There was a jukebox. A dance floor. We danced, on that height of reality that was ... incandescent. What *was* her name? I don't know. But I remember the song ... we danced to. [*Quietly, he speak-sings the lyrics, emphatically pronouncing a word here and there; a similar period song may be used.*] "Just kiss me once, then kiss me ... twice, then kiss me ... once again, it's been a ... long ... long ... time. Haven't felt like ... this ... my dear ... since can't remember when..." [*Voice fades out; he tries to sketch; gives it up.*] "When do you have to be back at the base?" I believe she asked me. "Not until tomorrow afternoon," I lied. "Stay with me." Did she say that? Yes. She did. "Stay with me." "I'd like that. Very much," I replied. Oh, yes. Ohhh, yes, yes, yes. I would like that very much. "The bus to San Diego is leaving in a few minutes," she said. "I have to say goodbye to my girlfriends," she said. "I'll meet you on the bus," she said. She moved her face closer to mine; her lips barely a breath away. "I'll be on the bus," I said, with all the manhood I could muster, getting up and running out ... getting on the bus that was jammed to the rafters with sailors and civilians and ... [*A pause; softly.*] Change pose.

[*POSE # 3:* ANGELICA *thinks of herself as* BROMBERG'*s young woman in Tijuana; her pose is as lovely and as simple as she can make it.* BROMBERG *turns page, sketches.*]

BROMBERG: [*Cont'd.*] My heart is beating so fast at this ... minute ... I feel like a fool. Anyway ... inside the bus, I waited for her, to get on, to join me, thinking, sweating, I should get off, I should find her, I should cry out, "Wait! I'm getting off! Excuse me! Excuse me!" But would you believe that the bus was already moving and she wasn't on it and I was traveling to San Diego ... without her? Would you believe ... that I never saw her again and up until this minute ... [*A sigh.*] I never told anyone about her. Not wife *numero uno*, wife *numero duo*, mistresses and lovers from *numero uno* to ... infinity. I told no one. From fear of embarrassment by the in-con-se-quen-ti-ality of that ... innocuous encounter. In Tijuana. Some fifty years ago. During the war to save democracy. What *was* her name? [*Shakes his head.*] I don't know. [*Sketches; laughs softly.*] You do think you're living a life. Peter, Peter, Richie, Richie. [*He laughs.*] You have no idea. What life could be. What life was. After ... After the war. Those who survived. We were in the center of the world. Right here. In this cesspool of a city. There was more happening within blocks of this studio, on canvas, than anywhere else in God's creation. Did you ever hear of a fellow named de Kooning? Pollock? Gorky? Rothko? Smith? Motherwell? My sweet, dear friend, Jimmy Ernst? Of course not! Why should you?

You know Oooostrovski! Maaaga-ne-tta! Wilber-*petomane*-quist!! Those fraudulent imitators of *neo-moderne* bile and excrement! [*Sharply.*] Change pose!

[*POSE # 4*: ANGELICA *is quite peeved by* BROMBERG'*s constant assault on her personal life. Her pose is mean-spirited, aggressive, defiant.* BROMBERG *sees through it; sharply:*]

BROMBERG: [*Cont'd.*] Change pose!

[*POSE # 5. She holds a particularly horrific pose.*

At once BROMBERG *responds.*]

BROMBERG: [*Cont'd.*] Change pose!

[ANGELICA *gives in. POSE # 6: a rather ordinary, innocuous one.*

BROMBERG *turns page, sketches, the charcoal scratching the paper.*]

BROMBERG: [*Cont'd.*] But then ... back then ... we were ... a community. What an endearing word that is. Community. How rich one felt being part of ... a ... community. Part of a group, a tribe, a band of brigands who congregated ... together. Every night partying at the Cedar's or San Remos's or downstairs at Louie's. Every day at our *ateliers*, showing one another what we were working on, talking about it, arguing about it, competing, putting down, raising up, but always respecting what was original, what was right, what was good. That, too, was ... together. [*A pause.*] In a city. In a country. Of endless opportunity. Burgeoning horizons. Supreme confidence. In the first full flush of being *numero uno*. [*Sketches a while.*] You had to be around in the sixties to know what I'm talking about. Free. Free at last. The pictures that run through my mind are those of naked, flower-haloed young people, celebrating under the crimson-tinted open sky. *Carpe diem*. Of thee I sing. [*A pause.*] What an unforgettable decade. So much happened. Was experienced. That's when making love was such a ... dance. Hedonism unbridled. Love on the run. Orgasm apotheosized. Ohhh, it does the heart wonders to reflect on it. [*Tone of voice gradually changes.*] But those are circumstances that young people nowadays have no way of knowing. Believe me, I am sorry for you. Do not mistake my ... outspokenness for a lack of compassion. For an expression of insensitivity. I truly pity you young people nowadays. A night of making love carries with it the horrendous onus of mortality. One forbidden excursion is potentially an act of suicide. How horrible the times. Guns and condoms in the gnarled, yellow beak of a bald-headed eagle. Oh, the horror of it all. [*A pause.*] I assume you practice safe sex. I assume you have sufficient intelligence to speak frequently on the subject with your Peter, Peter and Richie, Richie and whoever else you might be temporarily co-habitating with. [*Firmly.*] Change pose.

[*POSE # 7: the pose is in the main* ANGELICA *"mooning"* BROMBERG. BROMBERG *barks.*]

BROMBERG: [*Cont'd.*] Change pose!

[*POSE # 8: she juts her pelvis out towards him in a whorish pose.* BROMBERG *is intrigued by it; sketches, scratching charcoal on paper.*]

BROMBERG: [*Cont'd.*] There's so much that's screwed-up nowadays. It's an ideal age to grow old. One doesn't quite regret as much saying good-bye to the slime and disease and bloodletting that's drowning us. I wouldn't have liked, for anything, being old in the sixties, but being old in the nineties is something of a blessing. [*He smiles with the thought of it.*] One can stand on the side and observe the pathetic little lives lived by you ... people. I often wonder what it is you look forward to, what dreams and fantasies you have, what you believe in that makes all the ... horror of it worthwhile. I can't for the life of me imagine what it is. Marriage? Does that still exist for you young people? I understand the divorce rate is above fifty percent and that's not counting the number of husbands and wives who walk out the door, never to be heard from again. [*A pause.*] Family? Is that still a viable option? I would think as the years go by there'll be less and less of that. I would think we're witnessing the last vestiges of a worn-out social convention that has overstayed its usefulness. How many single mothers are there nowadays? How many couples live together without benefit of church or state? No, no, family is an impractical goal nowadays. Not very realistic. You'll probably end up with some jerk, you'll have his brats, he'll walk out and some other jerk will probably walk in to take his place. [*Sharply.*] Change pose ! [*He stops sketching; stares at Angelica, fixedly.*]

[*POSE # 9:* ANGELICA *has had it; she poses indifferently, repeating poses she's done previously, anticipating his call for a changed pose and posing anew even before he commands her to do so.*]

BROMBERG: [*Cont'd.*] Did you become impatient? Did you move in with somebody already? Richie, Richie? Peter, Peter? Ostrovski? Maganetta? One of the innumerable suitors who wait on your doorstep every morning? Change pose!

[*POSE # 10: a fantastical "in flight" pose, arms flung outwards, one leg raised.*]

BROMBERG: [*Cont'd.*] What about your mother? The one person I ever heard you say you had feelings for. Did you just leave her with your young sisters? Is that what she deserves from you? Change pose!

[*POSE # 11: another far-fetched pose.*]

BROMBERG: [*Cont'd.*] Change pose!

[*POSE # 12: and another.*]

BROMBERG: [*Cont'd.*] I thought you wanted more out of your life than a pinch on the ass and a quick lay! Change pose!

[*POSE # 13: and another.*]

BROMBERG: [*Cont'd.*] I thought you were interested in making something of yourself, of giving your life value, of ...

[ANGELICA *has had enough. Furiously, she moves to armchair, dresses quickly.*

BROMBERG *scrambles to pick up his cane; rises, continues, heedlessly.*]

BROMBERG: [*Cont'd.*] ... of becoming a productive, committed, caring human being! [*Shouts commandingly.*] Change pose!

[ANGELICA *pays him no mind.*

BROMBERG *shouts again.*]

BROMBERG: [*Cont'd.*] Change pose! Change pose! I thought you had a passion, a passion for books, a passion for painting and music and, and beautiful things! Was that all rot you were giving me? Were you lying, deceiving a man who trusted and believed in you? Is that how you treat people? Is that the extent of your humanitarianism? [*Pants for a beat or two.*] I did not dismiss you! I did not say you could go! I said you would be paid if you worked until the end of the day! the end of the day! Otherwise you don't get a penny from me! not a penny! Now get back on there and we'll ... we'll continue ... we'll ... go on ... [*Loudly; in despair.*] I cannot waste the day! No matter how much I'd enjoy kicking you out of here! I have ... my work ... to do! I have to ... Change pose! Change pose! Change ...

[*He swallows huge mouthfuls of air, watches, helplessly, as* ANGELICA *finishes dressing.*

She picks up her coat, scarf, knitted cap and is about to leave.

A whisper.]

BROMBERG: [*Cont'd.*] Angelica.

[*She turns to look at him.*

Softly.]

BROMBERG: [*Cont'd.*] Where were you last night? I wanted, very much, to talk to you. I felt ... not tired. I took the subway up to your neighborhood and I ... From a candy store I phoned you. I thought we'd have a cup of coffee *together* and ... talk *together*. I spoke to your mother. She said you were out. She didn't know where. So I ... I waited, on your doorstep. Until morning. Two ... three ... in the morning. You didn't show up. [*Forces a smile.*] I won't make that mistake again. I had no sleep. For a man my age ... that's a great ... sacrifice.

[ANGELICA *moves to him. She puts her arms around his waist and hugs him tightly, pressing her head to his chest.*

BROMBERG'*s hands are at his sides, one hand holding his cane.*

ANGELICA *raises her face and kisses him on the mouth, long and hard; passionately.*

BROMBERG *doesn't move, doesn't react.*

ANGELICA *backs away from him, her eyes on him.*

Abruptly, she turns and exits.

BROMBERG *stands stiffly, his eyes fixed on the offstage door for several beats.*

Using his cane, he makes his way to stand on the platform, center, facing front.

He drops his cane, unbuttons his shirt, takes it off, drops it on top of the cane.

He touches his naked chest with outspread hand, runs his hand over his chest, slowly, once, pressing hard, feeling his warm flesh under his fingers.

Hands at his sides, he inhales deeply, tasting the oxygen in his lungs. Exhales. He does this once again. Slowly. Deliberately. Clenching the sensation of breath in the fibers of his being.

Hands at sides, he raises them, slowly, over his head; his fingertips touch. Slowly he brings his hands down to his sides. He does this once again. Each movement felt throughout his body.

Lights begin to fade as he continues with his exercises.

Hands splayed on his hips, he moves his torso to the left. Then center. Then to the right. Then center. He does this once again. Slowly. Deliberately.

He stretches his arms out forward, slowly moves them perpendicular to his body. Etc.

Lights fade out.]

Jules Tasca

THE SPELLING OF COYNES

Jules Tasca

Jules Tasca has taught playwriting at Oxford University in England and he has performed with a commedia dell'arte group in central Italy. He is the author of eighty-four (twelve full-length, seventy-two one-act) published, produced plays, and he has written for radio and television as well. His *La Llorona* and *Maria* were produced on National Public Radio. Other one act pieces were broadcast in Los Angeles and abroad in Germany. He was the national winner in New York's Performing Arts Repertory Theatre playwriting contest for his libretto, *The Amazing Einstein*, which toured the country and played at the Kennedy Center in Washington, D.C. He has adapted the stories of Oscar Wilde, Guy DeMaupassant, Mark Twain, Robert Louis Stevenson, Saki, and has modernized Aristophanes' *Ecclesiazusae* (*Women in Congress*). His libretto for C.S. Lewis' *The Lion, the Witch and the Wardrobe* had its world premiere in California and played in London and New York and is currently touring nationwide. For his play *Theater Trip*, he was the recipient of a Thespie Award for Best New Play, and most recently, *Old Goat Song* won a drama critics award in Los Angeles.

CHARACTERS:

Louie Coynes, *a middle-aged housepainter*
Goldie Dibbs, *his middle-aged girlfriend*
Maria Soldo, *an old widow*
A Chorus of Men *and* **A Chorus of Women**, *represent unspoken thoughts of the characters*

SETTING:

A few chairs, a riser or two.
LOUIE, *when he is not in a scene, stands with the* MALE CHORUS. GOLDIE *and* MARIA, *when not on, stand and wait with the* FEMALE CHORUS.
A light comes up on GOLDIE DIBBS. *Music punctuates her appearance. She has grey hair and is hunched over for this opening moment.*

GOLDIE: [*Rubbing her back.*] I'm Goldie ... Goldie Dibbs. My back's not what it used to be. Louie Coynes, my boyfriend and me, we made a decision way back that changed both our lives. [*She removes the grey wig and straightens up to musical punctuation.*] It all started some years ago when I was full of health like this.

[MARIA SOLDO *crosses on from one side;* LOUIE COYNES *crosses on from the other.*]

GOLDIE: [*Cont'd.*] Old Maria Soldo's husband had died and Louie got the job to paint the Soldo Victorian house. [GOLDIE *crosses off to the* FEMALE CHORUS.]

LOUIE: [*Looking around.*] It's a big house. Real big.

MARIA: I want every room painted. I left it alone for one year after the mister died. Now ... now it's time to start anew, Mr. Coynes.

LOUIE: [*With a brochure in his hand.*] And these are the colors you want?

MARIA: Yes, please. All light, bright, airy shades. I want to make the house young again.

LOUIE: These are beautiful colors you checked off, Mrs. Soldo.

MARIA: Oh, call me Maria.

LOUIE: Only if you call me Louie.

MARIA: Lou. I'll call you Lou. I like that name. When can you start, Lou?

LOUIE: I can start tomorrow.

MARIA: Perfect.

FEMALE CHORUS: [*As they shake hands.*] God, he's such a handsome man.

MALE CHORUS: The poor old biddy. Life's done for her.

[*Music punctuates. MARIA and LOUIE cross to the FEMALE and MALE CHORUSES respectively.*]

MARIA: Bye.

LOUIE: See you bright and early.

[*GOLDIE crosses center*]

GOLDIE: But Maria Soldo, who promised herself a year of mourning felt not like a poor old biddy, but a new lion cub. She fell in love, in love with my Louie, before he'd done the second bedroom.

[GOLDIE *crosses back to the FEMALE CHORUS.* LOUIE *walks on wearing a painter's cap and holding a paint brush. As he looks at the imaginary walls to admire his work,* MARIA *crosses to him with a glass of iced tea.*]

MARIA: Why doncha stop for a rest? I made you this.

LOUIE: Iced-tea. That's so nice of you. It is.

MARIA: It's okay. I enjoy having you in the house. The smell of cigarette smoke. The sound of a man trudging up and down the stairs. The house breathes again.

LOUIE: Maria, you have to get out more.

MARIA: I haven't gone anywhere for a year. I do everything by phone: groceries, banking, business. I'd love to get out. I'm ready. I'd love to go out to lunch, just love it, Lou.

MALE CHORUS: She's asking me to take her out to lunch. *Me.*

FEMALE CHORUS: I wonder if he gets my drift?

LOUIE: You'll start getting out now. I know you will. I'd better start on that third bedroom.

FEMALE CHORUS: I've got to be more direct.

MARIA: No. You did such a bang-up job so far, Lou, I'm gonna buy you a nice lunch.

LOUIE: Mrs. Soldo ... I mean, Maria ... No.

MARIA: Oh, yes.

MALE CHORUS: Oh, no.

LOUIE: I mean, you don't have to.

MARIA: I want to. For the nice work you're doing.

LOUIE: You shouldn't feel you have to ...

MARIA: Not at all. Call it a bonus.

LOUIE: A bonus.

MARIA: It's settled. Please, Lou. Not another word.

MALE CHORUS: Oh, go get a free meal, dope.

LOUIE: Okay, lunch in half an hour then, my girl.

FEMALE CHORUS: [*As* LOUIE *crosses off.*] "My Girl." He called me "my girl." [*Music accompanies* MARIA *back to the* FEMALE CHORUS.] "Lunch in half an hour then, my girl."

[GOLDIE *and* LOUIE *cross on.*]

GOLDIE: And she paid for the lunch?

LOUIE: And what a lunch. Filet mignon. Wine. Mousse for dessert. During the cappuccino, she took my hand.

GOLDIE: [*Laughs.*] Oh, Louie.

LOUIE: "Lou," she said, "being here with you makes me feel like a young woman again."

GOLDIE: Oh, Lou, how sad.

LOUIE: It is, Goldie.

FEMALE CHORUS: He'd never fool with an old woman, not my Louie.

LOUIE: She got all flushed, I tell you, over eating lunch with me.

FEMALE CHORUS: Why did this pump him all up?

GOLDIE: That would've been a nice lunch for us.

MALE CHORUS: Too expensive for us.

LOUIE: Are you kidding? The bill was almost a hundred bucks. We couldn't afford that kinda lifestyle, not if we get rid of my apartment and your apartment here, not if we want to put a down payment on a house someday. Deferred gratification, they call that.

FEMALE CHORUS: [*As* GOLDIE *kisses him.*] How could I think he'd do something perverted with an old lady. Come on, Goldie.

GOLDIE: We don't wanna defer all gratification, do we?

[*He grabs her, kisses her again, and goes off with her.*]

MALE CHORUS: How do women get horny all of a sudden over nothing?

[*Music punctuates. Lights fade out. They come up on* MARIA *and* LOUIE. LOUIE *wears his painter's hat.*]

LOUIE: That's four bedrooms, the kitchen, the living room and dining room. Well, Maria, how do you like the new look?

MARIA: It's a new house. For a new life.

FEMALE CHORUS: And I want you to be part of it, Lou.

MARIA: It's rejuvenation pure and simple. I'm gonna get all new rugs and curtains too.

LOUIE: Now don't go spending your money all at once.

FEMALE CHORUS: He really doesn't know.

MARIA: Lou, money means nothing to me. I have plenty.

LOUIE: Oh?

MALE CHORUS: What is plenty in her mind? Enough to buy denture paste?

MARIA: Mr. Soldo left me okay. I stand fine.

LOUIE: Then you won't be upset about the bill. [*He hands her a bill.*]

MALE CHORUS: She'll change her tune now when she sees my price.

MARIA: Two thousand dollars. I'd say that was more than a fair price for … rejuvenation.

LOUIE: And I enjoyed working for you.

MALE CHORUS: I wonder how much she's got. She didn't blink.

FEMALE CHORUS: How should I begin? [*Pause.*]

LOUIE: What's the matter?

MARIA: Nothing, Lou … it's just … it's just that I'm gonna miss you traipsing through the house.

FEMALE CHORUS: [*As MARIA writes out a check.*] I can't let him go.

LOUIE: I live in the neighborhood. I'll be seein' you around.

MALE CHORUS: [*As she tears off the check.*] Sad old soul. But if she has money, she'll find someone.

MARIA: [*Handing him the check.*] You wait right here, Lou. I want to give you something. [*She puts the checkbook down.*]

FEMALE CHORUS: [*As MARIA crosses off.*] I know he'll take a peek. I would.

[LOUIE *picks up the checkbook and sneaks a look at her balance.*]

MALE CHORUS: *Je-sus! Je-sus!* This skinny old lady's fat! *Je-sus!* [MARIA *reenters with a wrist watch.* LOUIE *replaces the check book.*]

MARIA: Here you are, Lou.

LOUIE: [*Taking the watch.*] What is this, Maria?

MARIA: It was my husband's. I want you to have it.

LOUIE: This is a very expensive …

MARIA: And it'll do my heart good to know it's now beating on your wrist.

LOUIE: Maria, you don't have to …

MARIA: I want to, Lou. I hope you'll stop by once in a while.

LOUIE: Huh? Oh, yeah I will.

MALE CHORUS: When Goldie sees this, she's gonna think I did something perverted here.

LOUIE: We're friends now. Sure.

FEMALE CHORUS: More than friends, Lou.

MARIA: Tomorrow night come for supper.

LOUIE: Tomorrow night?

MARIA: I want to show off my cooking … please, Lou. [LOUIE *looks at the watch and sees her put her checkbook in her pocket.*] Roast lamb. Apple pie. Homemade apple pie.

MALE CHORUS: Just tell her about Goldie and you're out of it, Louie.

LOUIE: Tomorrow night? Let me think if I have any appointments …

MALE CHORUS: Louie …

LOUIE: Okay, tomorrow night. Say at six.

MALE CHORUS: Louie, Jesus …

MARIA: [*As LOUIE starts off.*] Lou.

LOUIE: Yes, Maria?

MARIA: You told me you're divorced. But I mean to say, you … you're not seeing anybody now, are you?

LOUIE: Me? No. Not now. No.

FEMALE CHORUS: Thank God.

MALE CHORUS: Louie Coynes, what in hell're you doing?!

MARIA: [*as LOUIE goes off.*] At six then.

[*Music punctuates.* GOLDIE *crosses on as* MARIA *and* LOUIE *go off.*]

GOLDIE: At the candle light — yes, candle light — that dinner, Maria Soldo prepared, the old lady had such a good time that she drank more than usual, and my Louie found out how much money the poor soul really had.

[LOUIE *crosses to* GOLDIE.]

LOUIE: Really? Really? Really, Maria? Really? That's what I kept saying, Goldie, like a stuck word. Really? She's got stocks, bonds, mutual funds, municipal holdings, two whole safety deposit boxes full of those gold coins, you know …

GOLDIE: Krugerrands?

LOUIE: Them. Yeah. And she's got jewelry, old stuff …

GOLDIE: Calm down, Louie.

LOUIE: Goes back to her grandmother.

FEMALE CHORUS: Pay some attention to me, Louie.

[GOLDIE *kisses him.*]

MALE CHORUS: Now? She wants sex now? While my head's filled with this adventure?

LOUIE: Not now, Goldie. Sorry. I'm still digesting all that food and apple pie. [*As he crosses over to the MALE CHORUS area.*] God, her silverware set is all handmade with stones set in the handles and the plates are etched. I ate apple pie from a work of art.

GOLDIE: [*To audience.*] Over the next week, he showed little interest in yours truly. All he talked about was this wealthy widow and her money. One night he fell asleep on my sofa, and I know he even dreamed of her money.

[*As GOLDIE crosses off to the FEMALE CHORUS, a deep golden light illuminates LOUIE's dream state. A telephone falls to him. Music punctuates to the monologue.*]

LOUIE and MALE CHORUS: Yes, Louie Coynes here. [*Pause.*] I want my Rolls Royce polished and I want the leather seats treated. I need it by seven this evening. [*Pause.*] Yes, I'm dining with the cover girl from the *Sports Illustrated* swim suit issue. [*Pause.*] That's right, Loose Lucy. [*Pause.*] You bet your poverty-stricken ass it's wonderful. It's wonderful to be rich. Everything I do is creamy, sexy, shiny, or made of leather. I'm Louie Coynes, the man with the big bucks [*Pause.*] Excuse me, my other line. Hello? [*Pause.*] This is Louie Coynes. [*Pause.*] Yes, yes, yes, the filthy rich Louie Coynes. [*Pause.*] Yes, well, I'm not surprised. I expected it. I donated two hundred thousand dollars to his campaign. But thank you anyway. [*Music punctuates as the phone is pulled up and off.*] Goldie?! ... Goldie, where are you?!

[GOLDIE *crosses to* LOUIE.]

LOUIE: [*Cont'd.*] Goldie ... Goldie ... I've just been made U.S. ambassador to the Bahamas!

[GOLDIE *gently shakes him awake as the deep golden lights fade to regular lighting.*]

LOUIE: [*Cont'd.*] Pack my swim suit and my snorkel! Goldie! Goldie ... you hear me?!

Goldie where are you? Goldie, I'm the ambassador ...

GOLDIE: Jesus, Louie, wake up. Wake up!

LOUIE: Huh? Who?

GOLDIE: Wake up. You're yelling in your sleep.

LOUIE: I am? Me? Really? Yelling what?

GOLDIE: Something about an ambassador and snorkeling.

LOUIE: Oh, yeah.

GOLDIE: A nightmare?

LOUIE: No. No. It was a dream. A dream. I dream weird dreams lately. Goldie ... Goldie, do you love me?

GOLDIE: More than I've loved anyone.

LOUIE: Do you trust me?

FEMALE CHORUS: Something's happened.

GOLDIE: Louie, what's going on in that head?

LOUIE: Let me ... let me run this by you.

GOLDIE: Run what by me?

MALE CHORUS: You've got to be a real salesman, Louie.

LOUIE: Just listen. This Maria Soldo is really, really hot for me.

FEMALE CHORUS: Has he gone daffy duck?

GOLDIE: We know that, Louie. It's a joke. We laughed over the poor old woman. It's a crush. It's kinda cute.

FEMALE CHORUS: Or is it?

GOLDIE: Louie, Your eyes ... they look all glassy.

LOUIE: Goldie, she's loaded.

GOLDIE: So she's got a few dollars put away.

LOUIE: A few dollars. She's got money up the kazoo.

GOLDIE: Louie.

MALE CHORUS: Make your pitch, Louie.

LOUIE: Don't say anything until I'm finished. Listen. Just listen. I ... I ... I ... I could ... I could get this Maria Soldo to ... to marry me, Goldie. [*Music punctuates.*]

FEMALE CHORUS: He's inhaling too much paint thinner!

GOLDIE: Marry?

LOUIE: Listen. I could get her to marry me. She's eighty-five years old. How long could she last? And when she passes on, I'll have that money for the two of us. I could get her to marry me. I know I could ... I know it.

GOLDIE: So you never told her about me?

MALE CHORUS: She's got you now, Louie.

LOUIE: I didn't tell her about you. No.

FEMALE CHORUS: Good God.

GOLDIE: Why not, Louie.

FEMALE CHORUS: You know why not, Goldie.

LOUIE: I ... I ... it ... it just never came up and she ...

GOLDIE: You never told her about me, because from the get-go, from the time you drooled on her checkbook, this idea slithered around in the back of your head and finally bit your brain.

LOUIE: Okay, I'm not gonna deny it.

GOLDIE: You're telling me you wanna marry an old crone?

LOUIE: Stop being a female for thirty seconds, okay? I don't love Maria Soldo.

FEMALE CHORUS: There's some hope then.

LOUIE: I have no amorous feeling for her, for Christ's sake. I'd hoped you'd look on this as a ... a ... a business venture.

FEMALE CHORUS: There's no hope. He's nuts.

GOLDIE: I never knew you were this crazy.

LOUIE: Why is it crazy?

MALE CHORUS: Why is a man with vision always called crazy? Why?

GOLDIE: Louie.

FEMALE CHORUS: Could he have a fetish for old ladies?

GOLDIE: You marry a business venture and what about yours truly?

LOUIE: *How long could she last?* A year or two? How long?

GOLDIE: You feel right thinking this? Is this something a good person would do?

FEMALE CHORUS: She's always had this annoying moral streak in her.

LOUIE: Maria Soldo showed me her entire portfolio. Laid all the old brown envelopes out on the dining room table. It took my breath away, Goldie.

GOLDIE: She's trying to buy you, Louie.

MALE CHORUS: She's already bought me! It's a done deal!

LOUIE: Yes. Yes. That's what loneliness can do to an old woman. It's sad.

GOLDIE: So sad.

LOUIE: So she's buying companionship. If I give her a year or two of happiness, isn't that an act of charity on my part, our part—to take her loneliness away.

GOLDIE: And her money.

FEMALE CHORUS: How can he think like this?

MALE CHORUS: I knew Goldie was going to be tough.

LOUIE: Anyone—anybody—any bum who marries her gets the money when she dies. Now that she's out of mourning, some banker, some lawyer, somebody with a sharp eye is gonna come along and take advantage of her. If I don't look out and take care of her, who will? Huh?

FEMALE CHORUS: A real guardian angel of the bank book.

LOUIE: Goldie, when she passes on we're rich. Rich!

GOLDIE: Rich. How much does she actually have? Can it be that much?

MALE CHORUS: There's a change in her tone of voice, Louie.

LOUIE: You don't breathe a word of this to anybody.

GOLDIE: You know you can trust me.

LOUIE: You want me to count the jewelry too?

GOLDIE: Count it all. What's she worth?

LOUIE: Goldie. Goldie. Goldie, not counting the Victorian mansion she lives in, which we can sell for two hundred and fifty thousand, Maria Soldo's worth one and a half million dollars.

FEMALE CHORUS: *Je-sus! Je-sus! Je-sus Christ!*

GOLDIE: That much? One and a half …

LOUIE: Million dollars.

FEMALE CHORUS: *Je-sus! Je-sus! Je-sus Christ!*

MALE CHORUS: One and a half million!

LOUIE: You see what I'm saying? Huh? Do you?

GOLDIE: One and a half million …

MALE CHORUS: Take her to climax now, Louie.

LOUIE: She and her husband invested in all good stuff. Safe stuff. Old stuff. Blue chip stuff. A lotta stuff.

GOLDIE: One and a half …

LOUIE: You understand now? Jesus Christ, you drive a school bus. And I paint friggin' houses. Oh, we'd always be happy because we had each other. But we'd never live anything but a life of scraping to pay bills. This way we defer gratification, and we wind up sitting in the middle of the easiest street ever paved, the street with no money worries. None. Money, Goldie. Money and all the things a human being could do, could be with money. You're not supposed to say it, but it's true: money makes the man.

MALE CHORUS: Money. Money. Money. Money.

FEMALE CHORUS: Money. Money. Money. Money.

GOLDIE: I guess ... I guess it'd be like you living with your granny for a spell.

LOUIE: Yes. Yes. That's all. That's all it is, Goldie. Rooming at Granny's that's all. Nothing so bad about just living with somebody. It's not like we planned to harm her or anything.

GOLDIE: And she's probably past the sex stage.

LOUIE: Come on. I'd marry her. But I'd never touch her. Eighty-five years old, Goldie. I make her closing days happy with a little companionship, that's all.

GOLDIE: How long could she last? [GOLDIE *kisses him.*] I think you're a wonderful man to want to help this old woman.

LOUIE: Oh, Goldie, a more understanding love a man never had.

[*They embrace.*]

MALE and FEMALE CHORUS: Money. Money. Money. Money! Money! Money! Money! *MONEY!*

[*Music punctuates.* LOUIE *crosses off. Lights change: the deep golden light that represented* LOUIE's *dream state now pours down on* GOLDIE.]

GOLDIE: I started to dream now myself ... [*Music punctuates to her speech.*] Mc. Goldie Dibbs. Golden Goldie Dibbs. A woman of means. With real money. With gold coins to spare. A gal with the extras that make a woman a great lady. Lady Goldie Dibbs. Or Lady Goldie Coynes. The right clothes. The pop-eyeing rings and necklaces. The restaurants where the waiters are servants—no slaves. A huge house so big that if I'm upstairs and Louie's downstairs, I'll have to call him on the phone. A tennis court. I'll learn to play. A pool. I'll learn to swim or I'll hire people to swim for me. And a gardener. Yes. And my dream of dreams—a live-in woman to cook and clean—duties a real lady can brag she never does.

FEMALE CHORUS: [*With musical accompaniment as* GOLDIE *moves in an orgasmic frenzy.*] Money. Money. Ah, money. Oh money. Sweet money. Owwww money. Blessed money! Ahhhh money! Saint money! Ohhhhhhhhhhh money! My money! More money. Money! Money! Money! *MONEY!* Ahhhhhhh! Ahhhhhhhhhhhhhhh! Ohhhhhhhhhhhhhhhhhh! *Ohhhhhhhhhhhhhhhhhhhhhhhhh!*

[*She drops to the floor as the* FEMALE CHORUS *brings the speech to a climax. Golden dream lights go out.* LOUIE *and* MARIA *cross on.*]

LOUIE: ... And these few weeks with you, Maria, have turned my life around.

MARIA: Oh, Lou. [*They embrace.*]

FEMALE CHORUS: I knew I could make him stay.

MALE CHORUS: I wonder if she believes me.

LOUIE: To have met a generous kind-hearted person like you, I'm really touched by heaven.

MARIA: Be honest with me, Lou.

LOUIE: Am I ever not?

MARIA: Would you be embarrassed to be seen with me?

LOUIE: What? What? What?

MALE CHORUS: Jesus, would I.

LOUIE: Why would I be embarrassed to be seen with a great lady like yourself.

MARIA: Because I'm so much older than you.

LOUIE: Maria, love's not about age.

FEMALE CHORUS: Good thing money makes me attractive.

LOUIE: Love's about deep feeling.

MARIA: Love? Oh, Lou. Love?

LOUIE: Yes, love. I love you and age has nothing to do with it.

MALE CHORUS: I didn't think a man could stoop this low.

MARIA: I've got goose bumps.

FEMALE CHORUS: Even if he is exaggerating a little.

LOUIE: Maria.

MARIA: What is it, Lou? Say what's in your heart.

MALE CHORUS: If anybody could hear this, I'd die!

LOUIE: Maria, I'm ... I'm ... I'm asking you to marry me.

MARIA: Marry. Oh, Lou. Oh, dear Lou ...

LOUIE: What's the matter, Maria?

MARIA: Everyone'll say you married that old so and so for her money. You'd be miserable.

LOUIE: I'd punch the face of anyone who'd think that.

MALE CHORUS: This is the lowest I've ever sunk.

LOUIE: All I want to know is do you believe I love you?

MARIA: Oh, I do believe it, Lou. I do. I do. I do.

FEMALE CHORUS: [*As* LOUIE *and* MARIA *embrace again.*] I know I'm buying him, but I don't care. What's money for?

MALE CHORUS: I feel real bad. I mean, I do like her. I won't let anyone take advantage of her.

FEMALE CHORUS: I don't want to lose him.

MALE CHORUS: And I don't want to quash this plan for Goldie and me. Hold your breath and kiss her, Louie.

[LOUIE *kisses* MARIA. *Music punctuates. Lights fade. When they come up,* MARIA *is off and* GOLDIE *runs on to* LOUIE.]

GOLDIE: Louie!

LOUIE: Goldie.

[*They hug each other and kiss passionately.*]

GOLDIE: Jesus, it's good to see you! How in hell did you get away from her?

LOUIE: She's at the dentist. They put her to sleep. That's the only reason I could get away. Goldie, I'm goin' outa my mind.

GOLDIE: So am I. I miss you so much.

LOUIE: Oh, Goldie. After sleeping with that broom stick, to hold real firm flesh in my hand, *Jesus*. Goldie ... Goldie ... Goldie, I'm thinking of throwing in the towel. I mean it.

GOLDIE: Throwing in ... It's only been six months since you married her.

LOUIE: I don't think I can go on with it.

GOLDIE: Remember the pre-nup, Louie. You divorce her, you get zilch.

MALE CHORUS: I thought Goldie would welcome this.

LOUIE: I know. But I don't care.

FEMALE CHORUS: He can't back out now. What about our money?

GOLDIE: You're willing to throw six months down the drain?

FEMALE CHORUS: I'm wealthy in my mind! It's all I live for!

GOLDIE: What is it, Louie?

LOUIE: Everything. She's an old woman. She sits and knits and talks about her friends who're all dead. I sit there horny for you. I sit there on her grandmother's 19th century furniture. It's like a funeral parlor, Goldie.

GOLDIE: And phone calls are all we can have? There's no way you can sneak over here once in a while?

LOUIE: You kidding? Huh? She won't let me go a second. She won't let me work, says there's no need for me to paint houses. If I go to the john, she walks up with me. And when we sleep at night, Goldie, there's no time when she's not wrapped around me. Those bony limbs like death coiled 'round me. When I wake up, I see that grey head of hers grinning at me. I'm in hell, Goldie! I'm in frigging hell!

FEMALE CHORUS: Poor Louie.

GOLDIE: But it was your decision.

MALE CHORUS: I had to tell somebody what it's like.

LOUIE: The bitch of it is that the money's increased.

GOLDIE: Oh?

LOUIE: She let me re-invest some of the big CD's that matured, and I got her some real estate by the lake. The money's worth up over two million now.

FEMALE CHORUS: *Je-sus!*

GOLDIE: Really?

FEMALE CHORUS: Two Million!

GOLDIE: Really?

LOUIE: Yeah. But is it worth it? Goldie, is it?

GOLDIE: I say stick it out. She'll be eighty-six next month.

FEMALE CHORUS: Don't be weak-kneed.

LOUIE: Yeah. But, Jesus ...

GOLDIE: You gonna let everything we planned go bust, Louie?

LOUIE: I don't want to ... but ... but ... Why'd I think this'd be so easy?

GOLDIE: Louie, stay. Do it for us. Deferred gratification. Remember. Come into the bedroom. Let Goldie give you some incentive.

LOUIE: [*As* GOLDIE *pulls him off.*] It'll have to be a quickie. She'll be coming out of the gas soon. Oh, Goldie.

[*Music punctuates. Lights fade. As they come up,* MARIA *crosses on but with a cane to support her now.*]

FEMALE CHORUS: [*singing.*]
   Happy Birthday to you.
   Happy Birthday to you.
   Happy Birthday, Dear Maria ...

[LOUIE *crosses over with a cake and candles.*]

MARIA: I'm ninety years old today. And I'm still a happy woman. I have my health. The love of my husband, Lou. And there's nothing I want for. Thank you all for coming to my surprise party. Lou, you shouldn't've done it. But I love you.

[*She kisses* LOU. *She blows out the candle.*]

FEMALE CHORUS: [*Finishing the song.*]
   Happy Birthday to you.

[*Music punctuates as* MARIA *and* LOUIE *exit and lights fade. When they come up,* LOUIE *has a touch of gray on his temples.* GOLDIE *paces angrily.*]

LOUIE: Now what's the matter?

GOLDIE: What's the matter? It's been thirty-five days since I last saw or even got a call from you.

LOUIE: We went to the Grand Canyon. She wanted to go. It's not my fault.

GOLDIE: And while you and your wife are living like millionaires and flying out to the Grand Canyon, I'm still driving a grand fucking school bus!

LOUIE: Goldie, this has been tough as it is. What the hell do you want from me?

GOLDIE: I want some money.

FEMALE CHORUS: I've got to start getting something out of this!

LOUIE: Some money!

GOLDIE: Yes, some money. I've been living in this cramped apartment for five years. Five years—five. I think I'm entitled to some money.

MALE CHORUS: Is there never any rest?

LOUIE: How much money?

GOLDIE: Twenty, twenty-five thousand.

LOUIE: Twenty, twenty-five …

GOLDIE: To start.

LOUIE: Goldie.

FEMALE CHORUS: I never go anywhere, do anything.

GOLDIE: I might want to take a trip someplace.

LOUIE: Goldie, come to your senses. The old fart controls the money. I can't just get twenty-five thousand dollars.

FEMALE CHORUS: He doesn't hear me!

GOLDIE: Louie, I've had it. We haven't been together for months, and you didn't even call.

MALE CHORUS: Women, Jesus, Women.

LOUIE: I couldn't call. I'm in the same hotel room at the Grand Canyon with her. Look, I'm sorry. She said she wanted to see the Grand Canyon before she died.

GOLDIE: *When* is she going to die?!

FEMALE CHORUS: When? When? When?

GOLDIE: When? I want a circle on the calendar!

LOUIE: I've never seen you so beside yourself.

GOLDIE: Because you're living up there like a king. You know what tomorrow is?

LOUIE: What?

GOLDIE: My fiftieth birthday! Look at me.

FEMALE CHORUS: Doesn't he see I'm getting old?

MALE CHORUS: You know she *is* aging.

LOUIE: You look fine. Don't even look forty.

GOLDIE: Fifty. And you turned fifty at the Grand Canyon. Look at us. I'm having hot flashes. You're getting bags under your eyes. Five years.

FEMALE CHORUS: Five fucking years!

LOUIE: Come on, Goldie. Settle your kettle, huh? We've had some good times. That week the old fart had her gall bladder out was like heaven for us. A whole week.

GOLDIE: That was three years ago. I'm lonely, Louie. Why don't you just tell her about me. Why don't you explain that … that you need a woman in your life beside her?

LOUIE: You cuckoo? She's jealous as a teenager. She won't let go my arm when the cleaning lady comes in on Wednesdays. You wanna blow this whole deal.

GOLDIE: I'm lonely, Louie.

MALE CHORUS: I'd like to kill myself and be rid of the whole mess!

GOLDIE: I'm even thinking of … of … dating.

LOUIE: Other men?

MALE CHORUS: This is *my* girl talking!

GOLDIE: I'm all alone down here.

LOUIE: And I'm all alone up there with granny. But, okay, you want to date, okay. Okay, go ahead, Goldie.

FEMALE CHORUS: I know he doesn't mean it.

LOUIE: Go ahead, but if you do … you're out. You understand? You're out of the deal. When that old fart goes, I get the three and a half million myself.

GOLDIE: She's worth three and a half million now?

FEMALE CHORUS: Three and a half? *Je-sus!*

LOUIE: Our accountant just gave us an update. We're worth three and a half million now.

GOLDIE: Who's *we're?*

LOUIE: That could mean me and Maria or it could mean you and me.

MALE CHORUS: I'll keep her in line with the money, that's all.

GOLDIE: You can't cut me out now. Jesus, Louie, I've waited so long.

LOUIE: I won't count you out if you just hold on a tiny bit longer.

[*As* LOUIE *and* GOLDIE *kiss.*]

MALE and FEMALE CHORUS: Three and a half million dollars.

GOLDIE: Louie, I want you to take off my clothes and bite me all over.

LOUIE: Okay. Okay. But we don't have so much time. The podiatrist is cutting her corns right now, so we'll have to stop talking and start biting.

[*Music punctuates. He runs off with her. Lights fade and come up on* MARIA *crossing on with the aid of a walker.*]

FEMALE CHORUS: [*Sings.*]
　　Happy Birthday to you.
　　Happy Birthday to you.
　　Happy Birthday, Dear Maria ...

[LOUIE , *with more gray in his hair, crosses to* MARIA *with a birthday cake and candles.*]

FEMALE CHORUS: [*Cont'd.*] I've kept my Louie by letting him have spending money, but I won't let him get his hands on any big money. Oh, I know what's keeping him faithful. But I still love having him.

MARIA: Yes, ninety-five years old today. I'm glad you could all come by and help me blow out the candles. Lou and his surprise parties.

[LOUIE *blows out the candles.*]

MARIA: [*Cont'd.*] Love you, Lou.

FEMALE CHORUS: [*Finishing the song.*]
　　Happy birthday to you!

[MARIA *crosses off. Lights dim.* GOLDIE *sneaks on stage to* LOUIE *who looks around fearfully.*]

LOUIE: [*Sotto.*] We're taking a big chance, you coming here to the house.

GOLDIE: I don't care. I want you.

LOUIE: And I want you.

[*They embrace.*]

MARIA: [*From offstage position.*] Lou! Oh Lou! Yoohoo, Lou. You coming up? Lou? I need my legs rubbed. Lou?

[GOLDIE *and* LOUIE *freeze in fright.*]

MARIA: [*Cont'd.*] Lou? Lou, if you're not coming up, I'm coming down.

[*Music punctuates.* GOLDIE *runs off.* LOUIE *runs off to* MARIA.]

MALE and FEMALE CHORUS: Jesus Christ, all I wanted to do was get laid!

[*Music punctuates. Lights come up full.* LOUIE *and* GOLDIE *cross back on. They pace.*]

LOUIE: Never ... Never ... I never thought we'd be having this conversation.

GOLDIE: Why not? We've been thinking it. Both of us've been thinking of it for years.

LOUIE: Louie Coynes is not a killer. I won't do it.

GOLDIE: Oh, no. What was the real reason for all those goddamned surprise parties you gave her?

MALE CHORUS: I'd hoped the shock would stop her heart!

GOLDIE: Louie?

LOUIE: I'm not a killer.

GOLDIE: Five million dollars. Five million, she's worth. We're worth. For five million dollars, I'd kill my own mother.

LOUIE: Don't say that, Goldie.

MALE CHORUS: She can't mean it.

LOUIE: Whatever we've done so far, we were always good people, nice people.

FEMALE CHORUS: He's afraid to do it, that's all.

LOUIE: You want us to become criminals?

GOLDIE: Then what do you suggest?

LOUIE: I can't kill her, Goldie. I can't. If she died a natural death from one of the surprise parties, okay. But I can't just ...

MALE CHORUS: God almighty, that we even utter the word.

LOUIE: Kill her. I admit it crossed my mind a few times.

MALE CHORUS: More than a few times.

LOUIE: But I've lived with her for ten years. *I can't kill her.*

FEMALE CHORUS: Is he a wimp or is he just more decent than I am?

GOLDIE: Then get authority over everything, so we can finally spend some money.

FEMALE CHORUS: I can taste the goddamned money!

LOUIE: She won't give me authority over anything. I can't sign for anything. She's not stupid.

GOLDIE: No. No, she's not. *We're stupid!*

FEMALE CHORUS: Us! I never should've listened to him.

GOLDIE: We gotta do something.

LOUIE: I will not kill her, Goldie. I wouldn't know how to kill somebody.

MALE CHORUS: I only wish I could.

LOUIE: [*Embracing* GOLDIE.] We … we … we still have some time while they're fitting her new hearing aid.

GOLDIE: I'm just not in the mood.

LOUIE: Not in the mood for sex? For biting, screaming, yelling out loud sex?

GOLDIE: Louie, listen to me. It's scary. I think I'm over the hill. I think I'm losing my interest in sex.

LOUIE: Goldie?

MALE CHORUS: How? How could anybody lose interest in sex?!

[*Music punctuates.* LOUIE *and* GOLDIE *go off.* MARIA *wheels herself on in a wheelchair.*]

FEMALE CHORUS: Happy Birthday to you.
   Happy Birthday to you.
   Happy Birthday, Dear Maria …

[LOUIE, *almost all grey now, crosses to* MARIA *with cake and candles.*]

MARIA: You live to be one hundred you get yer name in the paper and the president of the United States calls you on the phone. You know what happens when the president of the United States calls you? [*She takes* LOUIE'*s hand.*] It breathes new life into you!

FEMALE CHORUS: [*Finishing the song.*]
   Happy birthday to you!

[*Music punctuates.* LOUIE *blows out the candles.* MARIA *wheels herself off. Lights dim and come back on* LOUIE *and* GOLDIE.]

LOUIE: [*Looking at his watch.*] We have twenty-eight minutes to spend together. You wanna rub me down with alcohol?

GOLDIE: I don't want to do anything until I hear how you're gonna murder her. Are you sure you're going to murder her, or is this just another empty promise?

LOUIE: Am I sure? I almost did it last night. I almost pushed her wheelchair down the cellar stairs. I had my friggin' foot raised and on the back of the chair.

GOLDIE: So why didn't you push? One push and we'd be eight and a half million dollars rich.

MALE and FEMALE CHORUS: Eight and a half million dollars.

LOUIE: The investments I've made for that old bitch. [*He hugs* GOLDIE.]

MALE CHORUS: That fucking bitch! I hate her!

FEMALE CHORUS: She's living now just to spite us!

MALE and FEMALE CHORUS: Every breath she takes is an insult!

GOLDIE: We deferred gratification beyond the limits of deferred gratification. Why didn't you just push her down the steps?

LOUIE: I don't want the bitch's death to look violent. And suppose she survived the fall?

GOLDIE: Get some poison. Poison her skim milk.

LOUIE: Poison could be detected, Goldie. I want that eight and a half million without fear.

FEMALE CHORUS: I love it when he talks rich.

GOLDIE: Starve her. Starve her to death. Starve her, Louie.

LOUIE: An undertaker, a doctor could detect starvation.

MALE CHORUS: She's so sexy when she prods me to kill Maria.

GOLDIE: How then?

LOUIE: This isn't easy for me. She is my wife.

MALE CHORUS: She doesn't know the pressure I'm under.

LOUIE: I'm not a killer. My background is painting houses. I always liked people.

GOLDIE: And you like Maria too, but now enough's enough. How? How, Louie?

LOUIE: I want to suffocate the old twat with a pillow. It won't leave any marks. I'll do it in her sleep. She won't feel any pain.

MALE CHORUS: I know now why people murder other people.

FEMALE CHORUS: There's just no other way to get rid of them.

GOLDIE: She lived a hundred years. Christ, how much does she want?

LOUIE: Yeah. She's a pig. Give someone else a chance.

GOLDIE: As soon as you smother her, Louie, call me.

MALE and FEMALE CHORUS: Money.

GOLDIE: Think of it.

MALE and FEMALE CHORUS: Money.

LOUIE: I think of nothing but.

MALE and FEMALE CHORUS: Money.

GOLDIE: Louie.

MALE and FEMALE CHORUS: Money.

LOUIE: What is it? [She puts her arms around him.]

MALE and FEMALE CHORUS: Money.

GOLDIE: You getting up enough gumption to do in the bitch—

MALE and FEMALE CHORUS: Money.

GOLDIE: Well, it's made me horny as a buzz saw. Bzzzzzzz.

MALE and FEMALE CHORUS: Money.

LOUIE: It's too late now. In six minutes her cataract surgery'll be over. [*He kisses her goodbye.*]

MALE and FEMALE CHORUS: Money.

GOLDIE: Oh ... Oh, well ... I'll keep buzzing.

MALE and FEMALE CHORUS: Money.

LOUIE: [*As he runs off.*] I'll make her a good dinner, all her favorite foods, nice hot tea. Then after I tuck her in, I'll smother her.

GOLDIE: [*As LOUIE runs off.*] Have a nice time.

MALE and FEMALE CHORUS: Money. Money. Money. Money. Money.

[*Music punctuates. Lights fade out and come up on two wheelchairs. MARIA in one, LOUIE in the other. LOUIE stares straight ahead.*]

MARIA: His name is ... is ... is ...

FEMALE CHORUS: Oh, what the hell's his name?

MARIA: I donno. Anyway, it's a blessing he survived the stroke. You know stroke could kill a person.

MALE CHORUS: If only I had died.

FEMALE CHORUS: But look at him, the darling man ...

MARIA: I'm glad he's still with me. He's bright eyes still see me doting on him.

MALE CHORUS: This is a punishment from God, I know it.

FEMALE CHORUS: Bo? Bo. No ... that's not it. Lou. That's his name. Lou.

MARIA: I've got to keep saying it over and over so I won't forget it.

FEMALE CHORUS: Lou. Lou. Lou. Lou. Lou. Lou. Lou. Lou. Lou.

[GOLDIE *enters.*]

GOLDIE: Hello, Mrs. Coynes.

MARIA: Oh, hello there.

FEMALE CHORUS: Now what the hell's *her* name? Gilda ... No ... Goldie. That's what it is. I gotta say her name over and over too. Goldie.

GOLDIE: [*As FEMALE CHORUS sotto chants "GOLDIE. LOUIE. GOLDIE. LOUIE."*] Louie never got a chance to smother her. The stress of having to do the deed was too much for him. The stroke left him speechless and wheelchair bound. In the hospital, he wrote on a pad his wish that I come and care for them. So Maria hired me. Before you think me stupid, listen to the deal I got. [*Music punctuates.*]

He promised me in writing—a nurse signed as witness—he'd leave me everything if he died. And he promised me half of the millions as soon as that bundle of wrinkles and crooked fingers croaks. I have his will here. It's notarized and all. Oh, I thought about killing her myself. I even had the pillow up over her face one night. But I couldn't do it. I'm afraid I'd get caught and wind up with nothing. I see it this way: How long can she last?

[*Music punctuates. Lights fade out. In the darkness the* MALE *and* FEMALE CHORUS *sing "Happy Birthday" to* MARIA . *Lights come up with* GOLDIE *standing behind* MARIA's *wheelchair.* MARIA *is wrapped in a blanket.* GOLDIE *is grey now and hunched over as we saw her at the opening of the play.*]

GOLDIE: It was in all the papers. This bitch in a blanket turned 105. [*Music punctuates.*] 105!

FEMALE CHORUS: Was I ever married?

GOLDIE: She won't stop breathing.

FEMALE CHORUS: I think I was married a few times.

GOLDIE: It's stubbornness that's keeping her alive, that's all.

FEMALE CHORUS: The first one was ... I don't recall him.

GOLDIE: Die. Die, why don't you? Die, please, die.

FEMALE CHORUS: The second husband was ... did he die before the first one?

GOLDIE: Oh, don't feel sorry for her. She can't hear a damned thing.

FEMALE CHORUS: I think my second husband's just sick.

GOLDIE: And my back's not what it used to be. Lumbago ... My mother had it.

FEMALE CHORUS: I never see him around ... Maybe he ran off with somebody ... Some young chippy.

GOLDIE: Louie died last year. [*Music punctuates.*] After twenty years of this cadaver on wheels, he dies. Louie. My Louie.

FEMALE CHORUS: This old woman who lives with me and pushes my chair and puts me to bed ... what's her name?

GOLDIE: Louie and me, we never lived together one day—if you take away that week Mrs. Methuselah here had her gallbladder taken out. Louie's gone. I can't inherit a dime from him. I stay here because Mrs. Coynes promised to leave yours truly something when she kicks off. Lawyer's coming today to re-do the will.

FEMALE CHORUS: Whatever her name is she's a nice old woman. I'm gonna leave her my grandmother's sofa. Yep. Gotta remember that. Sofa ... sofa ... sofa ... Sofa for what's her name? ... Sofa for what's her name ...

GOLDIE: [*Pushing the chair off as the lights fade.*] Come on you old bitch in a blanket. It's time for your cereal and vitamins. Your lawyer's coming today. Isn't that nice? Huh? We'll dress you up in pink for your lawyer okay?

MALE AND FEMALE CHORUS: [*Singing.*]
Many more of them too!
Many more of them too!
Happy birthday Dear Maria,
Happy birthday to you!

Thornton Wilder

THE WRECK
ON THE
FIVE-TWENTY-FIVE

Thornton Wilder

Thornton Wilder was born in Madison, Wisconsin, April 17, 1897, the second son in a family of five. In 1906 the family moved to Hong Kong, where his father was appointed American Consul General, transferring later to Shanghai and remaining there until 1914. During these years Thornton attended schools in Hong Kong, Shanghai, China, and California. He went to Oberlin College for two years before transferring to Yale. Eight months of his junior year were spent in the Coast Artillery during the First World War before he graduated from Yale in 1920. A year followed at the American Academy in Rome, attending archeology courses and writing his first published novel, *The Cabala*.

From 1921–28 he taught French at the Lawrenceville School in New Jersey, taking out one year to get an M.A. in French Literature at Princeton and a second year tutoring abroad and writing *The Bridge of San Luis Rey*. During the years 1930–36 he taught part of the year at the University of Chicago; the other part he used to make cross-country lecture tours and to write. Later he taught for a year at Harvard, lectured and held seminars in European universities, and wrote the film *Shadow of a Doubt* for Hitchcock, starring Joseph Cotton.

He represented the U.S. at UNESCO conferences abroad and joined a State Department Cultural Mission to three South American contries in early 1941. During the Second World War he served three years in the Intelligence Branch of the Air Force through the ranks of Captain to Lt. Colonel, for which he was awarded numerous military honors. He has also, over the years, received many honorary degrees, medals, and other honors.

Publications include: the novels *The Cabala* (1926), *The Bridge of San Luis Rey* (1927, Pulitzer Prize), *Heaven's My Destination* (1935), *The Eighth Day* (1967), *Theophilus North* (1973); the plays *The Long Christmas Dinner and Other Plays in One Act* (1931), *Our Town* (1938, Pulitzer Prize), *The Merchant of Yonkers* (1939), *The Skin of Our Teeth* (1942, Pulitzer Prize), *The Matchmaker* (1957, a slightly revised version of *The Merchant of Yonkers*, which engendered the musical *Hello, Dolly!*); opera librettos; and essay collections.

Thornton Wilder died December 7, 1975.

CHARACTERS:
>   **Mrs. Hawkins**
>   **Minnie**
>   **Mr. Forbes**
>   **Hawkins**

SETTING:

> *Today. Six o'clock in the evening. MRS. HAWKINS, forty, and her daughter MINNIE, almost sixteen, are sewing and knitting. At the back is a door into the hall and beside it a table on which is a telephone.*

MRS. HAWKINS: Irish stew doesn't seem right for Sunday dinner, somehow. [*Pause.*] And your father doesn't really like roast or veal. [*Pause.*] Thank Heaven, he's not crazy about steak. [*Another pause while she takes some pins from her mouth.*] I must say it's downright strange—his not being here. He hasn't telephoned for years, like that,—that he'd take a later train.

MINNIE: Did he say what was keeping him?

MRS. HAWKINS: No ... Something at the office, I suppose. [*She changes pins again.*] He never really did like chicken, either.

MINNIE: He ate pork last week without saying anything. You might try pork-chops, mama; I don't really mind them.

MRS. HAWKINS: He doesn't ever say anything. He eats what's there.—Oh, Minnie, men never realize that there's only a limited number of things to eat.

MINNIE: What did he say on the telephone exactly?

MRS. HAWKINS: "I'll try to catch the six-thirty."

[*Both look at their wristwatches.*]

MINNIE: But, mama, papa's not cranky about what he eats. He's always saying what a good cook you are.

MRS. HAWKINS: Men! [*She has put down her sewing and is gazing before her.*] They think they want a lot of change,—variety and change, variety and change. But they don't really. Deep down, they don't.

MINNIE: Don't *what*?

MRS. HAWKINS: You know for a while he read all those Wild Western magazines: cowboys and horses and silly Indians ... two or three a week. Then, suddenly, he stopped all that. It's as though he thought he were in a kind of jail or prison.—Keep an eye on that window, Minnie. He may be coming down the street any minute.

[MINNIE *rises and, turning, peers through a window, back right.*]

MINNIE: No.—There's Mr. Wilkerson, though. He came back on the five-twenty-five, anyway. Sometimes papa stops at the tobacco shop and comes down Spruce Street.

[*She moves to the left and looks through another window.*]

MRS. HAWKINS: Do you feel as though you were in a jail, Minnie?

MINNIE: *What?!*

MRS. HAWKINS: As though life were a jail?

MINNIE: [*Returning to her chair.*] No, of course, not.—Mama, you're talking awfully funny tonight.

MRS. HAWKINS: I'm not myself. [*Laughs lightly.*] I guess I'm not myself because of your father's phone call,—his taking a later train, like that, for the first time in so many years.

MINNIE: [*With a little giggle.*] I don't know what the five-twenty-five will have done without him.

MRS. HAWKINS: [*Not sharply.*] And all those hoodlums he plays cards with every afternoon.

MINNIE: And all the jokes they make.

[MRS. HAWKINS *has been looking straight before her—through a window—over the audience's heads; intently.*]

MRS. HAWKINS: There's Mrs. Cochran cooking her dinner.

[*They both gaze absorbedly at* MRS. COCHRAN *a moment.*]

MRS. HAWKINS: [*Cont'd.*] Well, I'm not going to start dinner until your father puts foot in this house.

MINNIE: [*Still gazing through the window; slowly.*] There's Mr. Cochran at the door ... They're arguing about something.

MRS. HAWKINS: Well, that shows that he got in on the five-twenty-five, all right.

MINNIE: Don't people look foolish when you see them, like that,—and you can't hear what they're saying? Like ants or something. Somehow, you feel it's not right to look at them when they don't know it.

[*They return to their work.*]

MRS. HAWKINS: Yes, those men on the train will have missed those awful jokes your father makes.

[MINNIE *giggles.*]

MRS. HAWKINS: [*Cont'd.*] I declare, Minnie, every year your father makes worse jokes. It's growing on him.

MINNIE: I don't think they're awful, but—I don't understand *all* of them. Do you? Like what he said to the minister Sunday. I was so embarrassed I didn't want to tell you.

MRS. HAWKINS: I don't want to hear it,—not tonight. [*Her gaze returns to the window.*] I can't understand why Mrs. Cochran is acting so strangely. And Mr. Cochran has been coming in and out of the kitchen.

MINNIE: And they seem to keep looking at us all the time.

[*After a moment's gazing, they return to their work.*]

MRS. HAWKINS: Well, you might as well tell me what your father said to the minister.

MINNIE: I ... I don't want to tell you, if it makes you nervous.

MRS. HAWKINS: I've lived with his jokes for twenty years. I guess I can stand one more.

MINNIE: Mr. Brown had preached a sermon about the atom bomb ... and about how terrible it would be ... and at the church door papa said to him: "Fine sermon, Joe. I enjoyed it. But have you ever thought of this, Joe,"—he said—"Suppose the atom bomb didn't fall, what would we do then? Have you ever thought of that?"—Mr. Brown looked terribly put out.

MRS. HAWKINS: [*Puts down her sewing.*] He said that!! I declare, he's getting worse. I don't know where he gets such ideas. People will be beginning to think he's *bitter.* Your father isn't bitter. I know he's not bitter.

MINNIE: No, mama. People like it. People stop me on the street and tell me what a wonderful sense of humor he has. Like ... like ... [*She gives up the attempt and says merely:*] Oh, nothing.

MRS. HAWKINS: Go on. Say what you were going to say.

MINNIE: What did he mean by saying: "There we sit for twenty years playing cards on the five-twenty-five, hoping that something big and terrible and wonderful will happen,—like a wreck, for instance?"

MRS. HAWKINS: [*More distress than indignation.*] I say to you seriously, Minnie, it's just *self-indulgence.* We do everything we know how to make him happy. He loves his home, you know he does. He likes his work,—he's proud of what he does at the office. [*She rises and looks down the street through the window at the back; moved.*] Oh, it's not *us* he's impatient at: it's the whole world. He simply wishes the whole world were different,—that's the trouble with him.

MINNIE: Why, mama, papa doesn't complain about anything.

MRS. HAWKINS: Well, I wish he would complain once in a while. [*She returns to her chair.*] For Sunday I'll see if I can't get an extra good bit of veal. [*They sit in silence a moment. The telephone rings.*]

MRS. HAWKINS: [*Cont'd.*] Answer that, will you, dear?—No, I'll answer it. [MINNIE *returns to her work.* MRS. HAWKINS *has a special voice for answering the telephone, slow and measured.*]

MRS. HAWKINS: [*Cont'd.*] This is Mrs. Hawkins speaking. Oh, yes, Mr. Cochran. What's that? I don't hear you. [*A shade of anxiety.*] Are you *sure?* You must be mistaken.

MINNIE: Mama, what is it?

[MRS. HAWKINS *listens in silence.*]

MINNIE: [*Cont'd.*] Mama!—Mama!!—What's he saying? Is it about papa?

MRS. HAWKINS: Will you hold the line one minute, Mr. Cochran? I wish to speak to my daughter. [*She puts her hand over the mouthpiece.*] No, Minnie. It's not about your father at all.

MINNIE: [*Rising.*] Then what *is* it?

MRS. HAWKINS: [*In a low, distinct, and firm voice.*] Now you do what I tell you. Sit down and go on knitting. Don't look up at me and don't show any surprise.

MINNIE: [*A groan of protest.*] Mama!

MRS. HAWKINS: There's nothing to be alarmed about,—but I want you to *obey* me. [*She speaks into the telephone.*] Yes, Mr. Cochran ... No ... Mr. Hawkins telephoned that he was taking a later train tonight. I'm expecting him on the six-thirty.
—You do what you think best.
—I'm not sure that's necessary but ... you do what you think best.
—We'll be right here. [*She hangs up and stands thinking a moment.*]

MINNIE: Mama, I'm almost sixteen. *Tell* me what it's about.

MRS. HAWKINS: [*Returns to her chair; bending over her work she speaks as guardedly as possible.*] Minnie, there's probably nothing to be alarmed about. Don't show any surprise at what I'm about to say to you now. Mr. Cochran says that there's been somebody out on the lawn watching us—for ten minutes or more. A man. He's been standing in the shadow of the garage, just looking at us.

MINNIE: [*Lowered head.*] Is *that* all!

MRS. HAWKINS: Well, Mr. Cochran doesn't like it. He's ... he says he's going to telephone the police.

MINNIE: The police!!

MRS. HAWKINS: Your father'll be home any minute, anyway. [*Slight pause.*] I guess it's just some ... some *moody* person on an evening walk. Maybe, Mr. Cochran's done right to call the police, though. He says that we shouldn't pull the curtains or anything like that,—but just act as though nothing had happened.—Now, I don't want you to get frightened.

MINNIE: I'm not, mama. I'm just ... interested. Most nights *nothing* happens.

MRS. HAWKINS: [*Sharply.*] I should hope not!

[*Slight pause.*]

MINNIE: Mama, all evening I *did* have the feeling that I was being watched ... and *that* man was being watched by Mrs. Cochran; and [*Slight giggle.*] Mrs. Cochran was being watched by us.

MRS. HAWKINS: We'll know what it's all about in a few minutes.

[*Silence.*]

MINNIE: But, mama, what would the man be looking at?—just us two sewing.

MRS. HAWKINS: I think you'd better go in the kitchen. Go slowly—and don't look out the window.

MINNIE: [*Without raising her head.*] No! I'm going to stay right here. But I'd like to know *why* a man would do that—would just stand and look. I he ... a crazy man?

MRS. HAWKINS: No, I don't think so.

MINNIE: Well, say *something* about him.

MRS. HAWKINS: Minnie, the world is full of people who think that everyone's happy except themselves. They think their lives should be more exciting.

MINNIE: Does that man think our lives are exciting, mama?

MRS. HAWKINS: Our lives are just as exciting as they ought to be, Minnie.

MINNIE: [*With a little giggle.*] Well, they are tonight.

MRS. HAWKINS: They are all the time, and don't you forget it. [*The front door bell rings.*] Now, who can that be at the front door? I'll go, Minnie. [*Weighing the dangers.*] No, *you* go.—No, I'll go.

[*She goes into the hall. The jovial voice of* MR. FORBES *is heard.*]

MR. FORBES'S VOICE: Good evening, Mrs. Hawkins. Is Herb home?

MRS. HAWKINS'S VOICE: No, he hasn't come home yet, Mr. Forbes. He telephoned that he'd take a later train.

[*Enter* MR. FORBES, *followed by* MRS. HAWKINS.]

MR. FORBES: Yes, I know. The old five-twenty-five wasn't the same without him. Darn near went off the rails. [*To* MINNIE.] Good evening, young lady.

MINNIE: [*Head bent; tiny voice.*] Good evening, Mr. Forbes.

MR. FORBES: Well, I thought I'd drop in and see Herb for a minute. About how maybe he'd be wanting a new car,—now that he's come into all that money.

MRS. HAWKINS: Come into *what* money, Mr. Forbes?

MR. FORBES: Why, sure, he telephoned you about it?

MRS. HAWKINS: He didn't say anything about any money.

MR. FORBES: [*Laughing loudly.*] Well, maybe I've gone and put my foot in it again. So he didn't tell you anything about it yet? Haw-haw-haw. [*Confidentially.*] If he's got to pay taxes on it we figgered out he'd get about eighteen thousand dollars.—Well, you tell him I called, and tell him that I'll give him nine hundred dollars on that Chevrolet of his,—maybe a little more after I've had a look at it.

MRS. HAWKINS: I'll tell him.—Mr. Forbes, I'm sorry I can't ask you to sit down, but my daughter's had a cold for days now and I wouldn't want you to take it home to your girls.

MR. FORBES: I'm sorry to hear that.—Well, as you say, I'd better not carry it with me. [*He goes to the door, then turns and says confidentially:*] Do you know what Herb said when he heard that he'd got that money? Haw-haw-haw. I've always said Herb Hawkins has more sense of humor than anybody I know. Why, he said—"All window-glass is the same." Haw-haw—"All window-glass is the same." Herb! You can't beat him.

MRS. HAWKINS: "All window glass is the same." What did he mean by that?

MR. FORBES: You know: that thing he's always saying. About life. He said it at Rotary in his speech. You know how crazy people look when you see them through a window—arguing and carrying on—and you can't hear a word they say? He says that's the way things look to him. Wars and politics … and everything in life.

[MRS. HAWKINS *is silent and unamused.*]

MR. FORBES: [*Cont'd.*] Well, I'd better be going. Tell Herb that's real good glass—*unbreakable*—on the car I'm going to sell him. Good night, miss; good night, Mrs. Hawkins.

[*He goes out.* MRS. HAWKINS *does not accompany him to the front door. She stands a moment looking before her. Then she says, from deep thought:*]

MRS. HAWKINS: That's your father who's been standing out by the garage.

MINNIE: Why would he do that?

MRS. HAWKINS: Looking in.—I should have known it.

MINNIE: [*Amazed but not alarmed.*] Look! All over the lawn!

MRS. HAWKINS: The police have come. Those are their flashlights.

MINNIE: All over the place! I can hear them talking ... [*Pause.*] ... Papa's angry ... Papa's *very* angry.

[*They listen.*]

MINNIE: [*Cont'd.*] Now they're driving away.

MRS. HAWKINS: I should have known it. [*She returns to her seat. Sound of the front door opening and closing noisily.*] That's your father.—Don't mention anything unless he mentions it first.

[*They bend over their work. From the hall, sounds of* HAWKINS *singing the first phrase of "Valencia." Enter* HAWKINS, *a commuter. His manner is of loud, forced geniality.*]

HAWKINS: Well,—HOW are the ladies? [*He kisses each lightly on the cheek.*]

MRS. HAWKINS: I didn't start getting dinner until I knew when you'd get here.

HAWKINS: [*Largely.*] Well, *don't* start it. I'm taking you two ladies out to dinner.—There's no hurry, though. We'll go to Michaelson's after the crowd's thinned out. [*Starting for the hall on his way to the kitchen.*] Want a drink, anybody?

MRS. HAWKINS: No.—The ice is ready for you on the shelf.

[*He goes out. From the kitchen he can be heard singing "Valencia." He returns, glass in hand.*]

MRS. HAWKINS: [*Cont'd.*] What kept you, Herbert?

HAWKINS: Nothing. Nothing. I decided to take another train. [*He walks back and forth, holding his glass at the level of his face.*] I decided to take another train. [*He leans teasingly a moment over his wife's shoulder, conspiratorially.*] I thought maybe things might look different through the windows of another train. You know: all those towns I've never been in? Kenniston—Laidlaw—East Laidlaw—Bennsville. Let's go to Bennsville someday. Damn it, I don't know why people should go to Paris and Rome and Cairo when they could go to Bennsville. Bennsville! Oh, Bennsville,—

MRS. HAWKINS: Have you been drinking, Herbert?

HAWKINS: This is the first swallow I've had since last night. Oh, Bennsville ... breathes there a man with soul so dead—

[MINNIE'*s eyes have followed her father as he walks about with smiling appreciation.*]

MINNIE: I know a girl who lives in Bennsville.

HAWKINS: They're happy there, aren't they? No, not exactly happy, but they live it up to the full. In Bennsville they kick the hell out of life.

MINNIE: Her name's Eloise Brinton.

HAWKINS: Well, Bennsville and East Laidlaw don't look different through the widows of another train. It's not by looking though a train window that you can get at the *heart* of Bennsville. [*Pause.*] There all we fellows sit every night on the fine-twenty-five playing cards and hoping against hope that there'll be that wonderful beautiful—

MINNIE: [*Laughing delightedly.*] Wreck!!

MRS. HAWKINS: Herbert! I won't have you talk that way!

HAWKINS: A wreck, so that we can crawl out of the smoking, burning cars … and get into one of those houses. Do you know what you see from the windows of the train? Those people—those cars—that you see on the streets of Bennsville,—they're just dummies. *Cardboard.* They've been put up there to deceive you. What really goes on in Bennsville—inside those houses—*that's* what's interesting. People with six arms and legs. People that can talk like Shakespeare. Children, Minnie, that can beat Einstein. Fabulous things.

MINNIE: Papa, *I* don't mind, but you make mama nervous when you talk like that.

HAWKINS: Behind those walls. But it isn't only behind those walls that strange things go on. Right on that train, right in those cars,—The damnedest things. Fred Cochran and Phil Forbes—

MRS. HAWKINS: Mr. Forbes was here to see you.

HAWKINS: Fred Cochran and Phil Forbes—we've played cards together for twenty years. We're so expert at hiding things from one another— we're so cram-filled with things that we can't say to one another that only a wreck could crack us open.

MINNIE: [*Indicating her mother, reproachfully.*] Papa!

MRS. HAWKINS: Herbert Hawkins, why did you stand out in the dark there, looking at us through the window?

HAWKINS: Well, I'll tell you … I got a lot of money today. But more than that I got a message. A message from beyond the grave. From the dead. There was this old lady,—I used to do her income-tax for her—old lady. She'd keep me on a while—God, how she wanted someone to talk to … I'd say anything that came into my head … I want another drink. [*He goes into the kitchen. Again we hear him singing "Valencia."*]

MINNIE: [*Whispering.*] Eighteen thousand dollars!

MRS. HAWKINS: We've just got to let him talk himself out.

MINNIE: But, mama, why did he go and stand out on the lawn?

MRS. HAWKINS: Sh!

[HAWKINS *returns.*]

HAWKINS: I told her a lot of things. I told her—

MINNIE: I know! You told her that everything looked as though it were seen through glass.

HAWKINS: Yes, I did. [*Pause.*] You don't hear the words, or if you hear the words, they don't fit what you see. And one day she said to me: "Mr. Hawkins, you say that all the time; why don't you do it?" "Do what?" I said. "Really stand outside and look through some windows." [*Pause.*] I knew she meant my own … Well, to tell the truth, I was afraid to. I preferred to talk about it. [*He paces back and forth.*] She died. Today some lawyer called me up and said she's left me twenty thousand dollars.

MRS. HAWKINS: Herbert!

HAWKINS: [*His eyes on the distance.*] "To Herbert Hawkins, in gratitude for many thoughtfulnesses and in appreciation of his sense of humor." From beyond the grave … It was an order. I took the four o'clock home … It took me a whole hour to get up the courage to go and stand [*He points.*] —out there.

MINNIE: But, papa,—you didn't *see* anything! Just us sewing!

[HAWKINS *stares before him,—then changing his mood, says briskly:*]

HAWKINS: What are we going to have for Sunday dinner?

MINNIE: I know!

HAWKINS: [*Pinching her ear.*] Buffalo steak?

MINNIE: No.

HAWKINS: I had to live for a week once on rattlesnake stew.

MINNIE: Papa, you're awful.

MRS. HAWKINS: [*Putting down her sewing; in an even voice.*] Were you planning to go away, Herbert?

HAWKINS: What?

MRS. HAWKINS: [*For the first time, looking at him.*] You were thinking of going away.

HAWKINS: [*Looks into his glass a moment.*] Far away. [*Then again putting his face over her shoulder teasingly, but in a serious voice.*] There is no "away." … There's only "here."—Get your hats; we're going out to dinner.—I've decided to move to "here." To take up residence, as they say. I'll move in tonight. I don't bring much baggage.—Get your hats.

MRS. HAWKINS: [*Rising.*] Herbert, we don't wear hats anymore. That was in your mother's time.—Minnie, run upstairs and get my blue shawl.

HAWKINS: I'll go and get one more drop out in the kitchen.

MRS. HAWKINS: Herbert, I don't like your old lady.

HAWKINS: [*Turning at the door in surprise.*] Why, what's the matter with her?

MRS. HAWKINS: I can understand that she was in need of someone to talk to.—What business had she trying to make you look at Minnie and me *through windows?* As though we were strangers. [*She crosses and puts her sewing on the telephone table.*] People who've known one another as long as you and I have are not supposed to *see* one another. The pictures we have of one another are inside.—Herbert, last year one day I went to the city to have lunch with your sister. And as I was walking along the street, who do you think I saw coming toward me? From quite a ways off?—*You!* My heart stopped beating and I *prayed*—I prayed that you wouldn't see me. And you passed by without seeing me. I didn't want you to see me in those silly clothes we wear when we go to the city—and in that silly hat—with that silly look we put on our face when we're in public places. The person that other people see.

HAWKINS: [*With lowered eyes.*] You saw *me*—with that silly look.

MRS. HAWKINS: Oh no. I didn't look long enough for that. I was too busy hiding myself.—I don't know why Minnie's so long trying to find my shawl.

[*She goes out. The telephone rings.*]

HAWKINS: Yes, this is Herbert Hawkins.—Nat Fischer? Oh, hello, Nat. ... Oh! ... All right. Sure, I see your point of view. ... Eleven o'clock. Yes, I'll be there. Eleven o'clock.

[*He hangs up.* MRS. HAWKINS *returns wearing a shawl.*]

MRS. HAWKINS: Was that call for me?

HAWKINS: No. It was for me all right.—I might as well tell you now what it was about. [*He stares at the floor.*]

MRS. HAWKINS: Well?

HAWKINS: A few minutes ago the police tried to arrest me for standing on my own lawn. Well, I got them over that. But they found a revolver on me,—without a license. So I've got to show up at court tomorrow,—eleven o'clock.

MRS. HAWKINS: [*Short pause; thoughtfully.*] Oh ... a revolver.

HAWKINS: [*Looking at the floor.*] Yes ... I thought that maybe it was best ... that I go away ... a long way.

MRS. HAWKINS: [*Looking up with the beginning of a smile.*] To Bennsville?

HAWKINS: Yes.

MRS. HAWKINS: Where life's so exciting. [*Suddenly briskly.*] Well, you get that license, Herbert—so that you can prevent people looking in at us through the window, when they have no business to. Turn out the lights when you come.

Doug Wright

LOT 13: THE BONE VIOLIN
a Fugue for Five Actors

Doug Wright

Doug Wright's plays include *The Stonewater Rapture* (published in The *Best Short Plays of 1987*), *Interrogating the Nude*, *Dionosaurs*, *Lot 13: The Bone Violin*, *Watbanaland*, *Wildwood Park*, and a musical, *Buzzsaw Berkeley*, with songs by Michael John LaChiusa. His new play, *Quills*, based on the life of the Marquis de Sade, will open at New York Theater Workshop in 1996. His work has been performed at the Yale Repertory Theater, the WPA Theater, Lincoln Center Theater, the Mark Taper Forum New Work Festival, The Woolly Mammoth Theater in Washington, and The McCarter Theater in Princeton, New Jersey, among others. Television credits include four pilots for producer Norman Lear, and a three-hour adaptation of *The Arabian Nights* entitled *Scheherazade* for Home Box Office. He is a past recipient of the William L. Bradley Fellowship at Yale University, the Charles MacArthur Fellowship at the Eugene O'Neill Theater Center, an HBO Fellowship in playwriting, a McKnight Fellowship from the Playwright's Center, and the Alfred Hodder Fellowship at Princeton University. He received a bachelor's degree from Yale University in 1985, and an MFA in playwriting from NYU in 1987, and is a member of the Dramatists Guild, the Writer's Guild East, the Circle Rep Playwrights Unit, and New York Theater Workshop. He has taught playwriting at Princeton University.

Lot 13: The Bone Violin was originally produced by the Tweed New Work Festival at the Vineyard Theater. It was directed by Beth Schachter.

To Linda Raya, a valued teacher and beloved friend.

CHARACTERS:

The Auctioneer, *a no-nonsense professional*
The Mother, *a well-meaning woman overwhelmed by the enormity of life*
The Father, *pragmatic, Earth-bound, "No Frills"*
The Doctor, *a bespectacled woman in a lab coat, Aryan.*
The Professor, *supercilious, with discontent born of thwarted ambitions*

THE SETTING:

Downstage sits a table, about six feet in length, covered by a linen cloth.
Farther upstage are four stools with corresponding music stands.
Stage left, a podium.
In the distance, Paganini's Violin Concerto Number One.
Lights rise on THE MOTHER, THE FATHER, THE PROFESSOR, *and* THE DOCTOR. *They sit behind the four music stands, solemnly, their hands folded.*
THE AUCTIONEER *enters and takes his place behind the podium. He slams his gavel. The music abruptly stops. He announces in a loud voice:*

THE AUCTIONEER: LOT THIRTEEN.
[*The four other characters spring to life.*
They speak rapidly, their words trailing in and out of another, creating a kind of vocal symphony.
Most of the time, they address the audience directly. Occasionally, they speak among themselves. A few times, they re-enact snippets of dialogue from the past.]
THE MOTHER: I never wanted to play the violin. I don't even like classical music.
THE FATHER: The Stones. Led Zeppelin. To me, that's classic.
THE MOTHER: Psychologists say we're always thrusting our dreams onto the shoulders of our children. Well, I wanted to be a dog groomer.
THE DOCTOR: Nature or nurture?
THE MOTHER: No lie. A dog groomer.
THE DOCTOR: The chicken or the egg?
THE MOTHER: You dream bigger for your kids.
THE DOCTOR: The zygote? Andover?
THE MOTHER: I went to a genealogist once. He said one of my ancestors had been a harpsichordist. In Prague.

THE FATHER: Went back eight generations, just to come up with that.

THE DOCTOR: Ph.D. ...

THE MOTHER: If we were religious, we'd call it a gift from God.

THE DOCTOR: ... or D.N.A.?

THE MOTHER: When he was born, the first thing I noticed: his hands.

THE DOCTOR: The ovum, or the Ivy League?

THE MOTHER: Such elegant fingers for a baby.

THE DOCTOR: Molecules, or Montessori? Tanglewood or testes?

THE FATHER: He'd wrap those little mitts around my thumb, and I knew he wasn't going to wind up laying bricks.

THE DOCTOR: *Well ... ?*

THE MOTHER: It all started in nursery school, during Music Corner. *Peter and the Wolf.*

THE FATHER: Kid hummed it in the tub.

THE MOTHER: In his sleep.

THE FATHER: With his mouth full.

THE MOTHER: By his fourth birthday, he was hounding us for a violin.

THE FATHER: I bought him a baseball bat instead.

THE MOTHER: A mother expects certain milestones. Tying shoelaces. Scissors. But this?

THE FATHER: He took his pocket knife, and his brand new Louisville slugger ... the kid started whittling.

THE MOTHER: There were wood chips all over his dungarees.

THE FATHER: Scrape, scrape, scrape until ...

THE MOTHER: *Voila.* He'd carved a perfect bow.

THE FATHER: So much for Babe Ruth.

THE MOTHER: He stole his father's tennis racket. Stripped the frame and re-strung it with fishing line. A home-made violin.

THE FATHER: We should'a known then.

THE MOTHER: He had this remarkable gift for—what would you call it?

THE PROFESSOR: [*Dryly.*] Transformation.

[*Everyone regards* THE PROFESSOR *for a beat.* THE MOTHER *pauses, then opts to continue.*]

THE MOTHER: He'd go out back, to the old Chevy.

THE FATHER: It's on cinder blocks.

THE MOTHER: He'd sit in that car for hours.

THE FATHER: Scrap mostly, but the radio works.

THE MOTHER: Listening. Tune after tune.

THE FATHER: Only had to hear 'em once.

THE MOTHER: And he could play them right back. No, really.

THE FATHER: The kid was Memorex.

THE MOTHER: Note for note.

THE FATHER: Eerie.

THE MOTHER: I read Alice Miller. Ignore a child's creativity, and he'll grow up lopsided. Encourage it, and he slices off his ear, or drowns himself.

THE FATHER: It's a no-win situation.

THE MOTHER: Suppose you were in your garden, pulling weeds. Suppose for the first time, you noticed a beautiful rhododendron growing up through the crab grass. You'd water it, wouldn't you?

THE PROFESSOR: "Natural abilities are like natural plants; they need pruning by study." Sir Francis Bacon.

THE MOTHER: We found this college instructor. In town.

THE PROFESSOR: My last tutorial had ended badly. A tiny princess with a monstrous cello between her knees. Her parents made accusations so sinister and baroque I began to question their proclivities, never mind my own.

THE MOTHER: At first, he was skeptical.

THE PROFESSOR: I'd been an early bloomer myself. At twelve, you're a marvel. At thirty, you're lucky to be playing in summer bandshells. The score to *Gigi*. The best of Barry Manilow. Or, if you've a modicum of cleverness left over from your all-too distinguished adolescence ... you teach.

THE MOTHER: Still, he agreed to audition our mini concert master.

THE PROFESSOR: In strode a small boy, balancing a horrific instrument under his chin—all tennis string, and jagged wood. I handed him a few sheets of Strauss.

THE MOTHER: "Oh, he can't read music. He plays by ear."

THE PROFESSOR: I cringed. And then he lifted his bow. Two distinct versions of Beethoven's Sonata Number Eight. I recognized them both. The first was Zukerman's, an Angel recording circa 1974. The second was Isaac Stern's, performing with the Berliner Philharmoniker, Philips, 1986. The boy duplicated them with unerring accuracy;

each tremor, each trill. He would soon play a third and superior rendition. His own.

THE MOTHER: The professor was so *impressed*.

THE PROFESSOR: I know how Pope Julius felt when Michelangelo unveiled the Sistine ceiling. I know, because that's how I felt the first time I heard him play.

THE MOTHER: He offered a very generous scholarship.

THE PROFESSOR: My first violin was an Amati, bequeathed to me by my Italian grandfather. I, in turn, gave it to my new protege.

THE FATHER: The kid had one thing in his favor. He wasn't Japanese.

THE PROFESSOR: At five, he'd mastered Beethoven and Bruch. At six, he could perform Sarasate's *Zigeunenweisen* blindfolded. At seven, he was taxing my abilities as a teacher. As he played velvet phrase after velvet phrase, I'd doodle nervously on his sheet music, then offer some innocuous critique. I prayed that my feeble words wouldn't impugn his natural instincts.

THE MOTHER: If driving two hours three times a week to the university is a crime ...

THE PROFESSOR: He should've moved on.

THE MOTHER: If taking my child to his music lessons is an act of malice ...

THE PROFESSOR: A mentor worthy of his staggering gifts.

THE MOTHER: Go ahead.

THE PROFESSOR: But I was addicted.

THE MOTHER: String me up.

THE FATHER: Prof said our kid was a regular Perlman.

THE PROFESSOR: To him, I was vestigial. To me, he was the Grail.

THE FATHER: Who the hell's Perlman?

THE PROFESSOR: I was flying to New York for a music conference. I took the child to perform for a team of colleagues. Tchaikovsky's *Melancholique*. Every note—the plaintive sadness soaring into despair, the lilting cry of a broken heart—poured forth with volcanic force from the body of a seven-year old boy. I stood in the wings, reduced to tears. As he left the stage, he turned to me. "My bubble-gum," he said, "Give it back." I uncurled my fist, and he popped the pink wad into his mouth. I didn't know whether to embrace or throttle him.

THE FATHER: A man should support his children, not the other way around. But the car-pooling, the tuxedo fittings, the concert tours ...

THE MOTHER: I couldn't do it alone.

THE FATHER: I let the day job go.

THE MOTHER: At the supermarket, I'd hear the other mothers whispering. "Robbed of a normal childhood." People tend to say that of children with certain ... well ... advantages.

THE FATHER: I grew up normal. Look where it got me.

THE PROFESSOR: The artist is a willing casualty.

THE FATHER: A back-breakin' mortgage. Bifocals. Chronic gas pains.

THE PROFESSOR: His sacrifices as well as his skills catapult him beyond mere martyrdom into the realm of the divine.

THE FATHER: You can keep "normal."

THE MOTHER: When Dick hits a home-run or Jane sells the most cookies, those are achievements, too. They're just not worthy of the world's attention, that's all.

THE PROFESSOR: We toured for months. Venice. Dusseldorf.

THE MOTHER: I never dreamed I'd see Salzburg.

THE FATHER: We could'a planned a vacation. Put a little back each month.

THE MOTHER: I never knew I wanted to go, until I'd already been.

THE PROFESSOR: Soon, the parasites descended.

THE FATHER: I met Ray Charles backstage at Carson. And we got a two page lay-out in *Time*.

THE MOTHER: And that high-powered doctor.

THE DOCTOR: Is talent acquired ... or is it bred in the bone?

THE MOTHER: All those frozen test tubes.

THE DOCTOR: I first posed that question in an article entitled "Grafting the Muse," Genetic Engineering Journal, September 1984.

THE FATHER: All those I.Q. tests we had to take.

THE DOCTOR: Now I'm not one of those fanatics up in Cambridge who believe amino acids code our taste in wallpaper, and carry the names of our grandchildren. Environment plays a part. Still, the root of who we are ... our potential ... that's embedded.

THE FATHER: "The Institute for Genetic Predetermination."

THE DOCTOR: Highly misunderstood. "Master Race, neo-Nazi." We get that all the time.

THE FATHER: Some blue-ribbon sperm bank.

THE DOCTOR: I won't pretend our selection process is democratic. It's elitist, no question. But what the public fails to recognize—what they fail to admit, in their collective egoism—is that a born biophysicist benefits us all. A born Tolstoy benefits us all. And these people can be born.

THE MOTHER: Imagine. Designer children.

THE DOCTOR: What we needed was proof, on a grand scale. A scientific milestone with show-biz appeal.

THE FATHER: Three Nobel prize winners in the fridge, and they wanted our kid, too.

THE DOCTOR: Inside that boy's body swam countless incipient Mozarts. We were confident that, with him on our team, we could clone an entire orchestra.

THE FATHER: Hell, I was flattered.

THE MOTHER: He was more than a child. He was ... my baby was ...

THE DOCTOR: The necessary clue.

THE PROFESSOR: A pint-sized virtuoso with gargantuan coat-tails.

THE FATHER: A chip off some bigger, better block.

THE MOTHER: No. No. A miracle. He was a *miracle.*

THE DOCTOR: We sanitized a vial, sat back, and waited for the onset of pubescence.

[*They wait. Seconds tick by. Finally:*]

THE DOCTOR: [*Cont'd.*] The donation never occurred.

[*There is a brief pause.* THE PROFESSOR *tips his head toward* THE AUCTIONEER.]

THE PROFESSOR: [*To the* THE AUCTIONEER.] Psst.

[THE PROFESSOR *tips his head toward the downstage table.*]

THE MOTHER: Is it time for that? Already?

THE FATHER: Must be.

[THE AUCTIONEER *crosses to the table, and pulls off the linen cloth with a flourish, revealing a small mahogany coffin, about four feet in length. He returns to the podium. He pounds his gavel a second time.*]

THE AUCTIONEER: PAGE NUMBER SEVEN IN YOUR CATALOGUE.

[*Another brief rest.*]

THE FATHER: Kid never saw his tenth birthday.

THE DOCTOR: When we lost him, we lost funding.

THE FATHER: Had a bicycle in the garage, waiting.

THE MOTHER: His hands.

THE FATHER: Blue bicycle. With a horn.

THE MOTHER: I'll always remember his hands.

THE DOCTOR: One day, you're the darling of the Fords, the Mellons, the MacArthurs. The next day, you're staging phone-a-thons. Auctions. Even the occasional car-wash.

THE MOTHER: I wished I'd never heard the name Georg Solti.

THE PROFESSOR: I'd met Solti only once before, at the London Academy. We weren't formally *introduced*, but we did exchange words. Rub shoulders. Rumor has it he was in the room. And now he was requesting to perform with my prize pupil.

[THE MOTHER *pulls out a small concert programme.*]

THE MOTHER: I kept the programme.

THE PROFESSOR: Together, Solti and I would ruminate over every measure of music.

THE MOTHER: Still crisp. Unopened.

THE PROFESSOR: We'd dissect each piece with the same care and intensity a bomb technician employs when detonating explosives.

[THE MOTHER *reads from the programme:*]

THE MOTHER: "Paganini. *Concerto Number One.* The Chicago Symphony."

THE PROFESSOR: "Maestro," I'd offer, "perhaps we should conclude the evening with the *Perpetuum Mobile.*" "Please," he'd respond, "Call me Georg."

THE FATHER: Rehearsing the *Rondo.* That's when the kid cracked.

THE MOTHER: Perhaps it was exhaustion.

THE FATHER: Perhaps it was nerves.

THE DOCTOR: Perhaps it was a failed synapse.

THE PROFESSOR: Perhaps it was his own angry gesture of rebellion. The bow skidded, and the violin shrieked in pain. Like some torture victim refusing to comply.

THE FATHER: Our cat caught it's tail in the screen door. Made the same sound.

THE PROFESSOR: Solti suggested we begin again. But our little prodigy refused. Eyes flashing behind his tiny horn-rims. So much fury locked inside that elfin body, it shook.

THE FATHER: Concert was cancelled.

THE MOTHER: We took the first flight home.

THE FATHER: Kid didn't say a word.

THE MOTHER: Three hundred miles, not a peep.

THE FATHER: As soon as I opened the front door—whoosh, bang!—he ran upstairs, then a loud slam.

THE PROFESSOR: My reputation was wounded, to say the least.

THE MOTHER: If I'd only known ...

THE PROFESSOR: I wrote Sir Georg a long letter of apology, expressing the fervent hope we could collaborate again ...

THE MOTHER: If I'd had any idea ...

THE PROFESSOR: I received no reply.

THE MOTHER: ... that was the last time I'd ever see my angel.

THE DOCTOR: Without support from the private sector—in six, seven months—the Institute will be forced to close its doors.

THE PROFESSOR: When I heard of the boy's demise, in some dark, corroded corner of my mind—I felt vindicated.

THE MOTHER: That night ... alone in his room... high up at the top of the stairs ... he began to play.

[*The* Rondo *begins.*]

THE MOTHER: [*Cont'd.*] *Rondo* this. *Rondo* that.

THE FATHER: Forwards. Backwards. At triple speed.

THE MOTHER: It rang through the house like some terrible alarm.

THE FATHER: He was hell-bent on proving something.

THE MOTHER: But to who?

THE FATHER: Paga-whosit was turning cartwheels in his grave.

THE MOTHER: His door was locked.

THE FATHER: Windows, too. Shades drawn.

THE MOTHER: By evening, the neighbors complained.

THE FATHER: What was I 'sposed to do? Tear down a wall?

THE MOTHER: We felt foolish.

THE FATHER: Call out the fire department?

THE MOTHER: I was standing on the dining room table, pounding the ceiling with my shoe.

THE FATHER: Same damn piece, over and over and over and over and over ...

THE MOTHER: We started slipping sheet music under the door hoping he'd play something—*anything*—new.

THE FATHER: Even tried blue-grass.

THE MOTHER: I refused to cook for him. "When he's weak from hunger," I said, "he'll have to come down."

THE FATHER: Kid wouldn't budge.

THE MOTHER: We got used to it. That's the terrible truth.

THE FATHER: I'd be out, driving. I'd miss it.

THE MOTHER: It underscored our lives. Lunatic, I know. It became as natural to us as the sound of our own breathing. Then—when was it?

THE FATHER: Four a.m. in the middle of the third week.

THE MOTHER: He stopped playing.

[*The music stops.*]

THE MOTHER: [*Cont'd.*] Silence.

THE FATHER: It woke us up.

THE MOTHER: "Honey."

THE FATHER: "You go."

THE MOTHER: "We'll go together."

THE FATHER: I took a flashlight.

THE MOTHER: The stairs were so tall. The climb lasted hours.

THE FATHER: Door was ajar. In we went.

THE MOTHER: The flashlight rose and fell over the furniture. His trundle bed. His little red rocker. His music stand. No sign of him. Anywhere.

THE FATHER: Then we saw it.

THE MOTHER: It was lying in the center of the room.

THE FATHER: On the rug.

THE DOCTOR: Some days later, the parents brought it to me. Our lab performed a battery of tests.

THE PROFESSOR: I had to play it. What remarkable sound! Haunting tones more reminiscent of castrati than your conventional fiddle.

THE DOCTOR: Its cellular composition matched that of the child.

THE PROFESSOR: But it's appearance ... grotesque.

THE DOCTOR: Atom for atom. It matched the child.

THE FATHER: There ... on the rug... the thing was ...

THE MOTHER: Tell them.

THE FATHER: It was still warm.

[THE AUCTIONEER *crosses to the coffin and opens it. A hot white light pours forth from it, like the parched sheen of highly polished bone.* THE AUCTIONEER *returns to his podium.*

THE PROFESSOR *approaches the casket. Gingerly, he looks inside. He describes what he sees.*]

THE PROFESSOR: Hollow bone. The neck and scroll twist like a femur. The pegs resemble finger joints, and the ribs of the instrument are unnervingly authentic. The string, stretched taut across its pale white body, has the unmistakable consistency of human hair. The tuners are tiny molars laid out in a grin. But the bow. The bow is truly shocking. It has an almost spinal curve; the backbone of a child.

[THE DOCTOR *and* THE FATHER *step forward to meet* THE PROFESSOR. *Finally—with great hesitancy—*THE MOTHER *joins them.*

Solemnly, they all gaze into the coffin. The light illuminates them from beneath, casting an eerie glow across their faces.]

THE FATHER: We should'a known then.

THE PROFESSOR: Perhaps that's all he ever was. An instrument.

THE FATHER: Way back. We should'a known.

THE PROFESSOR: Are we to blame? For anthropomorphizing?

THE MOTHER: We never found him.

THE PROFESSOR: The violin is real. Did we imagine the child?

THE MOTHER: We never found our little boy.

[*Slowly,* THE MOTHER, THE FATHER, THE DOCTOR, *and* THE PROFESSOR *return to their music stands. The lights on them fade.*

Lights intensify on THE AUCTIONEER, *and on* THE BONE VIOLIN.

THE AUCTIONEER *pounds his gavel a third time.*]

THE AUCTIONEER: WE'LL START THE BIDDING AT TEN THOUSAND ...

[*Blackout.*]

BEST AMERICAN SHORT PLAYS
1993-1994

The Best American Short Play series includes a careful mixture of offerings from many prominent established playwrights, as well as up and coming younger playwrights. These collections of short plays truly celebrates the economy and style of the short play form. Doubtless, a must for any library!

Window of Opportunityby JOHN AUGUSTINE • Barry, Betty, and Bill by RENÉE TAYLOR/JOSEPH BOLOGNA • Come Down Burning by KIA CORTHRON • For Whom the Southern Belle Tolls by CHRISTOPHER DURANG • The Universal Language by DAVID IVES • The Midlife Crisis of Dionysus by GARRISON KEILLOR • The Magenta Shift by CAROL K. MACK • My Left Breast by SUSAN MILLER • The Interview by JOYCE CAROL OATES • Tall Tales from The Kentucky Cycle by ROBERT SCHENKKAN • Blue Stars by STUART SPENCER • An Act of Devotion by DEBORAH TANNEN • Zipless by ERNEST THOMPSON • Date With A Stranger by CHERIE VOGELSTEIN

$15.95 • Paper • ISBN 1-55783-199-8 • $29.95 • Cloth • ISBN 1-55783-200-5

BEST AMERICAN SHORT PLAYS
1992-1993

Little Red Riding Hood by **BILLY ARONSON** • Dreamers by **SHEL SILVERSTEIN** •Jolly by **DAVID MAMET** • Show by **VICTOR BUMBALO** • A Couple With a Cat by **TONY CONNOR** • Bondage by **DAVID HENRY HWANG** The Drowning of Manhattan by **JOHN FORD NOONAN** The Tack Room by **RALPH ARZOOMIAN** • The Cowboy, the Indian and the Fervent Feminist by **MURRAY SCHISGAL** • The Sausage Eaters by **STEPHEN STAROSTA** • Night Baseball by **GABRIEL TISSIAN** • It's Our Town, Too by **SUSAN MILLER** • Watermelon Rinds by **REGINA TAYLOR** • Pitching to the Star by **DONALD MARGULIES** • The Valentine Fairy by **ERNEST THOMPSON** • Aryan Birth by **ELIZABETH PAGE**

$15.95 • Paper • ISBN 1-55783-166-1 • $29.95 • Cloth • ISBN 1-55783-167-X

BEST AMERICAN SHORT PLAYS
1991-1992

Making Contact by **PATRICIA BOSWORTH** • Dreams of Home by **MIGDALIA CRUZ** • A Way with Words by **FRANK D. GILROY** • Prelude and Liebestod by **TERRENCE MCNALLY** • Success by **ARTHUR KOPIT** • The Devil and Billy Markham by **SHEL SILVERSTEIN** • The Last Yankee by **ARTHUR MILLER** • Snails by **SUZAN-LORI PARKS** • Extensions by **MURRAY SCHISGAL** • Tone Clusters by **JOYCE CAROL OATES** • You Can't Trust the Male by **RANDY NOOJIN** • Struck Dumb by **JEAN-CLAUDE VAN ITALLIE** and **JOSEPH CHAIKIN** • The Open Meeting by **A.R.GURNEY**

$12.95 • Paper • ISBN 1-55783-113-0 • $25.95 • Cloth • ISBN 1-55783-112-2